The name *Ann Pillsbury* has long been associated with what is best in baking. Countless tests performed in Pillsbury's Home Service Center have produced recipes that are easy to prepare and extra good to eat. Here for the first time are gathered more than 400 of the best *Ann Pillsbury* recipes. Included are 100 baking delights that won prizes in a National Baking Contest: *Old-Time Butter Sponge Cake* from Maryland, *Golden Dream Peach Pie* from Wisconsin, *Apple Candy Crisp* from Texas, *Pinwheel Dinner Rolls* from Massachusetts. With a baking book like this at hand you can't fail to bake rolls, cakes, cookies and pies that will win the admiration of your friends and family.

ILLUSTRATED WITH MORE THAN 35 DRAWINGS

Originally published by A. S. Barnes & Co.

Ann Pillsbury's

BAKING

BOOK

By ANN PILLSBURY

 POCKET BOOKS, INC., NEW YORK

The Printing History of

Ann Pillsbury's Baking Book

Barnes edition published December, 1950
1st printing ....December, 1950

POCKET BOOK edition published January, 1951
1st printing ....December, 1950
2nd printing ....December, 1950
3rd printing ....February, 1951
4th printing ....April, 1951

CONTENTS

INTRODUCTION

Baking is one of the most rewarding of all the arts.

The woman who bakes can feel a glow of accomplishment when she puts the finishing touches to a really beautiful cake, or takes a shapely loaf of bread from the oven. When she puts her own homemade baked things on the table, she can look forward to the warm satisfaction of compliments from her family and friends.

And the art of baking is not at all difficult to perfect!

The recipes in this book, for instance, are written in step-by-step form—so simple that even a beginner can follow them easily. They have all been tested again and again by the Ann Pillsbury Home Service Center, and are guaranteed to give you wonderful results.

You will find Ann Pillsbury's basic recipes for the traditional baked foods in this book. You will find "show-off" recipes, too, for the most intriguing foods that Ann Pillsbury and her staff have been able to create. You will also find 100 of the most famous recipes ever developed in home kitchens—the 100 prize-winning recipes from Pillsbury's First Grand National $100,000 Recipe and Baking Contest.

You'll notice that we've started right out with recipes for good foods to eat.

But don't miss what we've put into the back of the book. Notes on equipment, on freezing baked foods—lots of information that we use every day in our own kitchens. We hope these hints and notes will help you, too.

Happy baking!

Ann Pillsbury

ANN PILLSBURY'S
BAKING BOOK

CHAPTER ONE

Biscuits • Muffins • Pancakes
Waffles • Doughnuts
and other
Quick Breads

ALL *of these wonderful baked foods are simple to make. You can stir them up in a hurry and they turn even the plainest meal into something really special.*

Biscuits

IT CAN BE *so easy to make biscuits that are a joy to eat. Tender biscuits, with golden brown crust . . . the kind that break open in fluffy, flaky layers.*

How to Make Perfect Biscuits

HERE *are some of the biscuit-making tricks that we use in our kitchen.*

Mixing—The chief secret in making good biscuits is handling the dough lightly. Cut in the shortening until it is evenly distributed—the particles should be the size of small peas. Add the milk all at once and stir only until well blended. The dough should be quite soft.

Kneading—Place dough on lightly floured board or pastry cloth. Toss lightly to coat with flour. Knead gently 10

1

to 15 strokes to make dough smooth. Kneading helps give flaky texture and well-shaped, high biscuits. Over-kneading toughens the biscuits.

Rolling—Roll out or pat the dough to ½-inch thickness or half the desired height of baked biscuit.

Cutting—Dip cutter in flour before cutting. For well-shaped biscuits, cut straight up and down. Do not twist cutter. Cutting in squares or diamonds is quick and eliminates leftovers and rerolling.

Baking—Place on ungreased baking sheet—far apart for crusty biscuits, close together for soft biscuits. Biscuits should be baked in a hot oven; too low a temperature requires longer baking time and makes them dry.

HOT BISCUITS

If you like your biscuits Yankee-style (high and fluffy), roll the biscuit dough one-half inch thick. But if you like the way they make them in the South (thin and crusty), roll the dough only one-fourth inch thick. Either way, serve them piping hot, of course!

Makes 14 biscuits

Sift together _____ 2 cups sifted **enriched flour**
          3 teaspoons double-acting **baking powder**
          ½ teaspoon salt.

Cut in _____ ¼ cup **shortening** until mixture resembles coarse meal.

Add _____ ¾ cup **milk;** mix only until all flour is dampened. Knead gently on floured board or pastry cloth for a few seconds.

Roll _____ to ½-inch thickness and cut into rounds with 2-inch cutter. Place on ungreased baking sheet.

Bake _____ in hot oven (450°F.) 12 to 15 minutes.

BISCUIT VARIATIONS

ONE *of the nice things about biscuits is that you can make your biscuits just a little bit different from anyone else's. Add cheese or parsley . . . and when you are in a hurry, mix up a batch of drop biscuits.*

BUTTERMILK OR SOUR MILK BISCUITS

PREPARE Biscuits, decreasing baking powder to 2 teaspoons. Add ½ teaspoon soda and sift with flour and salt. Substitute ¾ cup sour milk or buttermilk for milk.

CHEESE BISCUITS

PREPARE Biscuits, adding ½ cup grated strong cheese to shortening and dry ingredients.

BACONETTE BISCUITS

PREPARE Biscuits, adding ½ cup crisp bacon, crushed, to shortening and dry ingredients.

PARSLEY BISCUITS

PREPARE Biscuits, cutting in ¼ cup chopped parsley with shortening.

ONION BISCUITS

PREPARE Biscuits, blending in 2 tablespoons browned onion with liquid ingredients.

DROP BISCUITS

PREPARE Biscuits, increasing milk to 1 cup. Drop by spoonfuls on greased baking sheet or fill greased muffin pans ⅔ full.

Muffins

NEXT TIME *you want to add a homey, thoughtful touch to a simple menu, make some muffins. Wonderful for breakfast, lunch or supper.*

How to Make Perfect Muffins

THE SECRET *of high, tender muffins is quick, light mixing. Too much mixing produces tough, peaked muffins with tunneled and uneven texture.*

Mixing—Sift the dry ingredients into a bowl and make a well in the center. Combine the melted and cooled shortening with the beaten egg and milk and add all at once to the dry ingredients. Stir with a fork only until the dry ingredients are moistened. Do not beat. The batter should be lumpy and rough.

Preparation for Oven—Drop the batter from a tablespoon into greased muffin pans as soon as it is mixed. Fill pans ⅔ full. The batter may be allowed to stand in pans a few minutes before baking.

Baking—Muffins are done when the tops are firm and delicately browned and the sides have shrunk slightly from the sides of the pan. Remove from pans immediately and serve hot.

FAVORITE MUFFINS

The quickest of all the quick breads to mix and put together.

Makes 10 to 12 muffins

Sift together _____ 2 cups sifted enriched flour
3 teaspoons double-acting baking powder

½ teaspoon salt
2 tablespoons sugar.
Beat ....1 egg until light; add
1 cup milk
¼ cup melted shortening or salad oil.
Add................liquid to dry ingredients all at once and
mix only until all flour is dampened.
Fill................well-greased muffin pans ⅔ full.
Bake................in hot oven (425°F.) 20 to 25 minutes.
Serve hot.

Muffin Variations

IN OUR KITCHEN, *of course, we have our own favorite kinds—
or variations—of muffins. Here are some of them. They are all
simple to make.*

NUT MUFFINS
PREPARE Muffins, adding ½ cup chopped nuts to dry ingredients.

CHEESE MUFFINS
PREPARE Muffins, adding ½ cup grated cheese to dry ingredients.

BLUEBERRY MUFFINS
PREPARE Muffins, adding 1 cup fresh blueberries to dry ingredients.

CHERRY MUFFINS
PREPARE Muffins, adding ¾ cup pitted, fresh cherries (halved) to muffin batter.

DATE MUFFINS
PREPARE Muffins, adding ½ cup chopped dates to dry ingredients.

BACON OR HAM MUFFINS

PREPARE Muffins, adding ⅓ cup coarsely chopped crisp bacon or finely cut ham to dry ingredients.

JELLY MUFFINS

PREPARE Muffins, dropping ½ teaspoon jelly or jam on batter in muffin pans before baking.

FESTIVE FRUIT MUFFINS

PREPARE Muffins, adding ½ cup raisins, chopped dried prunes or apricots to dry ingredients.

ORANGE MUFFINS

PREPARE Muffins, adding 2 teaspoons grated orange rind to dry ingredients.

LUNCHEON MUFFINS

Pillsbury Contest Winner by Mrs. Linda Flesh Born, Freeport, N. Y.

Mrs. Born developed these muffins from a recipe which had come to her as a gift. You'll find they have a color and seasoning that is quite out of the ordinary.

Makes 12 muffins

Sift together —1¾ cups sifted **enriched flour**

2 teaspoons double-acting **baking powder**

½ teaspoon **soda**

1 teaspoon **celery salt**

½ teaspoon **dry mustard**

¼ cup **sugar.**

Combine —————1 egg, well beaten

1 10-oz. can condensed **tomato soup**

1 tablespoon **onion juice**

¼ cup **salad oil.**

Add................to dry ingredients and mix only until all flour is dampened.

Fill................well-greased, 2-inch muffin cups ⅔ full.

Bake................in moderately hot oven (400°F.) 20 to 25 minutes. Serve hot.

CORN MEAL MUFFINS

These golden muffins have a crustiness all their own. And
they're full of wonderful sweet corn meal flavor. Bake this
batter in corn stick pans or in regular muffin tins. Serve
piping hot with lots of butter if you like.

Makes 10 to 12 muffins

Sift together —— 1¼ cups sifted **enriched flour**
                      3 teaspoons double-acting **baking powder**
                      1 teaspoon **salt**
                      ¼ cup sugar.
Add ——————— 1 cup **corn meal.**
Beat ——————— 1 **egg** until light; add
                      1¼ cups **milk**
                      ¼ cup melted **shortening** or salad oil.
Add ——————— liquid all at once to dry ingredients;
                      mix only until all flour is dampened.
Fill ——————— greased muffin pans ⅔ full.
Bake ——————— in hot oven (425°F.) 20 to 25 minutes.
                      Serve hot.

CORN STICKS

PREPARE Corn Meal Muffins, filling hot, greased corn stick pans
about ¾ full.

BRAN MUFFINS

These moist, even-textured muffins have a tender crust and
a good, wholesome, wheat-bran flavor.

Makes 12 muffins

Sift together ——— 2 cups sifted **enriched flour**
                      3½ teaspoons double-acting **baking powder**
                      1½ teaspoons **salt**
                      ⅓ cup sugar.

Blend in _____1 cup wheat bran.

Beat _____1 egg until light; add

      1½ cups milk

      3 tablespoons melted shortening or salad oil.

Add _____liquid to dry ingredients all at once; mix only until all flour is dampened.

Fill _____well-greased muffin pans ⅔ full.

Bake _____in moderately hot oven (400°F.) 25 to 30 minutes. Serve hot.

Popovers

GOLDEN BROWN, *crusty popovers are a quick bread gone "high hat." They look difficult to make—but they're really easy.*

How to Make Perfect Popovers

Mixing—Beat shortening, milk and eggs with flour and salt until batter is smooth. A rotary or electric mixer should be used—there is no need to worry about overbeating the batter.

Pan Preparation—Popovers may be baked in well-greased, preheated heavy iron pans or glass cups, or in well-greased unheated muffin pans. Fill pans ⅔ full.

Baking—Bake popovers in a hot oven for 30 minutes. The steam formed by the thin batter in the hot oven makes the popovers "pop." Prick popovers with fork or sharp knife to allow steam to escape and leave them in the oven about ten minutes longer to dry out. If popovers are not baked thoroughly, they will collapse when cool.

Serving—Popovers are usually served as a hot bread for breakfast, luncheon or dinner. We like them, too, as a "main course" filled with any of the creamed fillings given in Chapter Four. And some time, serve them with berries, ice cream or whipped cream — they make a festive dessert.

POPOVERS

These popovers "pop", beautifully every time!

Makes 10 to 12 popovers

Sift together —— 1 cup sifted **enriched flour**
½ teaspoon **salt**.

Add —————— 1 tablespoon melted **shortening** or salad oil
1 cup **milk**
2 **eggs**.

Beat —————— until smooth, using rotary or electric beater.

Fill —————— well-greased muffin or popover pans ⅓ to ½ full.

Bake —————— in hot oven (425°F.) 30 minutes. Turn off heat. Prick popovers with sharp fork. Let popovers remain in oven an additional 10 minutes to dry out. Serve hot.

Pancakes

GRIDDLE CAKES, *pancakes, flannel cakes, flapjacks . . . call them what you will. They all mean tempting, golden brown hot cakes, fresh from the griddle.*

You'll find that hot cakes make tasty, budget-wise meals, too.

They're always good for breakfast, of course. Try them, too, with a meat accompaniment for lunch or supper.

How to Make Perfect Pancakes

PANCAKES *are particularly easy to make, because they contain so few ingredients. However, you may want to note these pancake tips that we follow in our own kitchen.*

Mixing—Combine liquid and dry ingredients and stir only until flour mixture is dampened. Small lumps in batter disappear in baking. If mixture thickens on standing, add a little more milk.

Seasoning the Griddle—A new griddle should be seasoned before using. To season a griddle, preheat the iron, brushing it with unsalted fat. Once the griddle has been coated with a film of fat, it is not advisable to wash it.

Baking Pancakes—The pancake griddle is the correct temperature for baking when drops of water dance on the surface. The griddle does not need greasing if the batter contains 2 or more tablespoons of shortening for each cup of liquid. Use unsalted fat if it is necessary to grease the griddle. Drop batter from spoon on griddle. One-fourth cup medium-thick batter will make a 4½-inch cake. Turn pancakes when bubbles begin to break and the edges are slightly dry. Do not pat or smooth batter while baking. Turn only once.

When baking griddle cakes, rub the griddle frequently with a cheesecloth bag containing salt. This bag will clean the griddle of pieces of batter and will keep the cakes from sticking.

Serving—Pancakes are best when served really hot off the griddle.

PANCAKES

Some people like their pancakes thick. Some like them thin. This recipe makes medium-thick pancakes. If you want your pancakes thicker, use less liquid. If you want them thinner, add more liquid. It's as simple as that!

Makes seven 4¼-inch cakes

Sift together _____ 1 cup sifted enriched flour
2 teaspoons double-acting baking powder
½ teaspoon salt
2 teaspoons sugar.

Beat _____ 1 egg until light; add
¾ cup milk
2 tablespoons melted shortening or salad oil.

Add _____ liquid to dry ingredients, all at once; mix until well blended.

Bake _____ on hot griddle, turning only once. Serve immediately.

Pancake Variations

WHEN *you want to serve something fancier than just plain pancakes, why not try one of these ideas?*

CORN MEAL PANCAKES
PREPARE Pancakes, decreasing flour to ¾ cup and adding ¼ cup yellow corn meal.

DUTCH POTATO PANCAKES
PREPARE Pancakes, adding ½ cup finely grated raw potato, ½ teaspoon minced onion and 1 additional egg.

CORN KERNEL PANCAKES
PREPARE Pancakes, adding ½ cup whole kernel corn, drained.

APPLE PANCAKES

PREPARE Pancakes, adding ½ cup finely sliced apple. Before serving, spread with melted butter, cinnamon and brown sugar.

Waffles

GRANDMOTHER *really knew her quick breads. And waffles were among her favorites. We agree with grandmother's choice whole-heartedly—for breakfast, luncheon or supper.*

How to Make Perfect Waffles

WAFFLES *(like pancakes) contain only a few ingredients, and are easy to mix and bake. We find they turn out best when we follow these simple rules.*

Mixing—Combine liquid and dry ingredients, mixing until smooth. Eggs may be separated and the stiffly beaten whites folded in last. You may store waffle batter in the refrigerator for several hours, if you wish.

Baking—A waffle iron should be heated and greased with unsalted fat before it is used for the first time. Greasing is then unnecessary if the batter contains enough shortening.

Have the iron smoking hot before baking the first waffle. Do not lift the top of the iron during baking. The longer the baking period, the crisper and browner the waffles. Bake waffles until steam is no longer visible.

Brush the grids with a stiff brush to clean. Wipe off excess shortening or crumbs with paper toweling while iron is warm. Waffle irons bake better if they are not washed after they are well-seasoned. Always leave the cover open during cooling.

Serving—Waffles are best served hot. However, if waffles must be made in advance for a large group, they may be kept in a warm oven. Do not stack them, as they become soggy.

Serve waffles with maple syrup, jelly, brown-sugar syrup, corn syrup or other topping. For luncheon, creamed dried beef, shrimp, oysters, chicken or vegetables are delicious with waffles. Waffles may also be served for dessert with chocolate or caramel sauce, whipped cream or ice cream.

WAFFLES

This recipe makes medium-thick waffles. If you like your waffles fat and fluffy, make them with a little less liquid than this recipe calls for. And if you like them crisp and crunchy, use just a bit more liquid.

Makes 6 four-section waffles

Sift together _____ 2 cups sifted **enriched flour**
                    3 teaspoons double-acting **baking powder**
                    1 teaspoon **salt**
                    2 tablespoons **sugar.**

Combine _____ 2 **egg yolks,** well beaten
                    1¾ cups **milk**
                    ⅓ cup melted **shortening** or salad oil.

Add _____ liquid to dry ingredients all at once; mix until well blended.

Beat _____ 2 **egg whites** until stiff but not dry; fold gently into batter.

Bake _____ in preheated waffle iron until steaming ceases and waffle is golden brown.

Waffle Variations

THERE ARE *lots of ways to make different—and "special"—*

*kinds of waffles. We think these variations are especially
delicious.*

FRUIT WAFFLES

PREPARE Waffles, adding 1 cup fresh blueberries, raspberries
or finely chopped apple to batter.

SAVORY WAFFLES

PREPARE Waffles, adding ½ cup chopped crisp bacon or dried
beef to batter.

CHEESE WAFFLES

PREPARE Waffles, adding ½ cup grated cheese to batter.

CHOCOLATE WAFFLES

PREPARE Waffles, increasing sugar to 3 tablespoons and adding
2 squares melted chocolate to batter.

SOUR CREAM WAFFLES

**These waffles are rich and substantial . . . yet light and crisp.
Good served with bacon or sausage on the side.**

Makes 8 waffles

Sift together ———— 2 cups sifted enriched flour
2 teaspoons double-acting baking powder
½ teaspoon soda
1 teaspoon salt
2 tablespoons sugar.

Beat ———————— 4 egg yolks until light; add
2 cups sour cream.

Add ————————— liquid to dry ingredients all at once and
mix until well blended.

Beat ———————— 4 egg whites until stiff but not dry; fold
into batter.

Bake ————————— in preheated waffle iron until steaming
ceases and waffle is golden brown. Serve

immediately with butter, syrup, honey or jelly.

CRISPY CREAM WAFFLES

Pillsbury Contest Winner by Mrs. Leroy W. Hall, Oklahoma City, Okla.

Really crisp waffles that never, never wilt—that's what Mrs. Hall was looking for when she worked out this recipe. Quick to make—and delicious!

Makes 4 four-section waffles

Sift together ——1 cup sifted enriched flour

1½ teaspoons double-acting baking powder

½ teaspoon salt

1 tablespoon sugar.

Beat ——————2 egg yolks until thick and lemon colored.

Measure————½ pint (1 cup) whipping cream. Add to egg yolks and mix slightly.

Add——————dry ingredients all at once; beat only until smooth.

Blend in————2 tablespoons melted butter.

Beat —————2 egg whites until stiff but not dry. Fold gently into batter. The batter will be quite stiff.

Bake—————in preheated waffle iron until steaming ceases and waffle is golden brown.

Quick Breads

FRUIT-NUT SNACK BREAD

No fuss to make—this quick bread stays moist and fresh for days. It's so good, you'll want to try all the variations.

Makes 9x5x3-inch loaf

Sift together......2½ cups sifted **enriched flour**
4 teaspoons double-acting **baking powder**
1 teaspoon **salt**
1 cup **sugar**.

Cut in................¼ cup **shortening** until mixture resembles coarse meal.

Form....................a "well" in dry ingredients and add
1 cup **milk**
1 **egg**. Mix until all flour is dampened.

Blend in.............½ cup chopped **nuts**
½ cup finely-cut dried **apricots**, uncooked
½ cup finely-cut dried **prunes**, uncooked.

Pour into............well-greased 9x5x3-inch loaf pan. Spread batter into corners of pan, leaving the center slightly hollowed. For well-rounded loaf, allow to stand 20 minutes before baking.

Bake....................in moderate oven (350°F.) 1 hour. Remove from pan and cool. Store overnight before slicing.

DATE BREAD

PREPARE Fruit-Nut Snack Bread, substituting 1 cup finely-cut dates for apricots and prunes.

ORANGE-NUT BREAD

PREPARE Fruit-Nut Snack Bread, decreasing milk to ¾ cup
and omitting apricots and prunes. Add 3 tablespoons grated
orange rind and ¼ cup orange juice with nuts.

CANDIED ORANGE BREAD

Pillsbury Contest Winner by Mrs. Bess Atkinson, Brunswick, Ga.

*"Why not add candied orange peel to a quick bread," thought
Mrs. Atkinson—and this unusual loaf is the result! It's made
with whole wheat for extra flavor and texture.*

Makes 9x5x3-inch loaf

Sift together _____2 cups sifted enriched flour
            3 teaspoons double-acting baking powder
            1 teaspoon salt
            ¾ cup sugar.

Add _____1 cup whole wheat flour
            ¾ cup (3 oz.) candied orange peel, thinly
              sliced
            ½ cup chopped pecans.

*Combine*_____1 egg, well beaten
            1¼ cups milk
            ¼ cup melted shortening or salad oil.

*Add*_____liquid to dry ingredients and mix only
            until all flour is dampened.

*Pour*_____into well-greased 9x5x3-inch loaf pan.
            Push batter up into corners of pan, leav-
            ing the center slightly hollowed. Cut
            through batter with a spatula to break
            large air bubbles.

*Bake*_____in moderate oven (350°F.) 1 hour. Store
            overnight before slicing.

HOLIDAY CRANBERRY BREAD

Pillsbury Contest Winner by Mrs. Martin Stevlingson, Menomonie, Wis.

"Besides being delicious, it is very colorful for the holiday season," says Mrs. Stevlingson about this beautiful and fragrant fruit bread.

Makes 9x5x3-inch loaf

Sift together —— 2 cups sifted enriched flour
1 cup sugar
1½ teaspoons double-acting baking powder
½ teaspoon soda
1 teaspoon salt.

Combine —— juice and grated rind of
1 orange
2 tablespoons shortening and enough boiling water to make a total of ¾ cup.

Add —— 1 egg, well beaten.

Blend —— liquid into dry ingredients; stir only until flour mixture is dampened.

Add —— 1 cup nuts, chopped
1 cup raw cranberries, halved.

Pour —— into greased 9x5x3-inch pan. Push batter up into corners of pan, leaving the center slightly hollowed. For well-rounded loaf, allow batter to stand in pan 20 minutes before baking.

Bake —— in moderate oven (350°F.) 60 to 70 minutes. Cool thoroughly before slicing.

FLUFFY CORN BREAD

This fluffy, golden corn bread is a favorite with Northerners.
It's high, light and slightly sweet. Easy, quick to make and
very economical.

Makes 8x8x2-inch loaf

Sift together............1 cup sifted enriched flour
        3 teaspoons double-acting baking powder
        1 teaspoon salt
        2 tablespoons sugar.
Add ....1 cup corn meal.
Combine............2 eggs, slightly beaten
        1 cup milk
        ¼ cup melted shortening or salad oil
Add............liquid to dry ingredients, mixing only
        until all flour is dampened.
Pour............into well-greased 8x8x2-inch pan.
Bake............in moderately hot oven (400°F.) 30
        minutes. Serve hot with butter.

SOUTHERN CORN BREAD

Many Southerners like their corn bread creamy in color, crusty
and unsweetened. This recipe is very easy, quick and good.

Makes 12x8x2-inch loaf

Combine............2 cups corn meal
        1 teaspoon soda
        1 teaspoon salt.
Combine............1 egg, slightly beaten
        2 cups buttermilk or sour milk
        ¼ cup melted shortening or salad oil; add
        to dry ingredients. Beat until smooth.

Pour..................into hot, well-greased 12x8x2-inch pan.

Bake..................in hot oven (500°F.) 20 to 25 minutes.
Serve hot with butter.

CRACKLIN' BREAD

Pillsbury Contest Winner by Mrs. Herbert Leslie Evans, New Cumberland, W. Va.

A special kind of Southern corn bread . . . tender, tasty. Make
it with pork sausage or cracklings. Eat it hot, with or without
butter.

Makes 18 muffins or corn sticks

Brown ....¾ pound (about 1½ cups) bulk pork sausage. Drain and reserve drippings.
(Cracklings may also be used.*)

Sift together ....1 cup sifted **enriched flour**
2 cups **yellow corn meal**
3 teaspoons double-acting **baking powder**
1 teaspoon **soda**
1½ teaspoons **salt**
3 tablespoons **sugar.**

Add..................browned sausage or cracklings.

Combine..................2 **eggs,** well beaten
1 cup **buttermilk**
¼ cup **sausage drippings.**

Add..................to dry ingredients all at once; stir quickly only until all flour is dampened.

Fill..................well-greased muffin or corn stick pans
⅔ full.

Bake..................in moderately hot oven (400°F.) 12 to
15 minutes.

----

*Cracklings are the crisp, brown meat tissue left after lard is ren-
dered.

MARYLAND CORN BREAD

Pillsbury Contest Winner by Mrs. Lynn S. Strickler, Catonsville, Md.

Golden, fluffy corn bread . . . easy to make, and quick. Serve
it hot out of the oven.

Makes 9x9x2-inch loaf

Sift together ——1 cup sifted enriched flour
2 teaspoons double-acting baking powder
3 tablespoons sugar
1 teaspoon salt.

Add ——1 cup yellow corn meal.

Beat ——1 egg until light. Add
1 cup milk
¼ cup melted shortening or salad oil.

Add——liquid all at once to dry ingredients. Stir
only until all flour is dampened.

Pour——into well-greased 9x9x2-inch pan.*

Bake——in moderately hot oven (400°F.) 25 to
30 minutes. Serve warm.

———

*If desired, bread may be baked in a skillet on top of the stove.
Pour into heavy 10-inch skillet that is well greased and hot. Cover
tightly. Bake over low heat for 25 to 30 minutes.

SPOON BREAD

You bake this bread in a casserole and eat it with a fork or
spoon. It's soft and moist—a cross between bread and souffle.
Serve it hot, topped with butter, syrup or gravy.

Serves 6 to 8

Combine——1 cup corn meal and
1 cup cold water.

Add ——2 cups scalded milk; cook over boiling
water until thickened, about 5 minutes. Stir occasionally.

Combine——2 egg yolks, well beaten
1 teaspoon salt

	2 teaspoons double-acting baking powder
	2 tablespoons melted shortening or salad oil.
Add	to corn meal mixture; mix well.
Beat	2 egg whites until stiff but not dry; fold into batter.
Pour	into well-greased 2-quart casserole.
Bake	in slow oven (325°F.) 1 hour. Serve warm with butter or gravy.

SCOTCH SCONES

These rich biscuit-like scones are baked the modern way—in the oven instead of on a griddle. We often sprinkle our scones with a bit of grated lemon rind on top to add flavor. Serve them for breakfast, luncheon or afternoon coffee.

Makes 12 scones

Sift together	2 cups sifted enriched flour
	3 teaspoons double-acting baking powder
	1 teaspoon salt
	2 tablespoons sugar.
Combine	¼ cup melted shortening or salad oil
	1 egg, well beaten
	3 tablespoons milk
	½ cup sour cream blended with
	¼ teaspoon soda.
Add	liquid to dry ingredients, mixing only until all flour is dampened. Knead on floured board or pastry cloth 10 to 15 strokes.
Roll	dough to circular shape, ½ inch thick.
Sprinkle with	2 tablespoons sugar
	1 tablespoon grated lemon rind.
Cut	into 12 wedge-shaped pieces and place on greased baking sheet.
Bake	in hot oven (425°F.) 15 to 20 minutes.

Doughnuts

DOUGHNUTS *are almost an American tradition! Whether they're the cake-type made with baking powder or soda or the yeast-raised kind, they are always a favorite. In our Ann Pillsbury kitchen we have found the following "doughnut tips" helpful—we think that you will, too.*

How to Make Perfect Doughnuts

Mixing and Cutting—The dough for cake or quick dough-nuts should be soft. Chill the dough for ease in rolling. Cut the dough with a floured doughnut cutter. For variation, cut dough in strips about 1 inch wide and 3 inches long to make "Long Johns." Cake doughnuts should be allowed to stand about 15 minutes before frying.

Frying doughnuts.

Yeast-raised doughnuts should be handled much as other yeast breads. The doughnuts should rise in a warm place until almost double in bulk before frying.

Frying—Melt the shortening in a sturdy kettle. The kettle should be about half full. The temperature of the shortening is very important—it should be 375°F. If a 1-inch cube of bread browns in 60 seconds, the shortening is the correct temperature. A deep fat thermometer is very helpful in maintaining the correct temperature. When the temperature is too high, the doughnuts brown before they are thoroughly cooked—when too low, the doughnuts absorb the shortening.

Fry only a few doughnuts at a time or the shortening will cool too rapidly. Turn the doughnuts when they are brown on the underside—usually when they rise to the top of the shortening.

Drain on absorbent paper. Shake in a paper sack containing confectioners' or granulated sugar or frost with confectioners' sugar frosting.

HURRY-UP DOUGHNUTS

Cake doughnuts are the quickest kind of doughnuts to make. They taste best, of course, served hot, right out of the kettle.

Makes 2 dozen doughnuts

Sift together _____ 2 cups sifted enriched flour

2 teaspoons double-acting baking powder

½ teaspoon salt

½ teaspoon nutmeg

½ teaspoon cinnamon.

Combine _____ 2 eggs, well beaten

½ cup sugar

	2 tablespoons melted shortening or salad oil

2 tablespoons melted shortening or salad oil
1 tablespoon lemon juice
¼ cup milk.

Blend in..................dry ingredients; mix thoroughly.

Knead..................on lightly-floured board only enough to smooth surface.

Roll..................dough to ¼-inch thickness; cut with floured 2½-inch doughnut cutter.

Fry..................in deep hot fat (375°F.) until golden brown, about 2 to 3 minutes.

Drain..................on unglazed paper. Sprinkle with confectioners' sugar or brush with glaze while still warm.

ORANGE DOUGHNUTS

PREPARE Doughnuts, substituting 1 tablespoon orange juice for lemon juice and adding 1 teaspoon grated orange rind.

NUT DOUGHNUTS

PREPARE Doughnuts, adding ½ cup chopped nuts.

CHOCOLATE DOUGHNUTS

PREPARE Doughnuts, adding 1 square (1 oz.) chocolate, melted and cooled, ¼ teaspoon soda and substituting ⅓ cup sour milk or buttermilk for milk.

COUNTRY KITCHEN DOUGHNUTS

Pillsbury Contest Winner by Mrs. Ren Lyon, Cumberland, Ohio

Crisp, tender-crusted cake doughnuts . . . and they're made with mashed potatoes!

Makes about 3 dozen doughnuts

Sift together ____5 cups sifted enriched flour
4 teaspoons double-acting baking powder
1 teaspoon soda

1½ teaspoons salt
½ teaspoon cinnamon.

Measure................1 cup mashed potatoes into large bowl. Add
1½ cups sugar gradually and mix well.

Blend in................2 eggs
¼ cup melted butter; beat thoroughly.

Combine ....1 cup buttermilk or sour milk
1 teaspoon vanilla
½ teaspoon lemon extract
½ teaspoon grated lemon rind. Add alternately with sifted dry ingredients to mashed potato mixture. Blend well. Cover and let stand for 15 minutes.

Roll................dough on well-floured board to ½-inch thickness.

Cut................with 3-inch doughnut cutter.

Fry................in hot deep fat (375°F.) about 3 minutes or until golden brown on both sides. Drain on absorbent paper. Sprinkle with granulated or confectioners' sugar.

NO-KNEAD RAISED DOUGHNUTS

These light, delicate raised doughnuts are made by our simple No-Knead method. Just one rising period and no kneading. For something different, split fried doughnuts and toast under the broiler or in a hot oven. Really good!

Makes 2 dozen doughnuts

Combine ....½ cup scalded milk*
3 tablespoons shortening

---

*If desired, ½ cup scalded sour milk or buttermilk may be substituted for the sweet milk.

	¼ cup sugar
	1½ teaspoons salt.
Cool	to lukewarm by adding
	½ cup water†.
Add	1 cake compressed **yeast**, crumbled (or 1 package dry granular yeast dissolved as directed on package†); mix well.
Blend in	1 **egg**.
Add	3¼ cups sifted **enriched flour**; mix until well blended.
Roll out	on floured board to ¼-inch thickness.
Cut	with 2½-inch doughnut cutter and place on floured baking sheets.
Let rise	in warm place (85° to 90°F.) until double in bulk, about 1 hour.
Fry	in hot fat (375°F.) about 2 minutes on each side.
Drain	on absorbent paper; sprinkle with sugar or brush with glaze while still warm.

———

†The water used to dissolve dry yeast should be subtracted from water in recipe.

SPICY RAISIN DOUGHNUTS

PREPARE Doughnuts, blending in 1 cup raisins and ¼ teaspoon nutmeg before adding flour.

BISMARCKS

PREPARE Raised Doughnuts, cutting into rounds with 2½-inch round cutter. Place a heaping teaspoonful of jam or jelly in center of half of the rounds; top with remaining rounds. Seal edges well by moistening with water and pressing securely together so that none of filling will escape. Let rise and fry as for Raised Doughnuts.

COFFEE-TIME DOUGHNUTS

Pillsbury Contest Winner by Miss Loretto Yaeger, St. Louis, Mo.

"This doughnut recipe has been in my family for two genera-
tions, and is simply delicious," says Miss Yaeger. These yeast-
raised doughnuts are spiced with nutmeg.

Makes about 4 dozen doughnut strips

Dissolve..................1 cake compressed yeast (or 1 package dry
    granular yeast) in
    ¼ cup lukewarm water.

Combine..............½ cup boiling water
    2 tablespoons shortening
    ¼ cup sugar
    1½ teaspoons salt.

Cool........................to lukewarm by adding
    ½ cup fresh milk or diluted evaporated
    milk.

Blend in..............1 egg
    1 teaspoon nutmeg and dissolved yeast.
    Mix well.

Add ....3¾ cups sifted enriched flour. Mix to a soft
    dough.

Place........................dough in greased bowl, cover, and re-
    frigerate 2 to 3 hours or overnight.

Roll out..............on floured board or pastry cloth to ¼-
    inch thickness.

Cut............................into 1x3-inch strips or cut rounds with
    doughnut cutter.

Let rise..................in warm place (85° to 90°F.) until
    double in bulk, about 40 minutes.

Fry............................in hot fat (375°F.) about 2 minutes on
    each side. Drain on absorbent paper;
    sprinkle with sugar.

GOLDEN APPLE PUFFS

Pillsbury Contest Winner by Mrs. Helen Knoll, Houston, Texas

Here are apple fritters deluxe! They're golden-crusted, apple-filled puffs fried in deep fat and rolled in sugar. Eat them right away—when they're fresh and warm.

Makes about 2 dozen puffs

Sift together	2 cups sifted enriched flour
	2 teaspoons double-acting baking powder
	½ teaspoon salt
	½ teaspoon nutmeg.
Beat	2 eggs until light. Add
	1 cup milk
	½ teaspoon vanilla.
Blend in	sifted dry ingredients.
Add	1 cup peeled, diced apple.
Drop	rounded tablespoonfuls of batter into hot deep fat (375°F.) and fry on both sides until golden brown.
Drain	on absorbent paper. Roll in granulated or confectioners' sugar.

CHAPTER TWO

Yeast Breads

THERE IS *something romantic about homemade bread. Something reminiscent of grandmother's kitchen with its good fragrance of freshly-ground coffee and bread baking in the cook stove. And there aren't many things better in the way of eating than homemade bread, still warm from the oven!*

You know, contrary to what most people think, it's not hard to bake bread. We believe we have it down pat . . . down to an easy, quick method. And we've written our recipes accordingly . . . so you can take a fresh, golden-crusted loaf of bread from the oven and say, "Yes, I made it myself and it was easy!"

How to Make Perfect Yeast Breads

Mixing—When mixing the ingredients, one should remember that yeast is a plant. Hot temperatures kill yeast and cold temperatures retard its action. Combine compressed yeast with lukewarm liquids (80° to 85°F.). Dry granular yeast "works" at a higher temperature and may be dissolved in liquids of 98° to 120°F. The best way to test the temperature of the liquid is to use a candy thermometer. If one is not available, place a few drops of the liquid on the inside of the wrist. If it feels neither warm nor cold, it is about 80° to 85°F.

It is important that the yeast be evenly distributed

Fig. 1—Testing temperature of water.

throughout the dough. Blend the liquid mixture and the flour thoroughly.

No-Knead doughs are softer than kneaded doughs.

Kneading—Kneading helps to thoroughly mix the ingredients. It also develops the gluten of the flour to make light dough and, consequently, light bread.

Kneading consists of folding the dough over on itself and pushing it lightly with the palms of the hands. This process is repeated rhythmically until the dough feels satiny and smooth.

Yeast doughs are not delicate — handling actually helps to produce a finer-textured finished product.

No-Knead breads do not require kneading. This method was developed especially to eliminate kneading and was accomplished by carefully balancing the ingredients.

Fig. 2—Testing dough.

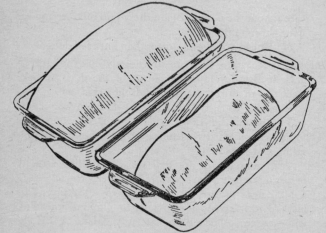

Fig. 3—Let dough rise until double in bulk.

Rising—The time needed for doughs to rise varies with the temperature of the rising place and the amount of yeast used.

Select a warm place, about 85° to 90°F., for dough to rise. Grease top of dough lightly and cover with waxed paper or a dry towel to prevent a crust from forming over the top.

Possible ways to maintain a steady warmth are:

1. Place covered bowl containing dough in a pan of warm water. Keep water warm during rising period.
2. Set a pan of hot water on bottom of unheated oven. Place dough on rack above. Keep water hot during rising.

   If your oven has a pilot light, place the covered dough in oven and keep the oven door open one or two inches.
3. Set the covered dough in a place free from drafts where there is a little warmth from a radiator or range.

The dough is light and has risen sufficiently when it appears to have doubled in bulk and one can plunge two fingers into it and the impression remains.

Shaping—Turn the dough out on a floured board or pastry cloth and mold into loaves of any desired shape. For easy handling, grease or flour hands.

When molding a loaf of bread, this procedure will help produce a well-shaped loaf:

1. Divide dough into loaf portions and shape into balls.
2. Flatten ball of dough by pressing and slapping with hands. Stretch dough in length and width.
3. Stretch dough to three times length of pan in which it is to be baked and three times the width.
4. Fold one side to center. ⎰ Press out air bubbles
5. Fold other side to overlap. ⎱ each time. This eliminates large air pockets in the bread.

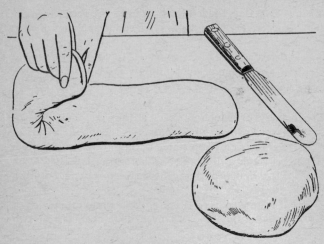

Fig. 4—Shaping the loaf (see steps 3-4).

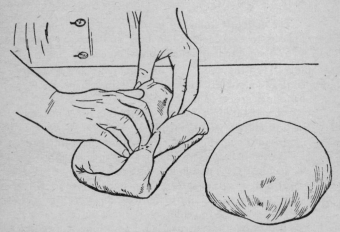

Fig. 5—Shaping the loaf (see steps 5-8).

6. Fold over both ends of dough—about ⅓ of length —and overlap in center. (Press out air bubbles.)

7. Press down and roll into loaf, sealing edge. (Press out air bubbles.)

8. Seal ends of loaf by pressing down sharply with side of hand and tucking edge under.

9. Place dough in greased pan and turn over to lightly grease all sides. Place seam-side down.

10. Dough should only half fill the pan.

Baking—Preheat oven to temperature specified in recipe before starting to bake yeast breads.

Always bake near the center of the oven and use only one rack if possible. If two racks are necessary, arrange racks as close to the center of the oven as possible, staggering and reversing position of pans during baking so all loaves brown evenly.

Bread foods are done when they are golden brown and sound hollow when thumped lightly. They should be removed from the pans when taken from the oven. The tops may be brushed lightly with shortening to prevent the crust from drying.

Storing—Cool breads thoroughly on a wire rack or across pans before placing in bread box. If desired, breads may be wrapped in waxed paper for storing.

Refrigerated Dough

ALL *No-Knead doughs and some of the other doughs in the other recipes in this book may be refrigerated. This is handy if it is not convenient to complete the baking immediately, or if one wishes to bake only half a batch.*

Dough should be mixed, then greased well, covered, and placed immediately in the refrigerator. For best results dough

*should be chilled at least two hours and not more than two days.
A constant temperature of 45° to 50° F. is most satisfactory.*

*Remove the dough from the refrigerator several hours before
serving time, for refrigerated dough requires a longer rising
period.*

HOMEMADE WHITE BREAD

**This is our own good, regular homemade bread—the kind that
requires kneading. We use this recipe again and again in our
kitchen. The rhythm of kneading is fun, once you've acquired
the knack. The bread is fine-textured, tender-crusted and
delicious.**

Makes 4 one-pound loaves*

Combine......................2 cups scalded milk
¼ cup sugar
2 tablespoons salt
¼ cup shortening.
Cool..............................to lukewarm by adding
1½ cups cold water.
Soften........................2 cakes compressed yeast (or 2 packages
dry granular yeast) in
½ cup lukewarm water. Add to milk mixture.
Blend in......11 to 12 cups sifted enriched flour.
Knead..............................dough on floured board. If dough sticks,
add a little flour to molding board. To
obtain a fine grain, knead about 5 minutes. Place dough in a greased bowl and
cover.
Let rise..........................in warm place (85° to 90°F.) until
double in bulk, about 1½ hours.
Punch down................dough by plunging the fist in center.

---

*For two loaves, divide recipe in half.

Fold edges toward center, turn upside down in bowl and cover.

Let rise................in a warm place about ½ hour.

Place................dough on floured board and divide into four pieces. Mold into balls; allow to rest, closely covered, for 15 minutes. Shape into loaves. Place in greased 9x4x3-inch bread pans and cover.

Let rise................in warm place until dough fills the pans and center is well above top, about 1¼ hours.

Bake................in moderately hot oven (375°F.) about 45 minutes.

WHOLE WHEAT BREAD

This whole wheat bread is extra good in flavor and nutrition.

Makes 2 one-pound loaves

Soften................1 cake compressed yeast (or 1 package dry granular yeast) in
1½ cups lukewarm water.

Add................2 cups sifted **enriched flour**
2 tablespoons sugar
1 tablespoon **salt**. Beat until smooth.

Let rise................in warm place (85° to 90°F.) until light and bubbly.

Combine................½ cup hot water
½ cup firmly packed **brown sugar**
3 tablespoons **shortening**. Cool to lukewarm and add to risen yeast mixture.

Add................4 cups unsifted **whole wheat** or graham flour; mix until smooth.

Knead	dough on floured board. To obtain a fine grain, knead about 7 minutes. Place dough in a greased bowl and cover.
Let rise	in a warm place (85° to 90°F.) about 1½ hours or until dough will retain the impression of finger.
Turn out	dough on well-floured board. Divide in half. Mold into two balls; let stand, closely covered, for 15 minutes. Shape into two loaves. Place in greased 9x4x3-inch bread pans and cover.
Let rise	in warm place until dough fills pan and center is well above top, about 1¼ hours.
Bake	in moderate oven (350°F.) 1 hour.

RYE BREAD

This bread has that true rye flavor. Sometimes, for a change, we add 1 to 2 tablespoons caraway seeds to the dough.

Makes 2 one-pound loaves

Combine	1 cup scalded milk 1 tablespoon salt 2 tablespoons shortening 3 tablespoons dark molasses. Cool to lukewarm.
Soften	1 cake compressed yeast (or 1 package dry granular yeast) in 1 cup lukewarm water. Add to cooled milk mixture.
Blend in	4½ cups sifted enriched flour 1½ cups unsifted rye flour.
Knead	dough on floured board. To obtain a fine grain, knead about 7 minutes. Place dough in a greased bowl and cover.
Let rise	in a warm place (85° to 90°F.) about

	1½ hours or until dough will retain the impression of finger.
Punch	dough down. Let rise in a warm place about ½ hour.
Turn out	dough on floured board and divide in half. Mold into two balls. Let stand, closely covered, for 15 minutes and shape into two long loaves. Place on greased baking sheet and cover.
Let rise	in warm place until dough is double in bulk, about 1 hour.
Brush	with egg white, diluted with 1 tablespoon water, to glaze. With sharp knife make three diagonal cuts across top of loaf.
Bake	in moderate oven (375°F.) about 45 min.

CRUSTY FRENCH BREAD

Pillsbury Contest Winner by Mrs. John Cabbell Roy, Birmingham, Ala.

"This recipe was coaxed out of a French chef in a small cafe on the road to Paris," says Mrs. Roy. "We enjoyed this bread so much that he broke down and told us his way of making this delicious, crispy, hard-crusted bread."

Makes 2 loaves

Measure	1 tablespoon shortening
	1 tablespoon salt
	2 teaspoons sugar into large bowl.
Add	1 cup boiling water; cool to lukewarm by adding
	1 cup cold water.*
Blend in	1 cake compressed yeast, crumbled (or 1 package dry granular yeast dissolved as directed on package*).

---

*The amount of water used to dissolve dry yeast should be subtracted from water specified in recipe.

Add gradually......6 cups sifted **enriched flour**; mix until dough is well blended.

Knead..................dough on lightly-floured board for 5 minutes; place in greased bowl and cover.

Let rise................in warm place (85° to 90°F.) until double in bulk, about 1½ hours.

Shape..................into long oblong loaves; place on greased baking sheet.

Let rise................until double in bulk, about 1 hour.

Brush..................with slightly beaten **egg white**. With sharp knife make three light diagonal cuts across top of loaf.

Bake..................in moderately hot oven (400°F.) 15 minutes, then at 350°F. for 45 minutes.

ITALIAN BREAD

This real Italian bread calls for only four ingredients. It's hard-crusted and delicious.

Makes 2 large loaves

Soften..................1 cake compressed **yeast** (or 1 package dry granular yeast) in
2 cups lukewarm **water**.

Add......................1 tablespoon **salt**.

Add gradually......6 cups sifted **enriched flour**; mix until dough is well blended.

Knead..................dough on lightly-floured board for 15 minutes; place in greased bowl and cover.

Let rise................in warm place (85° to 90°F.) until double in bulk, about 2 hours.

Knead..................dough for 5 minutes.

Divide..............into two pieces; shape into balls. Allow to stand closely covered for 10 minutes.

Shape..............into long oblong loaves, pointed at each end. Place on greased baking sheet.

Let rise..............in warm place until double in bulk, about 1 hour.

Bake..............in hot oven (425°F.) 10 minutes; reduce heat to moderate (350°F.) and bake for 50 minutes.

No-Knead Bread Method

WE *used to get many letters from women who said, "I'd bake bread more often if it didn't take such a long time to make!" That started us thinking. Why not develop a quick way to make good homemade bread?*

One member of our staff remembered a yeast-raised coffee cake that had been served in her home. It was an old-time recipe, one requiring no kneading. Maybe, we thought, we could adapt this no-knead method to bread baking.

Well, we did. We developed a new recipe and checked and improved it and checked it again. Now we call it a recipe for "No-Knead Bread."

It's a sweet, rich bread, more nutritious than bread made the old way. The crust is golden and tender. The moist crumb of the loaf has excellent keeping qualities and it makes rich, delicious toast. Best of all, it takes only two and one-half hours to make, from start to finish!

We developed other recipes using this quick No-Knead method, too. You'll find many of them in this chapter. They are recipes that have been tested and re-tested. Recipes that will save up to one-half of your baking time. We developed them especially for you—for easier, better, quicker bread baking. And we hope you will like them.

NO-KNEAD BREAD

This is our basic recipe for No-Knead bread. We think you'll like the beautifully shaped loaves, the rich creamy color inside and delicious flavor of this easily-prepared bread.

Makes 3 loaves

Combine............1½ cups scalded milk
   ½ cup shortening
   ¼ cup sugar
   4 teaspoons salt.

Cool............to lukewarm by adding
   1½ cups water.*

Add............3 cakes compressed yeast, crumbled (or 3 packages dry granular yeast dissolved as directed on package*); mix well.

Blend in............3 eggs

Add............9 to 10 cups sifted enriched flour; mix until well blended. Cover and let stand for 15 minutes. No-Knead dough may or may not be chilled. If dough is to be chilled, place in greased bowl, cover, and store in refrigerator at least 2 hours.

Shape............dough (chilled or unchilled) into three loaves on well-floured board. Place in greased 9x4x3-inch pans and cover.

Let rise............in warm place (85° to 90°F.) until double in bulk; allow about 1 hour for unchilled dough, about 1½ to 2 hours for chilled dough.

Bake............in moderate oven (350°F.) 1 hour.

---

*The water used to dissolve dry yeast should be subtracted from water in recipe.

Mixer Method—When using electric mixer, add half the flour to liquid ingredients and mix 1 minute at low speed. Add remaining flour and mix by hand.

NO-KNEAD PARTY BREAD

Nut, raisin, cheese, cinnamon or fruit . . . take your choice of these No-Knead breads. Quick to make; less than three hours turns the trick. These breads make excellent lunchbox sandwiches—for lunch or supper serve toasted slices of cheese bread with your favorite creamed vegetable or meat topping.

Makes 1 loaf

Combine ½ cup scalded milk
3 tablespoons shortening
1 tablespoon sugar
1½ teaspoons salt.

Cool to lukewarm by adding
½ cup water.*

Add 1 cake compressed yeast, crumbled (or 1 package dry granular yeast dissolved as directed on package*); mix well.

Blend in 1 egg
½ cup chopped nuts.

Add 3¼ cups sifted enriched flour; mix until well blended. Cover and let stand for 15 minutes.

Shape dough into loaf on well-floured board; place in greased 9x4x3-inch pan and cover.

Let rise in warm place (85° to 90°F.) until double in bulk, about 1 hour.

Bake in moderate oven (350°F.) 1 hour.

*The water used to dissolve dry yeast should be subtracted from water in recipe.

SPICY RAISIN BREAD

PREPARE Party Bread, omitting chopped nuts and blending in 1 cup raisins and 1 teaspoon cinnamon.

CHEESE BREAD

PREPARE Party Bread, omitting chopped nuts and blending in
1 cup grated cheese.

CINNAMON RAISIN BREAD

PREPARE Party Bread, omitting chopped nuts. Roll dough to
16x8-inch rectangle. Sprinkle with ¼ cup sugar, 1 cup raisins
and 2 teaspoons cinnamon. Roll as for jelly roll, starting with
8-inch edge; seal edges and place in greased 9x4x3-inch pan.

FESTIVE FRUIT BREAD

PREPARE Party Bread, decreasing chopped nuts to ¼ cup and
adding ¼ cup of each of the following: diced citron, raisins,
chopped candied cherries.

HONEY BRUNCH LOAF

*Bread and honey have never been better. Toast a few slices of
this loaf for breakfast—or serve with fruit salad for lunch.*

Makes 1 loaf

Prepare............................dough for No-Knead Party Bread, omit-
　　　　　　　　　　　　ting the chopped nuts.

Roll.................................dough to a 14x9-inch rectangle.

Spread............................1 tablespoon melted **butter**
　　　　　　　　　　　　2 tablespoons sugar
　　　　　　　　　　　　1 teaspoon **cinnamon** over dough.

Roll.................................as for jelly roll and place in well-greased
　　　　　　　　　　　　9½x5½x3-inch pan.

Slash..............................deep gashes crosswise almost to center
　　　　　　　　　　　　of loaf with greased knife. Cut about 1
　　　　　　　　　　　　inch apart. Then cut lengthwise through
　　　　　　　　　　　　center of loaf.

Combine.........................2 tablespoons strained **honey**
　　　　　　　　　　　　1 tablespoon melted **butter**.

Drip over loaf, filling gashes.

Let rise...............in warm place (85° to 90°F.) until double
in bulk, 45 minutes to 1 hour.

Bake...............in moderate oven (350°F.) 50 minutes.

NO-KNEAD WHOLE WHEAT BREAD

This simple recipe turns out wonderful, full-of-flavor whole
wheat bread. For variety, try substituting ¼ cup light molasses
for the ¼ cup brown sugar.

Makes 2 loaves

Combine...............1 cup scalded milk
⅓ cup shortening
¼ cup brown sugar
1 tablespoon salt.

Cool...............to lukewarm by adding
1 cup water.*

Add...............2 cakes compressed yeast, crumbled (or 2
packages dry granular yeast dissolved as
directed on package*); mix well.

Blend in...............2 eggs
3 cups unsifted whole wheat flour.

Add gradually...3½ cups sifted enriched flour; mix until
well blended. Cover and let stand for 15
minutes.

Shape...............dough into two loaves on well-floured
board. Place in greased 9x4x3-inch pans
and cover.

Let rise...............in warm place (85° to 90°F.) until double
in bulk, about 1 hour.

Bake...............in moderate oven (350°F.) 1 hour.

---

*The water used to dissolve dry yeast should be subtracted from water
in recipe.

NO-KNEAD RYE BREAD

This is one of the easiest and quickest recipes we know for making good old-fashioned rye bread.

Makes 1 loaf

Combine............½ cup scalded milk
2 tablespoons shortening
1 tablespoon molasses or brown sugar
2 teaspoons salt.

Cool............to lukewarm by adding
½ cup water.*

Add............1 cake compressed yeast, crumbled (or 1 package dry granular yeast dissolved as directed on package*); mix well.

Blend in............1 egg.

Add............1¾ cups sifted enriched flour
1½ cups unsifted rye flour; mix until dough is well blended. Cover and let stand for 15 minutes.

Shape............dough into a long loaf. Place on greased baking sheet and cover.

Let rise............in warm place (85° to 90°F.) until double in bulk, about 1 hour.

Brush............with egg white, diluted with 1 tablespoon water, to glaze. With sharp knife make three diagonal cuts across top of loaf.

Bake............in moderate oven (350°F.) 1 hour.

---

*The water used to dissolve dry yeast should be subtracted from water in recipe.

NO-KNEAD OATMEAL BREAD

You'll find this oatmeal bread moist, rich-flavored and excellent in keeping qualities.

Makes 2 loaves

Combine................2 cups boiling water*
                1 cup rolled oats
                ⅓ cup shortening
                ½ cup light molasses
                1 tablespoon salt. Cool to lukewarm.

Add................2 cakes compressed yeast, crumbled (or 2 packages dry granular yeast dissolved as directed on package*); mix well.

Blend in................2 eggs.

Add gradually...5½ cups sifted enriched flour; mix until well blended. Place dough in greased bowl and cover.

Store................in refrigerator at least 2 hours.

Shape................chilled dough into two loaves on well-floured board. Place in greased 9x4x3-inch pans and cover.

Let rise................in warm place (85° to 90°F.) until double in bulk, about 2 hours.

Bake................in moderate oven (350°F.) 1 hour.

*The water used to dissolve dry yeast should be subtracted from water in recipe.

NO-KNEAD PINWHEEL BREAD

Whole wheat dough makes dark swirls in the white part of this attractive bread. It's hard to believe, but it's really a simple matter to shape this loaf.

Makes 2 loaves

WHITE DOUGH

Combine————— ½ cup scalded milk
3 tablespoons shortening
1 tablespoon sugar
1½ teaspoons salt.

Cool—————to lukewarm by adding
½ cup water.*

Add—————1 cake compressed yeast, crumbled (or 1 package dry granular yeast dissolved as directed on package*); mix well.

Blend in—————1 egg.

Add—————3¼ cups sifted enriched flour; mix until well blended. Place in greased bowl, cover and store in refrigerator at least 2 hours.

WHOLE WHEAT DOUGH

Combine————— ½ cup scalded milk
3 tablespoons shortening
¼ cup dark molasses
1½ teaspoons salt.

Cool—————to lukewarm by adding
½ cup water.*

Add—————1 cake compressed yeast, crumbled (or 1 package dry granular yeast dissolved as directed on package*); mix well.

———————
*The water used to dissolve dry yeast should be subtracted from water in recipe.

Blend in	1 egg.
Add	3¼ cups unsifted whole wheat flour; mix until well blended. Place in greased bowl, cover and store in refrigerator at least 2 hours.

Directions for Making Pinwheel

Roll out	half of white dough to 12x8-inch rectangle. Roll out half of whole wheat dough to 12x8-inch rectangle and place on top of white dough.
Roll	as for jelly roll, beginning with 8-inch edge. Seal ends and place in greased 9x4x3-inch pan and cover. Repeat the process using the remainder of the white and whole wheat dough for second loaf.
Let rise	in warm place (85° to 90°F.) until double in bulk, about 2 hours.
Bake	in moderate oven (350°F.) 1 hour.

CHAPTER THREE

Dinner Rolls • Sweet Rolls
and
Coffee Cakes

Dinner Rolls

FRESH, HOT DINNER ROLLS, *right out of the oven, taste as good at a simple luncheon as they do at a formal dinner. Make easy pan rolls when you're in a hurry. When you have more time and want something fancy, try shaping knots, braids, crescents or cloverleafs.*

How to Reheat Rolls

ROLLS, PLAIN OR SWEET, *are best when they're served warm. When you've made a large recipe and have some left over, you may want to reheat them before serving again. You can place them in the top of a double boiler and heat over water until they are warmed through. Or, you can place the rolls in a dampened paper bag. Heat in a slow oven until the bag is dry. Of course, if you own a bun warmer . . . just follow suggestions given with the equipment.*

NO-KNEAD RICH DINNER ROLLS

Here are light, fine-textured dinner rolls you can make the No-Knead way. Dough may be kept overnight in the refrigerator. So you can make up a double recipe, if you like. Use one-half of the dough for one batch of rolls and refrigerate the rest of the dough for later baking.

Makes 14 to 16 rolls

Combine............½ cup scalded **milk**
¼ cup **shortening**
2 tablespoons **sugar**
1½ teaspoons **salt**.

Cool............to lukewarm by adding
½ cup **water**.*

Add............1 cake compressed **yeast**, crumbled (or 1 package dry granular yeast dissolved as directed on package*); mix well.

Blend in............1 **egg**.

Add gradually...3¼ cups sifted **enriched flour**; mix until well blended. Cover and let stand for 15 minutes. No-Knead dough may or may not be chilled. If dough is to be chilled, place in greased bowl, cover and store in refrigerator at least 2 hours.

Shape............dough (chilled or unchilled) on well-floured board into rolls. (See shaping suggestions, pages 54-57.)

Let rise............in warm place (85° to 90°F.) until double in bulk; allow about 1 hour for unchilled dough, about 1½ to 2 hours for chilled dough.

Bake............in moderately hot oven (400°F.) 15 to 20 minutes.

---

*The water used to dissolve dry yeast should be subtracted from water in recipe.

NO-KNEAD SPEEDY PAN ROLLS

You can think of these simple dinner rolls one minute . . .
serve them one and a half hours later. No kneading, of course.
Shape as directed on page 55.

Makes 2 dozen rolls

*Combine*_____1 cup lukewarm water*
⅓ cup melted shortening
1 tablespoon sugar
2 teaspoons salt.

*Add*_____2 cakes compressed yeast, crumbled (or 2
packages dry granular yeast dissolved as
directed on package*); mix well.

*Blend in*_____1 egg.

Add gradually...3½ cups sifted enriched flour; mix until
well blended. Cover and let stand for 15
minutes.

*Roll out*_____on well-floured board and fit into greased
12x8x2-inch pan.

*Cut*_____dough into 4x1-inch rectangles with
knife which has been dipped in melted
butter.

*Let rise*_____in warm place (85° to 90°F.) until
double in bulk, about 30 minutes.

*Bake*_____in moderately hot oven (400°F.) 20
minutes.

---

*The water used to dissolve dry yeast should be subtracted from water
in recipe.

REFRIGERATOR ROLLS

You can mix up these dinner rolls, store them in the refrigerator and have them all ready to bake for company the next day. Any of our ideas on pages 54-57 may be used for shaping.

Makes 18 medium-sized rolls

Combine................½ cup scalded milk
                      ¼ cup sugar
                      3 tablespoons shortening
                      1½ teaspoons salt.

Cool................to lukewarm by adding
                      ¼ cup water.

Dissolve................1 cake compressed yeast (or 1 package dry granular yeast) in
                      ¼ cup lukewarm water.

Add................1 egg and dissolved yeast to milk mixture.

Blend in................3½ cups sifted enriched flour. Mix until well blended.

Knead................on lightly-floured board about 5 minutes until dough is smooth and elastic. Place dough in greased bowl and cover.

Let rise................in warm place (85° to 90°F.) until double in bulk, about 1 hour.

Punch................dough down. Turn over in bowl and grease top lightly.

Cover................with waxed paper; tie securely.

Store................in refrigerator until needed (not longer than 2 days).

Shape................chilled dough as desired (see shaping instructions, pages 54-57). Cover and let rise in warm place until double in bulk, about 2 hours.

Bake................in moderately hot oven (400°F.) 15 minutes.

Fig. 1—HOW TO SHAPE SANDWICH SQUARES AND DINNER ROLLS

SQUARES: Roll or pat dough to 12x9 inch rectangle. Cut dough into twelve 3-inch squares with a greased knife. Place on greased baking sheet.
ROLLS: Shape each square into a round roll by tucking the corners under. Place in greased muffin pans.

Fig. 2—HOW TO SHAPE SPEEDY CLOVERS

Form dough into round balls, about 2 inches in diameter. Place in greased muffin pans. With scissors cut rolls in half, then in quarters, cutting almost to bottom of roll. Brush with butter.

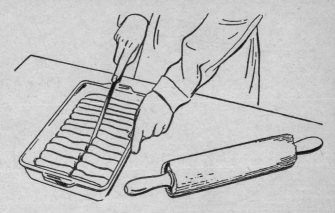

Fig. 3—HOW TO SHAPE SPEEDY PAN ROLLS

Roll or pat dough and fit into greased 12x8x2-inch pan. With greased knife cut crosswise at 1-inch intervals. Then cut lengthwise down center of dough.

Fig. 4—HOW TO SHAPE CLOVERLEAF ROLLS

Shape dough into small, round balls, about 1 inch in diameter. Place three balls in each cup of greased muffin pans. Brush with butter.

Fig. 1—HOW TO SHAPE PARKER HOUSE ROLLS

Roll dough on lightly floured board to ¼-inch thickness. Cut into rounds with 2½-inch cutter. Stretch each round slightly into oval; brush with melted butter. Fold over to make half circle; press edge to seal. Place on greased baking sheet.

Fig. 2—HOW TO SHAPE CRESCENTS

Divide dough into two parts. Roll each into circular shape, about ¼ inch thick. Cut each round into eight wedges. Roll each wedge, starting with wide end and rolling to point. Place on greased baking sheet, point side down, and curve ends to form crescent shape.

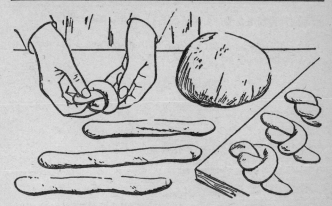

Fig. 3—HOW TO SHAPE KNOTS

Roll small pieces of dough into strips ½ inch in diameter, 9 inches long. Tie each strip into a loose knot. Place on greased baking sheet.

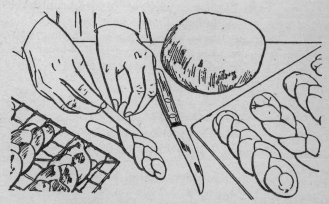

Fig. 4—HOW TO SHAPE BRAIDS

Roll dough to ¼-inch thickness. Cut into strips, ½ inch wide and 5 inches long. Seal ends of three strips; braid and fasten ends. Place on greased baking sheet.

NO-KNEAD CRUSTY SALAD ROLLS

These crusty hard rolls are tasty, filling, satisfying. Make them
dainty round balls or shape them into crusty bread sticks.

Makes 3 dozen rolls

*Soften*_____1 cake compressed yeast (or 1 package dry
granular yeast) in
1 cup lukewarm water.

*Add*_____¼ cup melted shortening
1 tablespoon sugar
2 teaspoons salt.

*Blend in*_____2 egg whites.

*Add gradually*___3½ cups sifted enriched flour; mix until
well blended. Cover and let stand for 15
minutes.

*Shape*_____dough into 3 dozen small, round balls.
Place on greased baking sheet.

*Let rise*_____in warm place (85° to 90°F.) until double
in bulk, about 1 hour.

*Fill*_____large, shallow pan with boiling water
and place on bottom shelf of oven.

*Bake*_____rolls in moderately hot oven (400°F.) 15
minutes.

HERB BREAD STICKS

PREPARE Crusty Salad Rolls, adding ½ teaspoon nutmeg, 1 teaspoon leaf sage and 2 teaspoons caraway seeds with shortening.
Divide dough into 3 dozen small pieces; roll each piece between
hands into cylindrical strips, 8 inches long. Place on greased
baking sheet, 1 inch apart. Let rise and bake as directed.

CRUSTY DINNER ROLLS

BEST OF CLASS WINNER
Pillsbury's 1st Recipe Contest
by Mrs. C. Arthur Reseland, Des Moines, Iowa

There's a crisp crust on the outside of these tender rolls.

Makes about 2 dozen rolls

*Measure*_____ 1 tablespoon sugar
1½ teaspoons salt
2 tablespoons shortening
½ cup boiling water into large bowl.

*Add*_____ ½ cup cold water.*

*Crumble in*_____ 1 cake compressed yeast (or add 1 package dry granular yeast dissolved in ¼ cup lukewarm water*).

*Add*_____ 1 cup sifted enriched flour
2 egg whites, stiffly beaten; mix thoroughly.

*Blend in*_____ 2¾ cups sifted enriched flour; mix thoroughly.

*Knead*_____ dough on lightly-floured board for 5 minutes; place in greased bowl and cover.

*Let rise*_____ in warm place (85° to 90°F.) until double in bulk, about 1 hour.

*Punch down*_____ dough by plunging the fist in center. Fold edges toward center, turn upside down in bowl and cover.

*Let rise*_____ again in warm place until double in bulk, about ½ hour.

*Shape*_____ dough on floured board into round or oval-shaped rolls.

*The water used to dissolve dry yeast should be subtracted from water in recipe.

Dip bottoms in corn meal and place on greased baking sheet.

Let rise............in warm place (85° to 90°F.) until double in bulk, about 1 hour.

Combine............1 egg yolk

2 teaspoons water; brush over tops of rolls.

Bake............rolls in moderately hot oven (400°F.) 20 to 25 minutes. (Place shallow pan filled with boiling water on bottom shelf of oven to give rolls crustiness.)

PINWHEEL DINNER ROLLS

Pillsbury Contest Winner by Mrs. Frank A. Grenier, Dorchester, Mass.

You shape these dinner rolls simply by rolling the dough jelly-roll style, and slicing. No trick to it!

Makes about 18 rolls

Combine............2 tablespoons sugar

1½ teaspoons salt

3 tablespoons shortening in large bowl.

Add............½ cup boiling water.* Stir until dissolved.

Cool............to lukewarm by adding

½ cup milk.

Add............1 cake compressed yeast, crumbled (or 1 package dry granular yeast dissolved in ¼ cup lukewarm water*); mix well.

Blend in............3 cups sifted enriched flour and mix thoroughly. Place in greased bowl; cover.

Let rise............in warm place (85° to 90°F.) until double in bulk, about 45 to 60 minutes.

Place............dough on lightly-floured board and knead about 20 strokes.

*The water used to dissolve dry yeast should be subtracted from water in recipe.

Roll out.................to 1-inch thickness and pound with rolling pin about 50 strokes.

Roll out.................to ½-inch thickness until about 18 inches long. Roll as for jelly roll, starting with 18-inch edge.

Cut.................into 1-inch slices. Place on greased baking sheet.

Let rise.................until double in bulk, about 30 to 45 minutes.

Bake.................in moderately hot oven (400°F.) 12 to 15 minutes.

OLD PLANTATION ROLLS

Pillsbury Contest Winner by Mrs. William Edwin Baker, Colorado Springs, Colo.

You don't have to knead these rich, tender, cloverleaf rolls. And you can store the dough in your refrigerator if you like ... then bake fresh rolls as needed.

Makes 24 large rolls

Combine.................1 cup scalded milk
¼ cup sugar
½ cup shortening.

Cool.................to lukewarm by adding
1 cup water.*

Add.................1 egg, unbeaten
1 cake compressed yeast, crumbled (or 1 package dry granular yeast dissolved as directed on package*); mix well.

Blend in.................3 cups sifted enriched flour; let stand 20 minutes.

Sift together.....2½ cups sifted enriched flour
1 teaspoon double-acting baking powder
½ teaspoon soda

---

*The water used to dissolve dry yeast should be subtracted from water in recipe.

1½ teaspoons **salt**. Add to soft dough. Place in lightly-greased bowl; cover.

Let rise................in warm place (85° to 90°F.) about 1 hour.

Shape................dough into 24 cloverleaf rolls. Place in greased muffin cups.

Let rise................in warm place until light, about 1 hour.

Bake................in moderately hot oven (400°F.) 15 to 20 minutes.

NO-KNEAD ENGLISH MUFFINS

Now you can make your own English muffins. No oven baking is required. Just bake on a griddle on top of the range. (English muffins keep well, too.) Split them—toast and serve with marmalade!

Makes 10 to 12 muffins

Combine...............½ cup scalded milk
                      ¼ cup shortening
                      1½ teaspoons salt
                      1 tablespoon sugar.

Cool...............to lukewarm by adding
                      ½ cup water.*

Add...............1 cake compressed yeast, crumbled (or 1
                      package dry granular yeast dissolved as
                      directed on package*); mix well.

Add...............3 cups sifted enriched flour; mix until well
                      blended. Cover, let stand 15 minutes.

Roll out...............on floured board to ¼-inch thickness.
                      Cut into rounds with 3½-inch cutter.

Place...............on baking sheet which has been sprin-
                      kled with 2 tablespoons corn meal.
                      Sprinkle tops of muffins with additional
                      2 tablespoons corn meal.

Let rise...............in warm place (85° to 90°F.) until
                      double in bulk, about 1 hour.

Bake...............slowly on hot ungreased griddle, about
                      7 minutes on each side.

Split...............muffins, toast cut sides and serve with
                      butter and marmalade.

---

*The water used to dissolve dry yeast should be subtracted from water
in recipe.

NO-KNEAD POTATO PUFF ROLLS

**These easy-to-make rolls are especially light and fluffy, tender
and delicious. (There really is potato in the dough.)**

Makes 2 dozen rolls

Combine...............1 cup scalded milk*

---

*The amount of water used to dissolve dry yeast should be subtracted
from milk specified in recipe.

                      3 tablespoons shortening
                      1 tablespoon sugar
                      2 teaspoons salt.
                      Cool to lukewarm.
*Add*_____1 cake compressed yeast, crumbled (or 1
                      package dry granular yeast dissolved as
                      directed on package*); mix well.
*Blend in*_____2 eggs
                      1 cup cooked, mashed potatoes.
*Add gradually*_____4 cups sifted enriched flour; mix until
                      well blended. Cover, let stand 15 min.
*Shape*_____dough into 2 dozen small, round balls.
                      Place on greased baking sheet.
*Let rise*_____in warm place (85° to 90°F.) until
                      double in bulk, about 1 hour.
*Bake*_____in moderately hot oven (400°F.) 15 to
                      20 minutes.

NO-KNEAD BRIOCHE

**You merely follow this recipe and you can turn out the French
pastry shop favorite—tender, rich, delicious brioche.**

Makes 18 rolls

*Combine*_____1 cup scalded milk*
                      ¼ cup shortening
                      ¼ cup sugar
                      2 teaspoons salt.
                      Cool to lukewarm.
*Add*_____1 cake compressed yeast, crumbled (or 1
                      package dry granular yeast dissolved as
                      directed on package*); mix well.
*Blend in*_____2 eggs.

----

*The amount of water used to dissolve dry yeast should be subtracted
from milk specified in recipe.

Add_____3½ cups sifted enriched flour; mix until well blended. Cover and let stand for 15 minutes.

Shape_____three-fourths of dough into 18 medium rolls. Place in greased muffin pans. Press large indentation in center of each roll and brush with melted shortening.

Divide_____remainder of dough into 18 equal parts; shape into small balls and press into indentations in rolls.

Let rise_____in warm place (85° to 90°F.) until double in bulk, about 1 hour.

Bake_____in moderate oven (375°F.) 20 minutes.

NO-KNEAD ORANGE-RAISIN BRAIDS

These braids are sweet enough to enjoy with your morning coffee, not too sweet to serve with a salad for lunch. They're easy to make the modern, No-Knead way!

Makes 18 braids

Combine_____½ cup scalded milk
¼ cup shortening
2 tablespoons sugar
1½ teaspoons salt.

Cool_____to lukewarm by adding
½ cup water.*

Add_____1 cake compressed yeast, crumbled (or 1 package dry granular yeast dissolved as directed on package*); mix well.

Blend in_____1 egg
2 tablespoons grated orange rind
¾ cup raisins.

_____
*The water used to dissolve dry yeast should be subtracted from water in recipe.

Add gradually...3¼ cups sifted enriched flour; mix until well blended. Cover and let stand for 15 minutes.

*Roll*_____dough to ¼-inch thickness.

*Cut*_____into ½-inch strips, 5 inches long. Seal top ends of three strips; braid and fasten ends. Place on greased baking sheet.

*Let rise*_____in warm place (85° to 90°F.) until double in bulk, about 1 hour.

*Bake*_____in moderately hot oven (400°F.) 15 minutes.

DATE-CARAWAY KNOTS

PREPARE Orange-Raisin Braids, omitting orange rind and raisins. Blend in ¾ cup dates, finely chopped, and 1 tablespoon caraway seeds with egg. Add flour and let stand as directed. Roll small pieces of dough into strips ½-inch in diameter, about 9 inches long. Tie in knots. Place on greased baking sheet. Let rise and bake as directed.

DANISH GINGER ROLLS

Pillsbury Contest Winner by Mrs. Edwin T. Tracy, Ogden, Utah

There's just a hint of ginger in these Parker House rolls—and a rich delicacy so often found in Scandinavian baking.

Makes about 18 rolls

*Dissolve*_____1 cake compressed yeast (or 1 package dry granular yeast) in
¼ cup lukewarm water.

*Beat*_____2 eggs in large bowl until light and fluffy.

*Blend in*_____½ cup milk
2 tablespoons melted butter or shortening
3 tablespoons sugar

	1½ teaspoons **ginger**
	1½ teaspoons **salt** and dissolved yeast. Mix well.
Add	3 cups sifted **enriched flour**. Mix to a soft dough. Place in greased bowl. Cover.
Let rise	in warm place (85° to 90°F.) until double in bulk, about 1 hour. Punch dough down.
Let rise	in warm place until double in bulk, about 30 minutes.
Roll	out on lightly floured board to about ¼-inch thickness. Cut into rounds with 3-inch cutter. Brush with melted **butter**. Mark a crease with dull edge of knife to one side of center of each round. Fold small part over large; press edge to seal. Place on greased baking sheet.
Let rise	in warm place about 30 minutes.
Bake	in moderately hot oven (400°F.) 15 to 20 minutes.

OLD-FASHIONED WHEAT ROLLS

Pillsbury Contest Winner by Mrs. Wallace Baker, Great Falls, Montana

This is a generous recipe for fluffy, fresh-from-the-oven wheat rolls. Refrigerate half the dough, if you wish, and bake it later.

Makes about 4 dozen rolls

Dissolve	2 cakes compressed **yeast** (or 2 packages dry granular yeast) in
	½ cup lukewarm **water**.
Combine	⅓ cup **shortening**
	½ cup **sugar**
	2 teaspoons **salt**
	¾ cup boiling **water**

	¾ cup evaporated milk (or omit water and use 1½ cups fresh, scalded milk). Cool to lukewarm.
Add	1 beaten egg and the dissolved yeast.
Blend in	2½ cups sifted enriched flour ¾ cup whole wheat flour or wheat germ. Beat until smooth.
Add	3 cups sifted enriched flour; mix thoroughly.*
Knead	dough on lightly-floured board until smooth, about 5 minutes. Place in greased bowl. Cover.
Let rise	in warm place (85° to 90°F.) until about double in bulk, 50 to 60 minutes.
Shape	dough into round or cloverleaf rolls. Place in greased pans or muffin tins.
Let rise	in warm place (85° to 90°F.) until about double in bulk.
Bake	in moderate oven (375°F.) 20 to 25 minutes for pan rolls, 15 to 20 minutes for cloverleaf rolls.

*If desired, part of the dough may be tightly covered and kept in refrigerator for later baking. For best results, do not refrigerate more than 2 days.

PARKER HOUSE WHEAT ROLLS

Pillsbury Contest Winner by Mrs. A. L. Morrison, New Orleans, Louisiana

The delicate brown of whole wheat adds flavor and texture to these delicious "pocketbook" rolls.

Makes 24 rolls

Combine	2 cups sifted enriched flour 1 cup whole wheat flour.
Cream	½ cup shortening ¼ cup sugar

	1½ teaspoons salt in large bowl.
Blend in	½ cup boiling water; cool to lukewarm.
Dissolve	1 cake compressed yeast (or 1 package dry granular yeast) in
	½ cup lukewarm water. Add to shortening-sugar liquid.
Blend in	1 egg, well beaten, and sifted dry ingredients; mix well. Place in greased bowl. Cover.
Let rise	in warm place (85° to 90°F.) until double in bulk, about 1 to 1½ hours.
Roll	out on lightly-floured board to ¼-inch thickness. Cut into rounds with 3-inch cutter and brush with melted butter. Mark a crease with dull edge of knife to one side of center of each round. Fold small part over large, press edges to seal and place in greased pan. Tops may be brushed with butter.
Let rise	in warm place until double in bulk, about 1 hour.
Bake	in moderately hot oven (400°F.) 12 to 15 minutes.

NO-KNEAD GOLDEN CORN MEAL ROLLS

Crisp on the outside, light and fluffy inside! These dinner rolls have a delightful crunchiness and color.

Makes 18 medium rolls

Combine	¼ cup corn meal
	¼ cup shortening
	1 tablespoon sugar
	1½ teaspoons salt.
Add	½ cup scalded milk.

*Cool*_____to lukewarm by adding
½ cup water.*

*Add*_____1 cake compressed yeast, crumbled (or 1 package dry granular yeast dissolved as directed on package*); mix well.

*Blend in*_____1 egg.

*Add gradually*_____3 cups sifted enriched flour; mix until well blended. Cover and let stand for 15 minutes.

*Shape*_____dough on well-floured board into 18 medium rolls. Dip rolls first in egg white, then in corn meal. Place in greased muffin pans.

*Let rise*_____in warm place (85° to 90°F.) until double in bulk, about 1 hour.

*Bake*_____in moderately hot oven (400°F.) 20 min.

---

*The water used to dissolve dry yeast should be subtracted from water in recipe.

CORN MEAL SANDWICH BUNS

ROLL dough on well-floured board to 16x8-inch rectangle. Cut into 16 small 4x2-inch rectangles. Place on greased baking sheet. Brush with unbeaten egg white; sprinkle with corn meal. Let rise in warm place (85° to 90°F.) until double in bulk. Bake in moderately hot oven (375°F.) 20 minutes.

THREE-WAY DINNER ROLLS

Pillsbury Contest Winner by Mrs. L. J. Wipperfurth, Madison, Wis.

You get a section of plain roll, wheat roll and corn meal roll in every one of these unusual cloverleafs.

Makes 24 rolls

*Combine*_____1 cake compressed yeast (or 1 package dry granular yeast) and

2 cups lukewarm water in large bowl. Stir until dissolved.

Add............⅓ cup sugar

1 tablespoon salt

⅓ cup melted shortening

2 beaten eggs

3 cups sifted enriched flour; beat until smooth.

Divide............dough into 3 equal parts.

Add TO FIRST PART: ½ cup yellow corn meal and

½ cup sifted enriched flour

TO SECOND PART: 1 cup whole wheat flour

TO THIRD PART: 1 cup sifted enriched flour.

Let rise............in warm place (85° to 90°F.) until double in bulk, about 1 hour. Punch dough down, then let rise about 30 min.

Shape............into cloverleaf rolls, placing one ball of each dough in greased muffin cups. Shape corn meal dough first, then whole wheat, then white dough.

Let rise............in warm place until double in bulk, about 1 hour.

Bake............in moderately hot oven (400°F.) 15 to 20 minutes.

NO-KNEAD ONION BARBECUE BUNS

Onions are chopped, browned and blended right into the dough for these buns. Perfect with hot dogs and hamburgers!

Makes 12 to 14 buns

Combine............½ cup scalded milk

¼ cup shortening

1 tablespoon sugar

1½ teaspoons salt.

*Cool*_____to lukewarm by adding
½ cup water.*

*Add*_____1 cake compressed yeast, crumbled (or 1 package dry granular yeast dissolved as directed on package*); mix well.

*Blend in*_____1 egg
¾ cup chopped onions lightly browned in butter.

*Add gradually*_____3 cups sifted enriched flour; mix until well blended. Cover and let stand for 15 minutes.

Square Buns_____Roll or pat dough to 12x9-inch rectangle. Cut into 12 three-inch squares. Place on greased baking sheet.

Round Rolls_____Roll or pat dough to 12x9-inch rectangle. Cut into 12 three-inch squares with greased knife. Shape each square into round roll by tucking corners under. Place in greased muffin pans.

Frankfurter Buns____Divide dough into 12 parts, then shape into long, narrow buns. Place on greased baking sheet.

*Let rise*_____in warm place (85° to 90°F.) until double in bulk, about 1 hour.

*Bake*_____in moderately hot oven (400°F.) 15 minutes.

_____
*The water used to dissolve dry yeast should be subtracted from water in recipe.

HERB PICNIC BUNS

PREPARE Onion Barbecue Buns, substituting ½ teaspoon celery seed, ½ teaspoon onion salt, ½ teaspoon dry mustard for browned onions.

CHEESE SANDWICH SQUARES

PREPARE Onion Barbecue Buns, substituting 1 cup grated cheese for browned onions.

HATTIE'S GARDEN CRESCENTS

Pillsbury Contest Winner by Mrs. Hattie Boutilier, Readfield, Me.

These tangy dinner rolls have vegetables and a speck of herb
blended right into the dough.

Makes about 16 crescents

*Dissolve*_____1 cake compressed yeast (or 1 package dry
granular yeast) in
¼ cup lukewarm water.

*Combine*_____¼ cup shortening
1 tablespoon sugar
1½ teaspoons salt
½ cup boiling water. Stir until dissolved.

*Cool*_____to lukewarm by adding
½ cup tomato juice.

*Blend in*_____1 tablespoon each: grated **onion, celery,
carrot**

½ teaspoon each: **garlic salt, sage.** Add dissolved yeast.

Measure————3½ cups sifted **enriched flour.** Add 2 cups of the flour and beat thoroughly. Then add remainder of flour and mix well.

Knead————dough 5 to 7 minutes on floured board.

Let rise————in warm place (85° to 90°F.) until double in bulk, 45 to 60 minutes.

Divide————dough into two parts. Roll each on lightly floured board to circular shape about ¼ inch thick.

Sprinkle with————grated **Parmesan cheese.**

Cut————each round into 8 wedges. If desired, 1 drop tabasco sauce may be added to each wedge. Roll each wedge, starting with wide end and rolling to point. Place on greased baking sheet, point-side down, and curve ends to form crescent shape.

Let rise————in warm place until light, about 45 to 60 minutes.

Bake————in moderately hot oven (400°F.) 12 to 15 minutes.

COCKTAIL TWIRL-UPS

The filling for these tiny hors d'oeuvres may be an olive spread or cheese, chopped nuts or deviled ham.

Makes 8 dozen twirl-ups

Soften————1 cake compressed **yeast** (or 1 package dry granular yeast) in

½ cup lukewarm **water.**

Add————¼ cup melted **shortening**

2 teaspoons **sugar**

1 teaspoon **salt.**

*Blend in*_____1 egg.

*Add gradually*__2¼ cups sifted **enriched flour**; mix until well blended. Cover and let stand for 15 min.

*Divide*_____dough into 3 equal parts. Roll each to 16x5-inch rectangle, ⅛ inch thick.

*Spread*_____with favorite sandwich spread and roll as for jelly roll starting with 5-inch side.

*Cut*_____into ½-inch slices and place on greased baking sheet. Flatten out slightly.

*Let rise*_____in warm place (85° to 90°F.) until double in bulk, about 45 minutes.

*Bake*_____in moderately hot oven (400°F.) 15 minutes.

Sweet Rolls

SWEET ROLLS, *rich and delicate, filled with fruit, spice, nuts . . . they're a wonderful, special treat. But they needn't be made only on special occasions, because here are sweet roll recipes that are especially easy. In fact, we predict that once you try them, you'll use them often—and you'll be serving your own home-made sweet rolls for breakfast or for a sweet snack with mid-morning or afternoon coffee.*

$50,000 NO-KNEAD WATER-RISING TWISTS

FIRST PRIZE WINNER
Pillsbury's 1st Recipe Contest
Mrs. Ralph E. Smafield, Detroit, Michigan

These sweet, tender nut rolls have a richness and delicacy all their own. The ease and speed of making them will delight you. Be sure to try the water-rising method, too. It's a very old but seldom-used way of submerging dough in water to let rise.

Makes 2 dozen twists

*Combine*_____½ cup shortening
3 tablespoons sugar
1½ teaspoons salt
1 teaspoon vanilla
½ cup scalded milk.*

*Add*_____2 cakes compressed yeast, crumbled (or 2
packages dry granular yeast dissolved in
¼ cup lukewarm water); mix well.

*Blend in*_____1½ cups sifted enriched flour and beat until
smooth. Cover and let rest for 15 min-
utes.

*Add*_____3 eggs, one at a time, beating well after
each addition.

*Blend in*_____1½ cups sifted enriched flour and mix thoroughly. The dough will be quite soft.

*Let rise*_____in only one of two ways: Either (1.) set
covered dough in warm place (80° to
90°F.) about ½ hour; or (2.) tie dough
in a tea towel, allowing space for dough
to rise. Then place in large mixing bowl
and fill with water (75° to 80°F.). Let
stand until dough rises to top of water,
about 30 to 45 minutes. Remove from
water. The dough will be soft and moist.

*Combine*_____¾ cup chopped nuts (any kind)
½ cup sugar
1 teaspoon cinnamon.

*Divide*_____dough into small pieces with a tablespoon. Roll each piece in sugar-nut mix-

*If dry yeast is used, decrease milk to ¼ cup.

ture; stretch to about 8-inch length. Twist into desired shape. Place on greased baking sheet. Let stand for 5 minutes.

Bake————————in moderate oven (375°F.) 12 to 15 min.

NO-KNEAD CINNAMON ROLLS

Cinnamon rolls are probably the most popular of all sweet rolls. These cinnamon rolls are made with no kneading and just one rising!

Makes 18 rolls

Combine————————½ cup scalded milk
3 tablespoons shortening
3 tablespoons sugar
1½ teaspoons salt.

Cool————————to lukewarm by adding
½ cup water.*

Add————————1 cake compressed yeast, crumbled (or 1 package dry granular yeast, dissolved as directed on package*); mix well.

Blend in————————1 egg.

Add gradually...3¼ cups sifted enriched flour; mix until well blended. Cover and let stand for 15 min.

Roll out————————dough on well-floured board to 18x12-inch rectangle. Spread with
2 tablespoons melted butter
¼ cup sugar
2 teaspoons cinnamon.

*The water used to dissolve dry yeast should be subtracted from water in recipe.

Roll_____as for jelly roll; cut into 1-inch slices and place in well-greased 12x8x2-inch pan or muffin pans.

Let rise_____in warm place (85° to 90°F.) until double in bulk, about 1 hour.

Bake_____in moderate oven (375° F.) 20 to 25 minutes.

NO-KNEAD CARAMEL PECAN ROLLS

These rich, light rolls have plenty of golden-brown butterscotch filling—and pecans—inside and out.

Makes 16 rolls

Prepare_____Cinnamon Roll dough. Cover and let stand for 15 minutes.

Combine_____½ cup firmly packed **brown sugar**
3 tablespoons light **corn syrup**
1 tablespoon melted **butter**
¼ cup **pecans.** Spread in bottoms of well-greased muffin pans.

Roll out_____dough on well-floured board to 16x12-inch rectangle. Spread with
¼ cup firmly packed **brown sugar**
1 teaspoon **cinnamon**
¼ cup chopped **pecans.**

Roll_____as for jelly roll; cut into 1-inch slices and place in prepared muffin pans over pecan mixture.

Let rise_____in warm place (85° to 90°F.) until double in bulk, about 1 hour.

Bake_____in moderate oven (375° F.) 20 minutes.

NO-KNEAD ORANGE ROLLS

If you like your sweet rolls—not too sweet, you'll like these orange rolls. They have a fresh flavor and are wonderful served warm.

Makes 16 rolls

Prepare_____Cinnamon Roll dough. Cover and let stand for 15 minutes.

Combine_____½ cup sugar

2 tablespoons melted butter

1 tablespoon grated orange rind

2 tablespoons orange juice. Spread in bottoms of well-greased muffin pans.

Roll out_____dough on well-floured board to 16x12-inch rectangle. Spread with

¼ cup sugar and

1 tablespoon grated orange rind.

Roll_____as for jelly roll; cut into 1-inch slices and place in prepared muffin pans over orange mixture.

Let rise_____in warm place (85° to 90°F.) until double in bulk, about 1 hour.

Bake_____in moderate oven (375°F.) 20 minutes.

NO-KNEAD DATE TWISTS

Dates, brown sugar and nuts make up the filling for these No-Knead rolls. They are easy to make, of course, and you'll find it is fun to shape them.

Makes 16 twists

Prepare_____Cinnamon Roll dough. Cover and let stand for 15 minutes.

Cook................1½ cups chopped **dates**
⅓ cup **water**
½ cup firmly packed **brown sugar** over low heat for 10 minutes. Cool and add
¾ cup chopped **nuts**.

Roll................out dough on floured board to an 18x12-inch rectangle. Spread with date filling.

Fold................dough over in thirds lengthwise. Cut into 16 strips. Twist each strip twice. Place on greased baking sheet.

Let rise................in warm place (85° to 90°F.) until double in bulk, about 45 minutes to 1 hour.

Bake................in moderate oven (375°F.) 15 to 20 minutes. Frost with confectioners' sugar icing.

NO-KNEAD LEMON TEA DROPS

**These dainty rolls have a delicious and tangy lemon topping.
So quick to make.**

Makes 2 dozen small rolls

Dissolve................1 cake compressed **yeast** (or 1 package dry granular yeast) in
½ cup lukewarm **water**.

Add................2 tablespoons melted **shortening**
2 tablespoons **sugar**
1 teaspoon **salt**.

Blend in................1 **egg**.

Add gradually........2 cups sifted **enriched flour**; mix until well blended. Cover and let stand for 15 min.

Fill................2-inch greased muffin pans ½ full.

Combine............½ cup sugar

                2 teaspoons lemon juice

                2 tablespoons grated lemon rind; sprinkle over rolls, allowing about 1 teaspoonful for each.

Let rise............in warm place (85° to 90°F.) until double in bulk, about 45 minutes.

Bake............in moderate oven (375°F.) 20 to 25 min.

NO-KNEAD KOLACKY

Delicious, fruit-filled kolacky are often called the national dessert of Bohemia. We thought they were so good, we developed this modern, simplified version—No-Knead kolacky.

Makes 24 kolacky

Combine............½ cup scalded milk

                3 tablespoons shortening

                3 tablespoons sugar

            1½ teaspoons salt.

Cool............to lukewarm by adding

                ½ cup water.*

Add............1 cake compressed yeast, crumbled (or 1 package dry granular yeast dissolved as directed on package*); mix well.

Blend in............1 egg.

Add............3 cups sifted enriched flour; mix until well blended. Cover and let stand for 15 min.

Roll............dough on well-floured board to ¼-inch thickness; cut into rounds with 2½-inch cutter. Place on greased baking sheet.

Let rise............in warm place (85° to 90°F.) until double in bulk, about 1 hour.

*The water used to dissolve dry yeast should be subtracted from water in recipe.

*Press*_____indentation in center of each bun.

*Place*_____pitted cooked prunes or apricots dipped in nuts in each indentation.

*Bake*_____in moderate oven (350°F.) 15 to 20 min.

*Combine*_____1 cup sifted confectioners' sugar
4 teaspoons warm milk
½ teaspoon vanilla; frost warm kolacky.

PEACH BASKETS

*Prepare*_____Kolacky dough, cut into rounds and let rise.

*Drain*_____1 No. 2½ can sliced peaches.

*Sprinkle*_____½ teaspoon almond extract over slices and blend thoroughly to distribute flavoring.

*Press*_____indentation in center of each roll. Fill the hollow with 3 or 4 peach slices. Top peaches with a teaspoon of jam.

*Bake*_____in moderate oven (375°F.) 15 to 20 minutes.

*Combine*_____1 cup sifted confectioners' sugar
4 teaspoons warm milk
½ teaspoon vanilla. Frost warm rolls.

PRUNE BRUNCH ROLLS

Pillsbury Contest Winner by Mrs. Joseph Rutkowski, Milwaukee, Wis.

Mrs. Rutkowski, too, was inspired by "Kolacky," the traditional Bohemian sweet roll. So she developed these prune and nut filled rolls. (You'll notice her method is modern, no kneading needed.)

Makes about 40 small rolls

*Dissolve*_____1 cake compressed yeast (or 1 package dry granular yeast) in
¼ cup lukewarm water.

Combine _____ ¼ cup shortening
⅓ cup sugar
1½ teaspoons salt
¾ cup scalded milk. Cool to lukewarm.

Blend in _____ 1 beaten egg and the dissolved yeast.

Add _____ 3 cups sifted enriched flour; mix until smooth. Place in greased bowl; cover.

Let rise _____ in warm place (85° to 90°F.) until double in bulk, about 1 hour.

Roll _____ dough on lightly floured board to ¼-inch thickness; cut into rounds with 2-inch cutter. Place on greased baking sheet.

Let rise _____ in warm place until double in bulk, about 1 hour.

Press _____ fingers in center of each round to form a tart shape. Spread a teaspoon of prune filling and a teaspoon of cheese filling in each hollow. Sprinkle with chopped nuts.

Bake _____ in moderate oven (375°F.) 15 to 20 minutes.

PRUNE FILLING

COMBINE 1 cup chopped, cooked, pitted prunes, 2 teaspoons grated orange rind, 3 tablespoons sugar and ¼ teaspoon cinnamon.

CHEESE FILLING

COMBINE 1 cup creamed cottage cheese, ¼ cup sugar and ½ teaspoon salt.

NO-KNEAD HOT CROSS BUNS

These hot cross buns are a favorite during Lent and early spring. This recipe is simple. It calls for no kneading and only one rising.

Makes 18 buns

*Combine*_____½ cup scalded milk
¼ cup shortening
1 tablespoon sugar
1½ teaspoons salt.

*Cool*_____to lukewarm by adding
½ cup water.*

*Add*_____1 cake compressed yeast, crumbled (or 1 package dry granular yeast dissolved as directed on package*); mix well.

*Blend in*_____1 egg
½ cup raisins
½ teaspoon cinnamon.

*Add gradually*_____3 cups sifted enriched flour; mix until well blended. Cover and let stand for 15 min.

*Shape*_____dough into 18 buns; place on greased baking sheet.

*Let rise*_____in warm place (85° to 90° F.) until double in bulk, about 45 minutes.

*Combine*_____1 egg white
2 tablespoons cold water; brush tops of buns with mixture.

*Cut*_____cross in top of each bun with scissors.

*Bake*_____in moderately hot oven (400° F.) 20 minutes.

*Combine*_____4 teaspoons milk
1 cup sifted confectioners' sugar
¼ teaspoon vanilla; drip over hot buns, filling cross.

_____
*The water used to dissolve dry yeast should be subtracted from water in recipe.

Coffee Cakes

COFFEE CAKES *seem to be made-to-order for entertaining. Here are rich, fragrant coffee cakes that you can cut in thin slices or thick wedges—serve plain or with butter. But always, of course, coffee cakes taste best when they are warm.*

If you have your own favorite topping or filling for coffee cake, you might try it with one of the basic coffee cake doughs in this chapter. Some of them are particularly rich and delicate.

NO-KNEAD CINNAMON COFFEE RING

Spicy and fragrant cinnamon rolls make up this novel coffee ring that's baked in a layer cake pan.

Makes 8-inch round coffee cake

*Combine*_____⅔ cup scalded **milk***
⅓ cup **shortening**
3 tablespoons **sugar**
1½ teaspoons **salt**. Cool to lukewarm.

*Add*_____1 cake compressed **yeast**, crumbled (or 1 package dry granular yeast dissolved as directed on package*); mix well.

*Blend in*_____1 **egg**.

*Add*_____2½ cups sifted **enriched flour**; mix until well blended. Cover and let stand for 15 min.

*Roll out*_____dough to 15x10-inch rectangle. Sprinkle with
4 tablespoons **sugar**
1½ teaspoons **cinnamon**.

*Roll*_____as for jelly roll; cut into 1¼-inch slices.

———
*The amount of water used to dissolve dry yeast should be subtracted from milk specified in recipe.

*Arrange*_____rolls in a ring in a greased 8-inch round layer cake pan. Place a biscuit cutter or custard cup in center of pan to keep dough in ring shape. If desired, rolls may be arranged on a baking sheet or in a ring mold pan.

*Let rise*_____in warm place (85° to 90°F.) until double in bulk, about 1 hour.

*Brush*_____top of rolls with
    1 tablespoon melted **butter.** Sprinkle with
    2 tablespoons sugar
    ½ teaspoon cinnamon.

*Bake*_____in moderate oven (350°F.) 30 to 35 minutes.

RICH BUTTER COFFEE RING

Pillsbury Contest Winner by Mrs. Frank J. Lakota, Philadelphia, Pa.

Rich, old-time coffee cake is made extra good with sour cream and eggs. Note—the water-rising method is used.

Makes two 8-inch rings

*Sift together*_____3 cups sifted enriched flour
    2 tablespoons sugar
    1 teaspoon salt.

*Cut in*_____2 tablespoons butter
    2 tablespoons shortening.

*Dissolve*_____1 cake compressed yeast (or 1 package dry granular yeast) in
    ¼ cup lukewarm water.

*Beat*_____1 egg and
    1 egg yolk.

*Make*_____a "well" in the dry ingredients and add beaten eggs and yeast mixture. Add
    ⅔ cup rich sour cream. Blend well.

Tie..................dough in a tea towel, allowing ample space for dough to rise. Place in large bowl filled with cool water (about 60° F.). Let stand until dough floats on top of water, about 1 hour. Remove from water.

Place..................dough on floured board. Cut into four pieces. Roll each piece between hands to about 14-inch length.

Twist..................two lengths together and seal ends to form a ring. Repeat with remaining two lengths. Place the rings on large greased baking sheet or in two greased 8-inch round layer cake pans.

Brush with..................3 tablespoons melted **butter**.

Let rise..................in warm place (85° to 90°F.) until light, about ½ hour.

Bake..................in moderate oven (375°F.) 25 to 30 minutes. Frost warm rings with almond icing.

ALMOND ICING

BEAT 1 egg white with fork. Blend in 1½ cups sifted confectioners' sugar. Add ½ teaspoon almond flavoring. Beat until smooth and glossy. Spread on warm coffee rings.

SNOW RING

Pillsbury Contest Winner by Mrs. Harold W. Bockstahler, East Lansing, Mich.

There are almonds, citron and currants between the braids of this coffee cake. The bread itself is wonderfully rich and good —made with eggs and butter. Mrs. Bockstahler suggests that it "may be decorated for seasonal holidays as desired, but is delicious by itself for any occasion."

Makes one large coffee cake

Dissolve..................1 cake compressed yeast (or 1 package dry granular yeast) in

                            2 tablespoons lukewarm water.
*Add*_____1 cup scalded milk, cooled to lukewarm
                            2 teaspoons sugar
                            1½ cups sifted enriched flour. Beat until
                               smooth.
*Let rise*_____in warm place (85° to 90°F.) until light,
                               about 30 minutes.
*Cream*_____½ cup butter (half shortening may be used)
                               with
                            1 cup confectioners' sugar. Beat in
                            1 egg
                            1 egg yolk and
                            1½ teaspoons salt. Add to risen yeast mix-
                               ture.
*Blend in*_____2½ cups sifted enriched flour. Beat for 2
                               minutes.
*Let rise*_____in warm place until light, about 1 hour.
                               Punch down dough with fist.
*Let rise*_____in warm place about 30 minutes.
*Divide*_____dough into three parts. Roll each part
                               between floured hands to make strips
                               about 18 inches long. Lay dough on
                               floured board and flatten slightly.
*Place*_____¼ cup blanched almonds down center of
                               one strip,
                            ¼ cup diced citron down center of next
                               strip,
                            ¼ cup currants down center of last strip.
                               Seal fillings into dough by pinching
                               edges together.
*Braid*_____the three strips of dough and form in a
                               circle on greased baking sheet. Insert
                            ¼ cup almonds in dough between strips.
*Let rise*_____in warm place until light, about 20 to 25
                               minutes.

Combine..............1 egg white

1 tablespoon water and brush over dough.

Bake..............in moderate oven (350°F.) 25 to 30 minutes. Sprinkle with confectioners' sugar while warm.

NO-KNEAD SWEDISH TEA RING

This attractive old-country specialty has a prune filling between rich, golden brown layers of sweet dough.

Makes 1 tea ring

Combine..............½ cup scalded milk

3 tablespoons shortening

2 tablespoons sugar

1½ teaspoons salt.

Cool..............to lukewarm by adding

½ cup water.*

Add..............1 cake compressed yeast, crumbled (or 1 package dry granular yeast dissolved as directed on package*); mix well.

Blend in..............1 egg.

Add gradually......3 cups sifted enriched flour; mix until well blended. Cover and let stand for 15 min.

Simmer..............1 cup cooked prunes, chopped

¼ teaspoon cinnamon

1 tablespoon lemon juice

¼ cup sugar

⅛ teaspoon salt until thickened.

Roll..............dough to 14x12-inch rectangle. Spread with cooled prune mixture.

Roll..............as for jelly roll; place on greased baking

*The water used to dissolve dry yeast should be subtracted from water in recipe.

	sheet and join ends together to form ring.
Cut	deep slits almost to center of ring with scissors. Cut about 1 inch apart. Turn each piece on its side, cut edge up.
Let rise	in warm place (85° to 90° F.) until double in bulk, about 45 minutes.
Bake	in moderate oven (350° F.) 30 minutes.
Combine	4 teaspoons warm milk

1 cup sifted confectioners' sugar

¼ teaspoon vanilla; frost warm ring.

TWO-WAY COFFEE BREAD

Pillsbury Contest Winner by Mrs. Henry Roeschlein, Chicago, Ill.

This one batch of dough makes both coffee cake and sweet rolls. Both of them have a luscious caramel pecan flavor!

Makes one 9-inch coffee ring and 12 large sweet rolls

Dissolve	2 cakes compressed yeast (or 2 packages dry granular yeast) in
	1 cup lukewarm water.
Cream	½ cup butter (half shortening may be used).
Blend in	2 eggs, one at a time
	1½ teaspoons salt
	¼ cup sugar
	grated rind of 1 lemon
	½ cup raisins.
Add	3¾ cups sifted enriched flour alternately with yeast mixture. Beat thoroughly after each addition.
Tie	dough in cheesecloth or tea towel, allowing ample space for dough to rise. Place in large bowl and fill with cool water. Let

stand until dough floats on top of water, about 1 hour. The dough will be soft and moist.

Prepare.................9-inch ring mold and 12 muffin cups by greasing well.

Combine.................¼ cup **light corn syrup**

½ cup firmly packed **brown sugar**

½ cup chopped **pecans**

2 teaspoons **cinnamon**. Spread in bottoms of pans.

Spread.................half of dough in ring mold over brown sugar mixture. Divide balance of dough into 12 muffin cups.

Let rise.................in warm place (85° to 90°F.) until double in bulk, about 45 minutes.

Bake.................in moderate oven (375°F.) 25 to 30 minutes. Turn out immediately on serving plate.

MERRY-GO-ROUND COFFEE CAKE

Pillsbury Contest Winner by Mrs. Howard Graham, Charlotte, North Carolina

This festive coffee cake is just the thing for special holidays. It's spiral-shaped with a colorful filling of fruit, nuts and jelly.

Makes 10-inch round coffee cake

Dissolve.................1 cake compressed **yeast**, crumbled (or 1 package dry granular yeast) in

2 tablespoons lukewarm **water**.

Combine.................½ cup scalded **milk**

2 tablespoons **shortening**

¼ cup **sugar**

1 teaspoon **salt**. Cool to lukewarm.

Add.................1 **egg**, unbeaten, and the dissolved yeast.

Blend in.................2½ cups sifted **enriched flour** to form a soft dough.

Knead................dough on floured board until smooth, about 3 minutes. Place in greased bowl; cover.

Let rise................in warm place (85° to 90°F.) until double in bulk, about 1 hour. Roll to a 20x9-inch rectangle.

Spread with........½ cup jelly
¼ cup mixed **candied fruit**, chopped
¼ cup **candied cherries**, chopped
¼ cup **raisins**
¼ cup **nuts**, chopped.

Roll................as for jelly roll, starting with 20-inch edge. Seal edge well.

Flatten................roll slightly. Cut lengthwise through center of roll into two 20-inch strips. Turn cut sides up.

Place................one strip on greased baking sheet. Loosely coil the strip pinwheel fashion, keeping cut edge up. Then join second strip to end of first strip and continue winding the dough to make a round coffee cake, about 9 inches in diameter.

Let rise................in warm place until light, 30 to 45 min.

Bake................in moderate oven (350°F.) 25 to 30 minutes.

NO-KNEAD ORANGE-COCONUT COFFEE CAKE

Orange-coconut topping makes this coffee cake unusual!

Makes 10-inch square coffee cake

Combine................½ cup scalded **milk**
2 tablespoons **sugar**
2 tablespoons **shortening**

	1 teaspoon salt.
Cool	to lukewarm by adding
	¼ cup water.*
Add	1 cake compressed yeast, crumbled (or 1 package dry granular yeast dissolved as directed on package*); mix well.
Blend in	1 egg
	½ cup raisins.
Add gradually	2¼ cups sifted enriched flour; mix until well blended. Cover and let stand for 15 min.
Spread	dough in well-greased 10x10x2-inch pan.
Combine	½ cup sugar
	1 tablespoon flour
	2 tablespoons grated orange rind.
Cut in	1 tablespoon butter; add
	1 cup shredded coconut.
Place	on top of dough. Sprinkle with
	¼ cup orange juice.
Let rise	in warm place (85° to 90°F.) until double in bulk, about 1 hour.
Bake	in moderate oven (375°F.) 25 minutes.

*The water used to dissolve dry yeast should be subtracted from water in recipe.

NO-KNEAD MINCEMEAT COFFEE TWIRL

You fold rich, spicy mincemeat inside this coffee cake.

Makes 1 coffee cake

| *Combine* | ⅔ cup scalded milk* |

*The amount of water used to dissolve dry yeast should be subtracted from milk specified in recipe.

> ¼ cup shortening
> 3 tablespoons sugar
> 1½ teaspoons salt. Cool to lukewarm.

Add............1 cake compressed yeast, crumbled (or 1 package dry granular yeast dissolved as directed on package*); mix well.

Blend in............1 egg
> 2 teaspoons grated lemon rind
> ½ teaspoon cinnamon.

Add............2½ cups sifted enriched flour; mix until well blended. Cover and let stand for 15 min.

Roll............dough on well floured board to a 15x10-inch rectangle.

Spread............½ cup cooked mincemeat in a strip on center third of dough.

Fold............one side of dough to overlap center and spread with additional
> ½ cup mincemeat. Fold opposite side to overlap; seal. Place on greased baking sheet.

Slash............across top of dough several times with sharp knife.

Let rise............in warm place (85° to 90°F.) until double in bulk, about 45 minutes to 1 hour.

Bake............in moderate oven (350°F.) 30 minutes. Frost with confectioners' sugar icing.

---

*The amount of water used to dissolve dry yeast should be subtracted from milk specified in recipe.

FESTIVE FRUIT BASKET

Spicy apricot filling is hidden beneath rich, golden braids of
dough. Over it is a confectioners' sugar frosting. Looks festive
and tricky—but, really, there's nothing to making it!

Makes 1 coffee cake

Prepare................dough for Mincemeat Coffee Twirl.
Cover and let stand for 15 minutes.

Simmer................1 cup cooked, chopped **apricots**
2 tablespoons **apricot juice**
½ cup **sugar**
⅛ teaspoon **salt**
¼ teaspoon **nutmeg** until thickened.

Roll................dough to a 12-inch square. Place on
greased baking sheet.

Spread................cooled apricot mixture in a strip on
center third of dough.

Cut................dough diagonally, herring-bone fashion,
on both sides of filling. Make cuts 3
inches deep at 1½-inch intervals.

Cross................alternate strips of dough over filling to
give braided effect. Join ends. Cover.

Let rise................in warm place (85° to 90° F.) until double
in bulk, about 45 minutes.

Bake................in moderate oven (350°F.) 30 to 35
minutes. Frost with confectioners' sugar
icing while still warm.

NO-KNEAD HASTY CARAMEL
COFFEE CAKE

For variety, you may wish to top this coffee cake with berries
and brown sugar, bake in a skillet, and serve warm as dessert.
You can mix, let rise, bake and serve in less than two hours.

Makes 9-inch square coffee cake

Combine................½ cup scalded milk
2 tablespoons shortening
2 tablespoons sugar
1 teaspoon salt.

Cool................to lukewarm by adding
¼ cup water.*

Add................1 cake compressed yeast, crumbled (or 1
package dry granular yeast dissolved as
directed on package*); mix well.

Blend in................1 egg.

Add gradually........2 cups sifted enriched flour; mix until well
blended. Cover and let stand for 15 min.

Spread................in well-greased 10-inch skillet or 9x9x2-
inch pan.

Prick................top of dough with fork and brush with
melted butter.

Combine................⅓ cup firmly packed brown sugar
3 tablespoons butter
2 tablespoons flour
¼ teaspoon cinnamon
½ cup chopped nuts; sprinkle over top of
dough.

Let rise................in warm place (85° to 90°F.) until double
in bulk, about 45 minutes to 1 hour.

Bake................in moderate oven (375°F.) 25 to 30
minutes.

*The water used to dissolve dry yeast should be subtracted from water
in recipe.

NO-KNEAD APRICOT BRAID

This apricot braid looks complicated, but it is really simple
to mix and shape. Even the creamy white icing and nut topping
are easy!

Makes 1 coffee cake

Combine................1 cup scalded milk
¼ cup shortening
¼ cup sugar
2 teaspoons salt
¼ cup water.* Cool to lukewarm.

*Add*_____1 cake compressed yeast, crumbled (or 1
package dry granular yeast, dissolved as
directed on package*); mix well.

*Blend in*_____1 egg
1 teaspoon grated lemon rind
½ cup chopped raisins
¼ cup chopped nuts
½ cup finely cut dried apricots.

Add gradually........4 cups sifted enriched flour; mix until well
blended. Cover and let stand for 15 min.

*Divide*_____dough into five equal parts and shape
each into an 18-inch strip.

*Place*_____three strips on greased baking sheet and
form into horizontal braid. Join ends together. Twist the two remaining strips
together and place on top of braid. Join
ends.

*Let rise*_____in warm place (85° to 90° F.) until double
in bulk, about 1 hour.

*Bake*_____in moderate oven (350° F.) 35 to 40
minutes. Frost with confectioners' sugar
icing and sprinkle with nuts.

_____
*The water used to dissolve dry yeast should be subtracted from water
in recipe.

RICH WALNUT COFFEE CAKE

Filled with walnuts and brown sugar crumbs, this coffee cake
is really rich and exceptionally good. This is a quick coffee
cake—not made with yeast. It requires no rising.

Makes 9-inch square coffee cake

Sift together......1½ cups sifted enriched flour
2 teaspoons double-acting baking powder
½ teaspoon salt
¾ cup sugar.

Add.................¼ cup shortening
½ cup milk.

Beat.................for 2 minutes, 300 strokes, until batter is
well blended. (With electric mixer blend
at low speed, then beat at medium speed
for 2 minutes.)

Add.................2 eggs, unbeaten.

Beat.................for 2 minutes.

Combine............2 tablespoons melted butter with
½ cup firmly packed brown sugar.

Add.................1 cup chopped walnuts
1 tablespoon flour
1 teaspoon cinnamon; mix well.

Spread..............half of cake batter in bottom of greased
9x9x1½-inch pan; sprinkle with half of
sugar-nut mixture. Add remainder of
batter and balance of sugar and nuts.

Bake.................in moderate oven (350°F.) 30 minutes.
Serve warm.

CHAPTER FOUR

Main Dishes

THERE ARE *so many ways to vary your meals!*

You can serve just one food in many, many ways. Take left-over meat, for instance. It can be combined with vegetables, and served creamed inside a crusty popover shell or a crisp cream puff. You can put it in a meat pie or make a biscuit shortcake.

We feel that homemakers needn't get into a menu rut. There are entirely too many exciting foods and so many unusual ways of serving them! Have you ever tried hot Italian pizza or pork and sweet potato casserole or maybe mid-week meat pie? Well, you'll find these recipes right here—in this chapter. We hope you will try them!

DEAUVILLE DUMPLINGS
BEST OF CLASS WINNER
Pillsbury's 1st Recipe Contest
by Mrs. Joseph F. Maley, Osborn, Ohio

Currants and onion are an unusual combination. Mrs. Maley got this winning recipe at a country ladies' aid dinner.

Makes 16 to 18 dumplings

*Sift together*_____1 cup sifted enriched flour
3 teaspoons double-acting baking powder
1 teaspoon salt.
*Cut in*_____1 tablespoon butter.

Add................½ cup dried currants
                  ¾ cup fine, dry bread crumbs.
Combine............1 egg, well beaten
                  ¾ cup milk
                  2 teaspoons grated onion. Add to dry in-
                  gredients; mix just enough to blend.
Dip...............tablespoon into cold water. Then drop
                  batter from spoon onto hot chicken or
                  meat stew. Cover tightly.
Steam.............for 20 minutes. Do not remove the cover
                  during steaming process. Serve imme-
                  diately with chicken or meat stew.

SHORT RIBS AND DUMPLINGS

Feather-light dumplings top off flavorful braised short-ribs and good brown gravy. (Remember, keep your dumplings covered tightly while they're steaming and they are sure to be light and fluffy.)

Serves 6

Combine...........¼ cup sifted enriched flour
                  1 tablespoon salt.
                  ⅛ teaspoon pepper
Dredge............3 pounds beef short ribs cut into indi-
                  vidual servings, in flour mixture.
Brown.............1 medium onion, minced, and meat in
                  3 tablespoons shortening in large skillet.
Add...............3 cups water; cover and simmer slowly for
                  1½ hours or until tender.
Top...............with parsley dumplings.

PARSLEY DUMPLINGS

Sift together........2 cups sifted enriched flour

3 teaspoons double-acting **baking powder**
1 teaspoon **salt.**

Cut in............1/4 cup minced **parsley**
1/4 cup **shortening** until mixture resembles coarse meal.

Combine............1 **egg**, slightly beaten
3/4 cup **milk.**

Add............to dry ingredients and mix only until all flour is dampened.

Drop............by spoonfuls on top of boiling short ribs; cover tightly. Steam for 12 minutes. **Do not remove cover during steaming process.** Serve immediately.

Note: These dumplings are also delicious with chicken or vegetable stew.

LOG CABIN CHICKEN PIE

Pillsbury Contest Winner by Mrs. Mason Parker, Kenney, Ill.

This recipe is a family "hand-me-down." Abraham Lincoln (so the story goes) stopped at Mrs. Parker's great, great grandparents' log cabin. This tasty chicken pie was served.

Makes 10-inch pie

Sift together............2 cups sifted **enriched flour**
1 teaspoon **salt.**

Cut in............2/3 cup **shortening** until particles are the size of small peas.

Blend together............1 slightly beaten **egg**
1 tablespoon **lemon juice.** Sprinkle over flour mixture, tossing lightly with fork.

Add............1 to 3 tablespoons cold **milk.** Toss until pastry is moist enough to hold together. Form into a ball.

Roll............out on floured board or pastry cloth to a 12-inch circle.

Fit............pastry loosely into a 10-inch pie pan. Fold edge to form standing rim; flute.

FILLING

Heat..............1 ½ cups rich **chicken stock.**

Blend..............3 tablespoons **flour** and
⅓ cup **water.** Add to chicken stock, stirring
constantly until thickened.

Add..............3 cups diced **chicken**; heat. Pour into unbaked shell.

TOPPING

Crush..............10 slices **dried bread** with rolling pin.

Add..............1 medium **onion,** grated
½ teaspoon each: **salt, pepper, poultry seasoning.** Blend well.

Moisten with..............1 cup hot **chicken stock.** Spread evenly
over top of filling.

Bake..............in hot oven (425°F.) 40 to 45 minutes.

CHICKEN PIE

**This is a good old-fashioned chicken pie, topped with tasty
onion biscuits.**

Serves 6

Brown..............½ cup finely chopped **onion** in
¼ cup **shortening** or chicken fat; reserve
half of browned onion for biscuit topping.

Blend in..............¼ cup sifted **enriched flour**
¼ teaspoon **pepper**
½ teaspoon **salt.**

Add gradually..............2 cups **chicken stock,** stirring constantly.
Cook until thickened.

Add .... 2 cups coarsely chopped, cooked **chicken**
½ cup cooked peas
½ cup diced, cooked **carrots**
¼ cup sliced, cooked **green pepper**
½ cup cooked **pearl onions**; cook for ten minutes.

Pour .... into deep 9-inch round baking dish or 10x6-inch pan.

Top .... with onion biscuits.

ONION BISCUITS

Sift together ..... 1½ cups sifted **enriched flour**
2 teaspoons double-acting **baking powder**
½ teaspoon **salt**.

Cut in .... ¼ cup **shortening** until mixture resembles coarse meal. Blend in reserved browned onions.

Add .... ⅔ cup **milk**; mix only until all flour is dampened. Knead gently on floured board or pastry cloth for a few seconds.

Roll .... to ¼-inch thickness and cut into rounds with 2-inch cutter. Place biscuits on top of hot meat filling.

Bake .... in hot oven (450°F.) 12 to 15 minutes.

PASTRY TOPPING

CHICKEN PIE may also be baked with a pastry topping. Prepare pastry according to recipe on page 308. Roll to fit top of baking dish. Cut slits to allow escape of steam. Place over hot meat filling; seal by moistening edge of casserole and fluting crust. Bake at 425°F. 15 to 20 minutes.

CURRY-CHICKEN CASSEROLE

There's savory goodness and hearty satisfaction in this appe-
teasin' company casserole . . . a deliciously different flavor
touch in the biscuit topping.

Serves 6

Melt................⅓ cup **shortening** or **chicken fat** in top of
double boiler over direct heat; blend in
½ cup **enriched flour.**

Add................3 cups **chicken stock** (or part milk), stirring constantly. Cook over hot water
until thickened. Season to taste.

Prepare................3 cups cooked **chicken,** cut in pieces
1½ cups cooked **celery,** diced
1½ cups cooked **carrots,** diced
1½ cups cooked **peas**
1½ cups cooked **potatoes,** diced.

Divide................chicken and vegetables into six individual casseroles allowing ½ cup chicken
and ¼ cup of each vegetable per casserole.* Cover with hot chicken gravy.

Top................with curry-biscuit lattice strips.

CURRY-BISCUIT LATTICE TOPPING

Sift together........2 cups sifted **enriched flour**
3 teaspoons double-acting **baking powder**
½ teaspoon **salt**
½ teaspoon **curry powder,** if desired.

Cut in................⅓ cup **shortening** until mixture resembles
coarse meal.

Add................¾ cup **milk;** mix only until all flour is

*If desired, a 3-quart casserole may be used.

	dampened. Knead gently on floured board or pastry cloth for a few seconds.
Roll	dough to ⅛ to ¼-inch thickness; cut into strips ½ inch wide. Arrange strips of dough lattice-fashion over hot filling.
Bake	in hot oven (425°F.) 12 to 15 minutes.

MEAL-IN-ONE CASSEROLE

This hearty main dish has parsley biscuit crust over a delicious tuna filling.

Serves 6

Brown	2 tablespoons chopped onion in ¼ cup butter.
Blend in	¼ cup sifted enriched flour 1 teaspoon salt ⅛ teaspoon pepper.
Add gradually	2 cups milk; cook until thickened, stirring constantly.
Add	1 cup cooked celery 1 7-oz. can tuna fish 2 tablespoons chopped pimiento 2 sliced, hard-cooked eggs.
Pour	into 1½-quart casserole and top with biscuits.

PARSLEY BISCUITS

Sift together	1½ cups sifted enriched flour 2 teaspoons double-acting baking powder ½ teaspoon salt.
Cut in	3 tablespoons minced parsley and ¼ cup shortening until mixture resembles coarse meal.
Add	⅔ cup milk all at once; mix only until all flour is dampened.

Roll...................to ¼-inch thickness and cut into rounds
with 2-inch biscuit cutter.

Place...................an overlapping circle of biscuits at outer
edge of casserole.

Bake...................in hot oven (425°F.) 20 to 25 minutes.

MID-WEEK MEAT PIE

**The meat and vegetables are prepared as for stew. The flaky
cheese pastry topping adds a party touch.**

Serves 4 to 6

Brown...................½ pound cubed veal shoulder and
½ pound cubed pork shoulder in
2 tablespoons shortening.

Add...................3 cups water
1 bay leaf
2 teaspoons salt
¼ teaspoon each: pepper, garlic salt, thyme
4 small, whole onions; simmer for about
30 minutes.

Add...................1 cup coarsely diced carrots
1 cup green beans
1½ cups cubed potatoes. Cook until vegetables are tender.

*Blend together*___ ¼ cup enriched flour and
¼ cup water to form a smooth paste; add to
hot stew and stir constantly until thickened.

Turn into...............1½-quart casserole or 12x8x2-inch baking
dish. Top with pastry.

CHEESE PASTRY TOPPING

Sift together——1½ cups sifted enriched flour
¾ teaspoon salt.

Cut in————½ cup shortening and
½ cup grated cheese until particles are the size of small peas.

Sprinkle————4 to 5 tablespoons cold water over mixture, tossing lightly until dough is moist enough to hold together. Form into a ball.

Roll————————dough to fit top of baking dish; cut slits to allow escape of steam. Place on hot stew; seal by moistening edge of casserole and fluting crust.

Bake————————in hot oven (450°F.) 15 to 20 minutes.

DE LUXE MEAT PIE

This is a complete meal with meat, vegetables and biscuits in one casserole.

Serves 6

Brown————————½ cup finely chopped onion in
¼ cup shortening; reserve half of browned onion for biscuit topping.

Add————————1 pound ground beef
1 teaspoon salt
⅛ teaspoon pepper; cook until meat is lightly browned.

Add————————1 cup tomato juice
3 stalks celery, chopped
2 medium-sized carrots, diced
3 drops tabasco sauce; simmer five to ten minutes.

*Blend together*___½ cup **tomato juice**
⅓ cup **enriched flour**
½ cup **catsup**; add to cooked mixture. Stir
until thickened.

*Pour*_____into deep 9-inch round baking dish or
10x6-inch pan.

*Top*_____with onion biscuits, recipe on page 103.

*Bake*_____in hot oven (450°F.) 12 to 15 minutes.

CHEESEBURGER UPSIDE-DOWN PIE

A hearty meat filling is covered with flaky biscuit crust.
There's cheese on top of the filling, too, for added flavor.

Serves 4 to 6

*Brown*_____1 pound **ground beef** and
2 tablespoons chopped **onion** in
2 tablespoons **shortening**.
Season with
1 teaspoon **salt**
¼ teaspoon **pepper**.

*Sift together*___1½ cups sifted **enriched flour**
2 teaspoons double-acting **baking powder**
½ teaspoon **salt**.

*Cut in*_____¼ cup **shortening** until mixture resembles
coarse meal.

*Add*_____⅔ cup **milk**; mix only until all flour is
dampened. Knead gently on floured
board or pastry cloth for a few seconds.

*Spread*_____hamburger mixture evenly in bottom of
a greased 8-inch round casserole. Top
with
½ cup **catsup**.

*Sprinkle with*___1 cup grated **cheese**.

Roll............................biscuit dough to fit top of baking dish; cut slits to allow escape of steam. Place on hot meat filling.

Bake............................in hot oven (450°F.) 20 to 25 minutes.

CRUSTY CORN PIE

In this quick casserole, luncheon meat is baked with vegetables, and topped with corn meal biscuits.

Serves 6

Brown............................1 cup cubed ham or luncheon meat in
2 tablespoons shortening in 10-inch skillet.

Add............................½ cup finely diced onion
1 cup finely diced celery
¼ cup finely diced green pepper; cook until partially tender.

Blend in............................1½ teaspoons salt
¼ teaspoon pepper
2 tablespoons flour.

Add............................2 cups canned tomatoes
½ cup drained whole kernel corn; cook until thickened. Top with corn meal biscuits.

CORN MEAL BISCUITS

Sift together............................¾ cup sifted enriched flour
2½ teaspoons double-acting baking powder
½ teaspoon salt.

Blend in............................¾ cup corn meal.

Cut in............................¼ cup shortening until mixture resembles coarse meal.

Add............................¾ cup milk all at once; stir only until all flour is dampened. Drop by spoonfuls onto meat and vegetable mixture.

Bake............................in moderately hot oven (400°F.) 35 to 40 minutes.

PORK AND SWEET POTATO CASSEROLE

Onion biscuits top a pork and vegetable casserole. (Sweet potatoes add extra flavor.)

Serves 6

Brown............1 pound (2 cups) cubed pork in
2 tablespoons shortening.

Add............2 cups water or stock; cook until tender.

Blend together....5 tablespoons enriched flour
1 tablespoon salt
¼ teaspoon pepper
1 cup cold water; mix until smooth. Pour into stock and stir constantly until thickened.

Add............1½ cups diced, cooked sweet potatoes
1 cup cooked peas
1 cup cooked small onions
1 cup diced, cooked carrots; simmer about 2 minutes.

Pour............into deep 9-inch round baking dish or 10x6-inch pan.

Top............with onion biscuits, recipe on page 103.

Bake............in hot oven (450°F.) 15 to 20 minutes.

PORK PIE WITH SWEET POTATO BISCUITS

PREPARE Pork Pie, omitting sweet potatoes. Top with the following sweet potato biscuits.

Sift together....1½ cups sifted enriched flour
2 teaspoons double-acting baking powder
2 teaspoons salt.

Cut in————————¼ cup **shortening** and
¼ cup cooked, mashed **sweet potatoes** until mixture resembles coarse meal.

Add————————½ cup **milk**; mix only until all flour is dampened. Knead gently on floured board or pastry cloth for a few seconds.

Roll————————to ½-inch thickness and cut into rounds with 2-inch cutter.

Place————————biscuits on top of hot meat-vegetable mixture.

Bake————————in hot oven (425°F.) 25 minutes.

MAN-COOKED MEAL

Pillsbury Contest Winner by Houston James Newman, St. Louis, Mo,

This meal-in-one has man-appeal. It should have—it originated with one of the men contestants in our contest!

Serves 6

Combine————————¼ cup chopped **celery**
1 small **green pepper**, chopped
1 large **onion**, chopped
1 **clove garlic**, chopped. Sauté in
2 tablespoons **shortening**.

Add————————1 pound **hamburger**; brown thoroughly.

Add————————1 cup cooked **rice** (or 2 medium potatotes, boiled and diced)
2 teaspoons **chili powder**
1 8-oz. can **tomato sauce**
2 teaspoons **salt**
⅛ teaspoon **pepper**; simmer while mixing topping.

Sift together————————1 cup sifted **enriched flour**
¾ cup **yellow corn meal**
2 teaspoons double-acting **baking powder**

½ teaspoon **soda**
1 teaspoon each: **salt, sugar.**

Combine........................1 cup **buttermilk**
¼ cup melted **shortening**
2 **eggs**, well beaten.

Add........................liquid all at once to dry ingredients, stirring only until dampened.

Spread........................hamburger mixture evenly in 9x9x2-inch pan. Pour corn bread mixture over meat.

Bake........................in hot oven (425°F.) 45 min. Serve with tomato sauce.

PATIO PICNIC CASSEROLE

Pillsbury Contest Winner by Mrs. Earl Raymond Broadwell, Santa Barbara, Calif.

Spices and black olives add a real Western touch to this meatless main dish. It's inexpensive and easy to make.

Makes one 2-quart casserole

Sift together........½ cup sifted enriched **flour**
1 cup yellow **corn meal**
1½ teaspoons **chili powder**
2 teaspoons **salt**
¼ teaspoon **pepper.**

Combine........................3 cups canned **cream-style corn**
1 8-oz. can **tomato sauce**
1 cup **milk**
½ cup melted **shortening** or salad oil
2 **eggs**, well beaten.

Blend........................dry ingredients into corn mixture; mix well.

Add........................2 tablespoons grated **onion**
1 cup **black olives.** Pour into greased 2-qt. casserole.

Bake........................in slow oven (325°F.) 2 hours.

PARSLEY SUPPER RING

While your No-Knead bread ring is baking—make up one of
your favorite meat and vegetable fillings—and you have almost
a complete meal ready for the table.

Serves 8

Soften............1 cake compressed yeast (or 1 package dry
granular yeast) in
1 cup lukewarm water.

Add............3 tablespoons melted shortening
2 teaspoons sugar
1½ teaspoons salt.

Blend in............1 egg.

Add gradually............3 cups sifted enriched flour; mix until well
blended. Cover and let stand for 15 min.

Turn............dough into greased 9-inch ring mold.

Let rise............in warm place (85° to 90° F.) until double
in bulk, about 45 minutes.

Bake............in moderately hot oven (400°F.) 25
minutes.

Cut............into thick slices, spread generously with
parsley or garlic butter and serve with
the following.

CREAMED MEAT AND GREEN BEANS

MELT ¼ cup shortening in skillet. Blend in 1 cup cubed luncheon meat or any cooked meat or fish, ¼ cup sifted enriched flour,
1 teaspoon salt, ⅛ teaspoon pepper and 2 cups milk. Cook until
thickened, stirring constantly. Add 2 cups cooked, green beans.
Serve hot with buttered ring.

CHEESE AND HAM SUPPER RING

Here's ham à la king served over thick slices of tangy cheese
bread.

Serves 8

*Combine*_____½ cup scalded milk
                  3 tablespoons shortening
                  1 tablespoon sugar
                  1½ teaspoons salt.

*Cool*_____to lukewarm by adding
                  ½ cup water.*

*Add*_____1 cake compressed yeast, crumbled (or 1
                  package dry granular yeast dissolved as
                  directed on package*); mix well.

*Blend in*_____1 egg
                  1 cup grated cheese.

*Add*_____3 cups sifted enriched flour; mix until
                  dough is well blended. Cover and let
                  stand for 15 minutes.

*Turn*_____dough into greased 9-inch ring mold.

*Let rise*_____in warm place (85° to 90°F.) until light,
                  about 45 minutes.

*Bake*_____in moderately hot oven (375°F.) 25
                  minutes.

*Cut*_____into thick slices, spread with butter and
                  serve with the following.

HAM À LA KING

MELT ¼ cup butter in saucepan. Blend in ¼ cup sifted enriched
flour. Add gradually 2 cups milk, stirring constantly until thickened. Add 2 cups cooked, diced ham, 1 cup chopped mush-
rooms, 2 hard-cooked eggs, diced, 1 tablespoon chopped green

---

*The water used to dissolve dry yeast should be subtracted from water
in recipe.

pepper, 1 tablespoon pimiento, ¼ teaspoon pepper or paprika, ½ teaspoon salt. Serve hot with buttered ring.

CHEESE AND EGG SUPPER RING

PREPARE Cheese and Ham Supper Ring. Serve with curried eggs and peas, recipe page 120.

TUNA RING

Creamed tuna and vegetables make the sauce for this bread ring. You make the bread the easy No-Knead way.

Serves 8

Sauté————½ cup chopped celery in
1 tablespoon shortening. Remove from heat.

Blend in————1 cup (7 oz. can) flaked tuna fish
2 tablespoons chopped pimiento
1 egg, slightly beaten
few grains pepper
½ teaspoon salt
½ teaspoon lemon juice.

BREAD RING

Combine————½ cup scalded milk
3 tablespoons shortening
1 tablespoon sugar
1½ teaspoons salt.

Cool————to lukewarm by adding
½ cup water.*

Add————1 cake compressed yeast, crumbled (or 1 package dry granular yeast, dissolved as directed on package*); mix well.

*Amount of water used to dissolve dry yeast should be subtracted from water in recipe.

*Blend in*_____1 egg.

*Add*_____3 cups sifted **enriched flour**; mix until well blended. Cover and let stand for 15 min.

*Roll*_____dough to 14x12-inch rectangle. Spread tuna mixture over rolled dough.

*Roll*_____as for jelly roll; place on greased baking sheet and join ends together to form ring.

*Cut*_____deep slits almost to center of ring about 1 inch apart. Turn each piece on its side, cut edge up.

*Let rise*_____in warm place (85° to 90°F.) until double in bulk, about 45 minutes.

*Bake*_____in moderate oven (375°F.) 20 to 25 minutes. Serve warm with creamed eggs and peas.

CREAMED EGGS AND PEAS

BLEND together 4 tablespoons melted butter and 4 tablespoons flour. Add gradually 2 cups milk, stirring until thickened. Add 1 teaspoon salt, ⅛ teaspoon pepper, 2 cups cooked peas and 3 hard-cooked eggs, diced. Serve over Tuna Ring.

LUNCHBOX FOLDOVERS

These sandwiches have the filling baked in. Easy to make and easy to eat!

Makes 18 foldovers

*Combine*_____½ cup scalded milk
                    3 tablespoons **shortening**
                    2 teaspoons **sugar**
                    1½ teaspoons **salt**

                    ¼ cup water.*
                    Cool to lukewarm.

Add................1 cake compressed yeast, crumbled (or 1
                    package dry granular yeast dissolved as
                    directed on package*); mix well.

Blend in...........2 eggs
                    1 cup grated cheese.

Add................3 cups sifted enriched flour; mix until well
                    blended. Cover and let stand for 15 min.

Divide.............dough in half. Roll each half on well-
                    floured board to a 12-inch square. Cut
                    into nine 4-inch squares.

Brown..............2 tablespoons chopped onion in
                    1 tablespoon shortening.

Add................2 cups ground, cooked meat
                    1 teaspoon salt
                    ¼ teaspoon pepper
                    2 tablespoons catsup
                    ¼ cup chopped pickle
                    few drops Worcestershire sauce.

Place..............a tablespoonful of meat mixture in one
                    corner of each square. Fold diagonally
                    to make a triangle. Seal edges.

Slit...............folded edge of each triangle two or
                    three times to allow escape of steam.
                    Place on greased baking sheet.

Let rise...........in warm place (85° to 90° F.) until double
                    in bulk, about 45 minutes.

Bake...............in moderately hot oven (400° F.) 12
                    minutes.

---

*The water used to dissolve dry yeast should be subtracted from water
in recipe.

DEVILED EGGS IN BISCUIT RINGS

This flaky, tasty biscuit ring can be served with almost any
meat or vegetable filling. This recipe calls for deviled eggs—
but try other fillings with it, too!

Serves 4

*Sift together*_____1 cup sifted enriched flour
1½ teaspoons double-acting baking powder
½ teaspoon salt.

*Cut in*_____¼ cup shortening until mixture resembles
coarse meal.

*Add*_____⅓ cup milk; mix only until all flour is
dampened. Knead gently on floured
board or pastry cloth for a few seconds.

*Roll*_____to 12 x 5-inch rectangle ¼ inch thick.
Cut into four 12-inch strips. Place on
ungreased baking sheet. Twist each strip
several times and shape into a ring.
Seal ends.

*Bake*_____in hot oven (425°F.) 12 to 15 minutes.
Fill rings with hot deviled eggs. Serve
with hot cheese sauce.

DEVILED EGGS

HALVE 4 hard-cooked eggs lengthwise. Remove yolks and mash
with fork. Blend in 2 tablespoons mayonnaise, 1 teaspoon vinegar, ½ teaspoon prepared mustard, ¼ teaspoon salt, few grains
pepper. Refill egg whites with yolk mixture.

CHEESE SAUCE

MELT 3 tablespoons shortening in top of double boiler over
direct heat. Blend in 3 tablespoons flour, ½ teaspoon salt, few
grains pepper. Add gradually 1½ cups milk, stirring constantly until thickened. Place over boiling water. Blend in 1 cup
grated cheese; stir occasionally until melted.

CHICKEN SHORTCAKE

Flaky biscuit shortcake served with generous sized pieces of chicken in rich cream sauce.

Serves 6

SHORTCAKE ROUNDS

Sift together........2 cups sifted **enriched flour**

3 teaspoons double-acting **baking powder**

½ teaspoon **salt.**

Cut in................½ cup **shortening** until mixture resembles coarse meal.

Add................¾ cup **milk** and mix until all flour is dampened.

Roll................dough to ¼-inch thickness; cut with 3¾-inch cutter, making six to eight rounds. Place on baking sheet.

Bake................in hot oven (425°F.) 12 to 15 minutes. Serve with the following.

CHICKEN TOPPING

Brown................¼ cup chopped **green pepper** and

¼ cup chopped **onion** in

¼ cup **shortening.**

Blend in................¼ cup **enriched flour**

⅛ teaspoon **pepper**

½ teaspoon **salt.**

Add gradually......2 cups **chicken** stock or milk, stirring constantly. Cook until thick and smooth.

Add................2 cups coarsely chopped, cooked **chicken**

½ cup cooked **peas**

½ cup coarsely diced, cooked **carrots.**

Cook................ten minutes and serve hot between and on top of split shortcake rounds.

SEAFOOD SHORTCAKE

Prepare................Shortcake Rounds.

Melt................3 tablespoons **shortening** in top of double boiler over direct heat.

Add................2 tablespoons chopped **green pepper** and sauté for 2 minutes.

Blend in................3 tablespoons **flour**
1 teaspoon **salt**
dash of **pepper**.

Add gradually...1½ cups **milk**, stirring constantly. Cook until thickened. Place over boiling water.

Add................1 cup flaked **salmon**, tuna, shrimp or other seafood
2 hard-cooked **eggs**, diced
1 tablespoon chopped **pimiento**.

Heat................thoroughly. Serve hot between and on top of split shortcake rounds.

HAM SHORTCAKE

PREPARE Shortcake Rounds. Serve with creamed ham or luncheon meat, substituting ham for seafood in Seafood Shortcake recipe.

CURRIED EGGS AND PEAS

Prepare................Shortcake Rounds.

Combine................¼ cup sifted **enriched flour**
1 teaspoon **salt**
½ teaspoon **sugar**.

Melt................¼ cup **shortening**.

Add................1 teaspoon **curry powder**

1 tablespoon minced **onion**, stirring constantly until onion is tender.

Blend in..................flour mixture, stirring until smooth.

Add..................½ teaspoon **lemon juice**

2½ cups **liquid** (milk and juice from peas)

Cook..................about 5 minutes, stirring constantly.

Add..................2 cups cooked **peas**

6 hard-cooked **eggs**, sliced.

Heat..................thoroughly and serve between and on top of split shortcake rounds.

LUNCHEON POPOVERS

PREPARE Popovers, recipe on page 9. Fill warm popovers with any of above creamed combinations.

SUPPERTIME WAFFLES

PREPARE Waffles, recipe on page 13. Serve with any of above creamed combinations.

CHICKEN ON CORN BREAD SQUARES

PREPARE Corn bread, recipe on page 19. Cut into 2-inch squares. Serve with Chicken Topping.

SALMON PUFFS

Golden-brown puffs are filled with rich creamed salmon. You can easily make them up in 45 minutes. For variety, fill with creamed tuna or chicken.

Serves 8

Sift together..........½ cup sifted **enriched flour**

¼ teaspoon **salt**

⅛ teaspoon **pepper.**

Melt..................¼ cup **shortening in**

½ cup **boiling water.**

Add............2 tablespoons chopped **pimiento**

2 tablespoons chopped **green pepper** and dry ingredients to boiling liquid all at once, stirring constantly.

Cook............until mixture leaves sides of pan in a smooth compact ball. Remove from heat and cool for about 1 minute.

Add............2 eggs, one at a time, beating vigorously after each addition until mixture is smooth again.

Drop............by rounded tablespoonfuls 1½ inches apart on greased baking sheet.

Bake............in hot oven (450°F.) 10 minutes, then at 400°F. for 15 to 20 minutes. Cut opening in each puff and fill with the following.

CREAMED SALMON

SAUTE ½ cup chopped celery, 1 tablespoon chopped green pepper and 1 tablespoon chopped pimiento in 1 tablespoon fat. Melt 6 tablespoons shortening in top of double boiler over direct heat. Add 6 tablespoons flour and mix well. Add gradually 3 cups milk, stirring constantly. Cook until thick and smooth. Place over boiling water. Add 2 cups (1 lb. can) flaked salmon, 1 teaspoon salt, ⅛ teaspoon pepper and the celery mixture. Cook for about 5 minutes or until thoroughly heated.

ITALIAN PIZZA

You can serve it hot from the oven. Or you can make it up ahead of time, and warm it, just before you put it on the table. (Cut pizza in big, wide wedges—to be eaten with fingers or forks.)

Makes two pizzas

Combine............½ cup scalded milk

¼ cup **shortening**

1 tablespoon **sugar**

	1½ teaspoons salt.
Cool	to lukewarm by adding ½ cup water.*
Add	1 cake compressed **yeast**, crumbled (or 1 package dry granular yeast dissolved as directed on package*); mix well.
Add	3 cups sifted **enriched flour**; mix until dough is well blended. Grease top of dough and cover.
Let rise	in warm place (85° to 90°F.) until double in bulk, about 45 minutes to 1 hour.
Divide	dough in half. Roll into two rounds to fit 9 or 10-inch greased pie pans, or into two 12x8-inch rectangles and place on greased baking sheets.
Brush with	salad oil or olive oil.
Spread	the dough with the following, using half of the ingredients on each round of dough:

2 cups well-drained **tomatoes** (two No. 2½ cans)

¼ cup chopped **onion**

¼ teaspoon **thyme** or oregano

¼ cup chopped **parsley**

½ teaspoon **salt**

few grains of **black pepper**

1 pound cooked **pork sausage**†

½ cup grated **Parmesan cheese** or other strong cheese.

| *Bake* | immediately in moderately hot oven (400°F.) 15 to 20 minutes. |

---

*The water used to dissolve dry yeast should be subtracted from water in recipe.

†If desired, 4 oz. coarsely chopped anchovy fillets or ⅓ lb. Italian sausage, cut in small strips, may be substituted for the pork sausage.

CORN FRITTERS

Crispy, crusty fritters are filled with golden bits of corn, and served with syrup.

Makes about 20 fritters

Sift together............2 cups sifted **enriched flour**
3 teaspoons double-acting **baking powder**
1 teaspoon **salt**
dash of pepper and paprika, if desired.

Combine............2 cups **cream style corn**
2 eggs, well beaten
2 tablespoons melted **shortening** or salad oil.

Add............liquid to dry ingredients; mix well.

Drop............by heaping tablespoonfuls into deep hot fat (375°F.) and fry until golden brown, about 2 to 3 minutes on each side.

Drain............on unglazed paper. Serve warm with crisp bacon and warmed syrup or honey.

CHEESE SOUFFLÉ

Use either mild or tangy cheese in this high-handsome souffle.

Serves 6

Melt............¼ cup **butter** or margarine in top of double boiler over direct heat. Remove from heat.

Blend in............¼ cup sifted **enriched flour**
1 teaspoon **salt**
1¼ cups milk; cook over boiling water until thickened, stirring constantly.

Add	½ pound (1 cup) **cheese**, sliced; stir until melted; remove from heat.
Add	4 **egg yolks**, slightly beaten, to thickened sauce.
Beat	4 **egg whites** until stiff but not dry; gradually fold cheese mixture into egg whites.
Pour	into 2 quart casserole.
Bake	in pan of hot water in a slow oven (325°F.) 1 hour. Serve immediately.

BAKED-IN FRANKFURTERS

Here's an easy way to have your "hot dogs" complete with
mustard and chili sauce—baked right inside a layer of tender
biscuit dough. (Quick and easy.)

Makes 12

Sift together	2 cups sifted **enriched flour**
	3 teaspoons double-acting **baking powder**
	½ teaspoon **salt**.
Cut in	¼ cup **shortening** until mixture resembles coarse meal.
Add	¾ cup **milk** and mix only until all flour is dampened. Knead gently on floured board or pastry cloth for a few seconds.
Roll out	to a 13x9-inch rectangle and cut into ½-inch strips.
Split	12 frankfurters lengthwise, taking care not to completely separate the halves. Spread with prepared mustard and chili sauce.
Wrap	each wiener spirally with a strip of dough, leaving 1 inch exposed at each end. Fasten ends of dough with toothpicks. Place on baking sheet.
Bake	in hot oven (450°F.) 15 minutes. Serve with tomato sauce.

CHAPTER FIVE

Cakes • Frostings and Fillings

Cakes

ANY WOMAN *who bakes is happy and proud to serve a lovely cake—one that's delicate, light as a feather, velvet grained and beautiful to look at. Maybe it's because a glamorous cake is the focus of admiration at a table. The lady who baked the cake glows with pride when she says, "Why, yes, I baked it myself." Maybe cake baking is important because cake fits in so well with other desserts—ice cream, fresh fruits, sauces—or just coffee. Maybe it's because cake baking is such fun. Or maybe it's just because a cake is so very good to eat.*

There's a secret to making a perfect cake. It isn't a matter of luck. It doesn't make any difference whether you're a "born cook" or not. The secret is in following the rules. And we've listed a few hints and rules for you on the next few pages. Following the rules is important in almost any type of baking. But it's most important of all in cake baking, since cake ingredients are so carefully balanced.

How to Make Perfect Cakes

Ingredients—If you wish high, light, delicate cakes you must use high-quality ingredients. All ingredients should be at room temperature unless otherwise specified.

Standard Measuring Equipment—Cake recipes—more than most other recipes for baked foods — are delicately

balanced. For that reason all ingredients must be measured accurately. Level measurements in standard size
measuring cups and spoons are a necessity. Always sift
flour before measuring.

Size of Cake Pans—For best results, use the size of pan specified in the recipe. If the wrong size is used, the cake may
hump, crack or fall. If the pan is too large, the cake will
be thin.

The following pans are equivalent in size and may be
used interchangeably. If a cake recipe specifies one size
pan, one of the other sizes may be substituted.

Two 8-inch round layer cake pans =
    9x9x2-inch square pan,
    12x8x2-inch oblong pan or
    about 24 medium cupcakes.
Two 9-inch round layer cake pans =
    two 8-inch square layer pans or
    13x9x2-inch oblong pan.

Measuring all ingredients.

Measuring Cake Pans—Measure the top inside length and width and the inside perpendicular depth.

Preparing Cake Pans—For shortening-type cakes, grease bottom of pan well and then coat lightly with flour. Do not grease sides of pan. If desired, bottom of pan may be lined with waxed paper or ungreased wrapping paper.

For sponge-type cakes, do not grease the pan.

Pouring Batter in Pan—After the batter has been poured into the cake pan, cut gently through the batter several times with a spatula in order to break any large air pockets.

Baking Cakes—Always preheat oven to temperature stated in recipe before starting to bake a cake.

Placing Pans in Oven—Bake cake on a rack which is centered in the oven. Pans should not touch each other or the sides of the oven.

If you are baking three layers, arrange two racks as close to the center of the oven as possible. Stagger the pans so one pan is not directly above another and the heat can circulate freely.

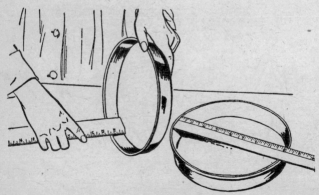

Fig. 1—How to measure pans.

Baking in Oven Glassware—Decrease the oven temperature 25°F. when using oven glassware as glass pans absorb more heat than metal pans.

Testing When Cake is Done—A cake is baked when it springs back without leaving an impression when touched lightly in center. Also, the cake will recede slightly from sides of pan.

Removing Cakes From Pans—Cool cakes 10 to 15 minutes before removing from pans. Then run spatula around sides of pans to release cake; turn cake out on a wire rack to cool. Cake racks are very useful in turning out layer cakes. If cake is cooled on a plate or board, the bottom surface will become soggy.

Conventional Method Shortening Cakes

MANY OF THE CAKES *in this chapter are made by the conventional method—that is, the shortening and sugar are creamed thoroughly, and the dry and liquid ingredients are added alternately.*

Fig. 2—Pouring batter into pans.

Cakes made this way are light and fluffy—if you remember these pointers:

Cream the shortening and sugar thoroughly—"Quick-Mix" or hydrogenated shortenings need no creaming. Butter, margarine or lard should be at room temperature for easy creaming. The sugar should be gradually added to

Testing when cake is done.

Removing layers from pans.

the shortening until the mixture is very light and fluffy. An electric mixer can do this very quickly. A wooden spoon is good for creaming by hand.

Eggs may be added unbeaten or beaten separately, according to the recipe. If unbeaten, add one at a time and combine thoroughly with other ingredients. If eggs are separated, fold the stiffly beaten whites into the batter just before pouring into pan.

Add the liquid and flour mixture alternately—First add about ⅓ of the flour mixture, then about ½ of liquid. Beat only until batter is smooth. Add another ⅓ of flour, then balance of milk. Always begin and end with flour. The batter may curdle if the liquid is added first. Blend well after each addition, but *do not overbeat* after the liquid and flour have been added.

Quick-Mix Method Cakes

THE QUICK-MIX METHOD *is a relatively new but very popular way of making shortening cakes. The cakes are light, velvety and even-textured. But best of all—they can be made more quickly than conventional method cakes and they're delicious! There's no creaming of shortening and sugar, no beating of eggs separately. All the ingredients are mixed together in just one bowl.*

We've tested hundreds of Quick-Mix cakes in our Ann Pillsbury Kitchen and here are a few suggestions we'd like to pass on to you:

Follow the recipe accurately—for the ingredients in Quick-Mix cakes are delicately balanced. Do not make substitutions. It is important that ingredients be at room temperature.

Use a high grade "Quick-Mix" or hydrogenated shortening

—either animal or vegetable. These types of shortenings are recommended for Quick-Mix cakes. Butter, lard or margarine may also be used—the general rule when using them is to decrease each cup of milk by 2 table-spoons.

Beat the batter—the full amount of time given in the recipe, 150 strokes per minute. If an electric mixer is used blend at low speed to avoid spattering, beat at a medium speed (about the middle of the dial if indicated by numbers) for the length of time given in the recipe.

Quick-Mix batters are generally thinner than conventional method cake batters.

White Cakes

SNO WHITE CAKE

Quick-Mix Method

This cake is high and light as a feather. It is beautiful frosted with fluffy white icing, and it can be decorated in countless ways. Sometime try the lime delight variation—or make it a birthday cake.

Makes two 8 or 9-inch round layers

All ingredients must be at room temperature.

*Sift together*____2¼ cups sifted enriched flour
                    3¼ teaspoons double-acting baking powder
                    1 teaspoon salt
                    1½ cups sugar.
*Add*_____½ cup shortening
                    ¾ cup milk.
*Beat*_____for 2 minutes, 300 strokes, until batter is well blended. (With electric mixer, blend at low speed, then beat at medium speed for 2 minutes.)

Add............................¼ cup milk
                  ½ cup egg whites, unbeaten
                  1 teaspoon vanilla.
Beat..........................for 2 minutes.
Pour..........................into two well-greased and floured 8 or 9-inch layer pans, at least 1¼ inches deep.
Bake..........................in moderate oven (350°F.) 30 to 35 minutes. Cool and frost with fluffy white frosting, page 215.

LIME DELIGHT

MAKE Sno White Cake as directed above. Place lime filling, page 222, between layers. Frost with 1 egg white fluffy white frosting, page 216. For festive occasions, decorate cake with coconut which has been tinted a pale green.

BIRTHDAY CAKE

MAKE Sno White Cake as directed above. Fill and frost with fluffy peppermint frosting, page 217. Decorate with crushed peppermint stick candy and candles.

LADY BALTIMORE CAKE

Quick-Mix Method

This queenly cake has the traditionally rich, fruit-nut Lady Baltimore filling and frosting.

Makes two 8-inch round layers

All ingredients must be at room temperature.

*Sift together*____1¾ cups sifted enriched flour
                  3 teaspoons double-acting baking powder
                  1 teaspoon salt
                  1¼ cups sugar.
Add..........................½ cup shortening
                  ½ cup milk.

Beat................for 2 minutes, 300 strokes, until batter is well blended. (With electric mixer blend at low speed, then beat at medium speed for 2 minutes.)

Add................¼ cup **milk**
3 **egg whites**, unbeaten
1 teaspoon **vanilla.**

Beat................for 2 minutes.

Pour................into two well-greased and floured 8-inch layer pans, at least 1¼ inches deep.

Bake................in moderate oven (350°F.) 25 to 30 minutes. Cool and frost with Lady Baltimore frosting, page 216.

COCONUT SURPRISE CAKE

Quick-Mix Method

You blend shreds of coconut right into this creamy cake batter. And what a luscious cake it makes . . . rich and chewy with coconut, delicately flavored with almond. Cover it with fluffy frosting—or any of your favorite frostings.

Makes two 8-inch round layers

All ingredients must be at room temperature.

Sift together........1¾ cups sifted **enriched flour**
3 teaspoons double-acting **baking powder**
1 teaspoon **salt**
1¼ cups **sugar.**

Add................½ cup **shortening**
½ cup **milk.**

Beat................for 2 minutes, 300 strokes, until batter is well blended. (With electric mixer blend at low speed, then beat at medium speed for 2 minutes.)

Add................¼ cup **milk**

3 **egg whites,** unbeaten
½ teaspoon **vanilla**
½ teaspoon **almond extract.**

Beat .... for 2 minutes.

Fold in .... 1 cup shredded **coconut.** (Chop slightly if shreds are long.)

Pour .... into two 8-inch layer pans, at least 1¼ inches deep, which have been greased and lined with waxed paper.

Bake .... in moderate oven (350°F.) 30 to 35 minutes. Cool and frost with fluffy white frosting, page 215, and sprinkle with shredded coconut.

BANQUET LAYER CAKE

Pillsbury Contest Winner by Mrs. O. A. Ornburn, Moberly, Mo.

This is a truly regal white cake. Frost with a 3-egg white fluffy frosting. It's a large cake to serve when a crowd's coming.

Makes three 9-inch round layers

All ingredients must be at room temperature.

Sift together .... 3 cups sifted **enriched flour**
3½ teaspoons double-acting **baking powder**
1 teaspoon **salt.**

Cream .... 1 cup **butter** (half shortening may be used); add gradually
1½ cups **sugar,** creaming well.

Combine .... 1¼ cups **milk**
1 teaspoon **vanilla**
1 teaspoon **almond extract.** Add alternately with dry ingredients to creamed mixture, beginning and ending with dry ingredients. Blend thoroughly after each

addition. (With electric mixer use low speed.)

Beat................7 **egg whites** until stiff but not dry.
Add gradually
½ cup **sugar**, beating until stiff. Fold gently into batter.

Pour................batter into three well-greased and floured 9-inch round layer pans.

Bake................in moderate oven (350°F.) 30 to 35 minutes. Cool; frost with 3-egg white fluffy white frosting, page 216, reserving ⅓ of frosting for filling. Fold in ¼ cup drained, chopped maraschino cherries, ½ cup coconut and ½ cup chopped nuts. Spread between cooled layers.

SWING-YOUR-PARTNER CAKE

Pillsbury Contest Winner by Mrs. Roger Slick, Waynesboro, Penna.

Quick-Mix Method

Here is a really showy cake with fluffy white frosting and a special "turkey-in-the-straw" topping, which was Mrs. Slick's own idea.

Makes two 8-inch round layers

All ingredients must be at room temperature.

Sift together................2 cups sifted **enriched flour**
3 teaspoons double-acting **baking powder**
1 teaspoon **salt**
1¼ cups **sugar.**

Add................½ cup **shortening**
¾ cup **milk**
1 teaspoon **vanilla**
1 teaspoon **almond** extract.

Beat................for 2 minutes, 300 strokes, until batter is

	well blended. (With electric mixer blend at low speed, then beat at medium speed for 2 minutes.)
Add	3 **egg whites,** unbeaten.
Beat	for 2 minutes.
Pour	into two well-greased and floured 8-inch round layer pans, at least 1¼ inches deep.
Bake	in moderate oven (350°F.) 30 to 35 minutes. Cool and frost with fluffy white frosting, page 215. Top with turkey-in-the-straw topping.

TURKEY-IN-THE-STRAW TOPPING

COMBINE ½ cup corn soya cereal and ½ cup shredded coconut. Sprinkle over top of frosted cake. Cut a slit in each of 6 green maraschino cherries. Cut 1 red maraschino cherry into 6 strips, inserting one strip into the slit in each green cherry to make "turkeys." Stand "turkeys" in corn soya-coconut "straw."

GRANDMOTHER'S ALMOND SNOW CAKE

Pillsbury Contest Winner by Mrs. Elisabeth H. Tinkler, Maitland, Fla.

High, light and snow-white . . . a dainty old-fashioned cake with a delicate almond flavor. Frost with a pretty fluffy frosting.

Makes two 8-inch round layers

All ingredients must be at room temperature.

Sift together	2 cups sifted **enriched flour**
	3 teaspoons double-acting **baking powder**
	1 teaspoon **salt.**
Beat	4 **egg whites** until foamy. Add gradually ¼ cup **sugar** and beat until stiff but not dry.

Cream..............½ cup **butter** (half shortening may be
used); add gradually
1 cup **sugar**, creaming well.

Combine..............¾ cup **milk**
½ teaspoon **almond extract**. Add alternately
with dry ingredients to creamed mixture, beginning and ending with dry ingredients. Blend thoroughly after each
addition. (With electric mixer use low
speed.)

Fold in..............beaten egg whites.

Pour..............into two well-greased and floured 8-inch
round layer pans, at least 1¼ inches
deep.

Bake..............in moderate oven (350°F.) 30 to 40 minutes. Cool and frost with seven-minute
frosting, page 217.

DUTCH RIDGE RECEPTION CAKE

Pillsbury Contest Winner by Mrs. J. V. Orlett, West Portsmouth, O.

**"This cake is my favorite for birthdays, parties and church
festivals, and it always brings top prices at a bake sale," says
Mrs. Orlett. "It has an old-fashioned something that appeals."**

Makes two 8-inch round layers

All ingredients must be at room temperature.

Sift together..............2 cups sifted **enriched flour**
1½ teaspoons double-acting **baking powder**
½ teaspoon **soda**
1 teaspoon **salt**.

Cream..............½ cup **shortening**; add gradually
1 cup **sugar**, creaming well.

Combine..............¾ cup **buttermilk** or sour milk
1 teaspoon **vanilla**
1 teaspoon **almond extract**. Add alternate-

ly with dry ingredients to creamed mixture, beginning and ending with dry ingredients. Blend thoroughly after each addition. (With electric mixer use low speed.)

Beat — 4 egg whites until stiff but not dry. Add ¼ cup sugar gradually. Fold gently but thoroughly into batter.

Pour — into two well-greased and floured 8-inch round layer pans, at least 1¼ inches deep.

Bake — in moderate oven (350°F.) 35 to 40 minutes. Cool and frost with fluffy white frosting, page 215.

TEXAS HOSPITALITY CAKE

Pillsbury Contest Winner by Mrs. P. C. Campbell, Houston, Tex.

The perfect cake for church suppers and family reunions. It is easy to carry, cuts to advantage and has a pleasing pecan flavor. Frost with pecan fondant frosting.

Makes 13x9x2-inch cake

All ingredients must be at room temperature.

Sift together — 3 cups sifted enriched flour
3 teaspoons double-acting baking powder
1 teaspoon salt

Cream — ¾ cup butter (half shortening may be used); add gradually
1¾ cups sugar, creaming well.

Combine — ½ cup milk
½ cup water
1 teaspoon vanilla
¼ teaspoon almond extract. Add alternate-

	ly with dry ingredients to creamed mixture, beginning and ending with dry ingredients. Blend thoroughly after each addition. (With electric mixer use low speed.)
Add	¾ cup chopped pecans.
Beat	3 egg whites until stiff but not dry. Fold gently but thoroughly into batter.
Pour	into well-greased and floured 13x9x2-inch pan.
Bake	in moderate oven (350°F.) 40 to 45 minutes. Cool and frost with pecan fondant frosting, page 219.

Yellow and Gold Cakes

GOLDEN GLOW CAKE

Quick-Mix Method

Here's a basic 2-egg cake that's good to the last, delicious crumb. Any one of your favorite frostings will go well with this cake. Notice the cake variations, too. You can make an orange, cocoa or spice cake from this same basic recipe.

Makes two 8-inch round layers

All ingredients must be at room temperature.

Sift together	2 cups sifted enriched flour
	3 teaspoons double-acting baking powder
	1 teaspoon salt
	1¼ cups sugar.
Add	½ cup shortening
	¾ cup milk.
Beat	for 2 minutes, 300 strokes, until batter is well blended. (With electric mixer blend at low speed, then beat at medium speed for 2 minutes.)

Add	¼ cup milk
	2 eggs
	1 teaspoon vanilla.
Beat	for 2 minutes.
Pour	into two well-greased and floured 8-inch layer pans, at least 1¼ inches deep.
Bake	in moderate oven (350°F.) 35 to 40 minutes. Cool and frost as desired.

ORANGE CAKE

PREPARE Golden Glow Cake as directed above, adding 1 tablespoon grated orange rind to shortening.

COCOA CAKE

PREPARE Golden Glow Cake as directed above, reducing flour to 1½ cups. Add ⅓ cup cocoa and sift with dry ingredients.

SPICE CAKE

PREPARE Golden Glow Cake as directed above, sifting 1 teaspoon cinnamon, 1 teaspoon allspice, ½ teaspoon nutmeg and ½ teaspoon cloves with dry ingredients. Decrease sugar to ¾ cup and add ½ cup firmly packed brown sugar with shortening and milk.

ONE-EGG CAKE

Quick-Mix Method

This quick, easy cake makes a delicious base for fruit short-cakes. Good, too, frosted with your favorite icing.

Makes 8x8x2-inch cake

All ingredients must be at room temperature.

Sift together	1¼ cups sifted enriched flour
	2 teaspoons double-acting baking powder
	½ teaspoon salt
	¾ cup sugar.
Add	¼ cup shortening

½ cup milk

2 teaspoons grated orange rind.

Beat................................for 2 minutes, 300 strokes, until batter is well blended. (With electric mixer blend at low speed, then beat at medium speed for 2 minutes.)

Add................................1 egg, unbeaten

1 teaspoon vanilla.

Beat................................for 2 minutes.

Pour................................into well-greased and floured 8x8x2-inch pan or 9-inch round layer cake pan.

Bake................................in moderate oven (350°F.) 30 to 35 minutes. Cool and frost as desired.

CHURCH SUPPER CAKE

When it's your turn to bring the cake—this cake is a wise choice. You will find it is easy to carry and easy to cut. Good with almost any kind of frosting, but we suggest the fluffy white kind.

Makes 13x9x2-inch cake

Sift together......2½ cups sifted enriched flour

3 teaspoons double-acting baking powder

1 teaspoon salt.

Blend together.....⅔ cup shortening

1 tablespoon grated orange rind.

Add gradually..1½ cups sugar, creaming well.

Add................................3 eggs, one at a time. Beat for 1 minute.

Combine................................1⅛ cups milk and

1 teaspoon vanilla. Add alternately with dry ingredients to creamed mixture, beginning and ending with dry ingredients. Blend thoroughly after each addition. (With electric mixer use low speed.)

Pour .... into well-greased and floured 13x9x2-inch pan.

Bake .... in moderate oven (350°F.) 40 to 45 minutes. Cool and frost as desired.

LAZY-DAISY CAKE

Quick-Mix Method

This caramel-flavored cake is especially easy to make. You mix it the Quick-Mix way, and the frosting is "baked on" under the broiler.

Makes 13x9x2-inch cake

All ingredients must be at room temperature.

Sift together .... 2½ cups sifted **enriched flour**
4½ teaspoons double-acting **baking powder**
1 teaspoon **salt**
¾ cup **sugar.**

Add .... ¾ cup firmly packed **brown sugar**, sieved
¾ cup **shortening**
1 cup **milk.**

Beat .... for 2 minutes, 300 strokes, until batter is well blended. (With electric mixer blend at low speed, then beat at medium speed for 2 minutes.)

Add .... ¼ cup **milk**
3 **eggs**, unbeaten
1 teaspoon **vanilla.**

Beat .... for 2 minutes.

Pour .... into well-greased and floured 13x9x2-inch pan.

Bake .... in moderate oven (350°F.) 40 to 45 minutes.

Combine .... ¼ cup **butter**, melted

½ cup firmly packed **brown sugar**
¾ cup **shredded coconut**
3 tablespoons **cream.**

Spread................on warm cake; place under broiler and brown lightly.

YELLOW DAISY CAKE

Pillsbury Contest Winner by Mrs. C. C. Holloman, Saratoga Springs, N. Y.

"In my family," says Mrs. Holloman, "we make this cake along with an angel food, utilizing the many egg yolks that would be left over."

Makes 9-inch tube cake

All ingredients must be at room temperature.

Sift together........2¼ cups sifted **enriched flour**
3 teaspoons double-acting **baking powder**
½ teaspoon **salt.**

Beat................9 **egg yolks** until very thick and lemon colored.

Cream................½ cup **butter** (half shortening may be used); add gradually
1½ cups **sugar**, creaming well. Add egg yolks; mix well.

Combine................1 cup **milk**
1 teaspoon **lemon extract.** Add alternately with dry ingredients to creamed mixture, beginning and ending with dry ingredients. Blend thoroughly after each addition. (With electric mixer use low speed.)

Pour................into well-greased 9-inch tube pan. Cut through batter with spatula to break large air bubbles.

Bake——————in slow oven (325°F.) 55 to 60 minutes. Cool a few minutes before removing from pan. Cool and frost with lemon butter frosting, page 211.

SALLY'S HURRY-UP CAKE

Quick-Mix Method

Pillsbury Contest Winner by Mrs. Sally Clark, Santa Maria, Calif.

No frosting needed—no fuss to make this Quick-Mix cake. It packs well in lunchboxes and is delicious at coffee parties or for after-school snacks.

Makes 12x8x2 or 10x10x2-inch cake

All ingredients must be at room temperature.

Sift together——2¼ cups sifted **enriched flour**

3 teaspoons double-acting **baking powder**

1 teaspoon salt

1½ cups **sugar**.

Add——————½ cup **shortening**

½ cup chopped **nuts**

3 eggs, unbeaten

1 cup **milk**

1 teaspoon **vanilla**

grated rind of 1 **orange**.

Beat——————for 2 minutes, 300 strokes, until batter is well blended. (With electric mixer blend at low speed, then beat at medium speed for 2 minutes.)

Pour——————into greased and floured 12x8x2 or 10x10x2-inch pan.

Sprinkle with——¼ cup chopped **nuts**.

Bake——————in moderate oven (350°F.) 45 to 55 min.

CANDY KISSES CAKE

Pillsbury Contest Winner by Mrs. H. Hartman, West Bend, Wis.

There are dates, nuts and milk-chocolate candy kisses in this cake.

Makes 9-inch tube cake

All ingredients must be at room temperature.

*Sift together*____3½ cups sifted **enriched flour**

3½ teaspoons double-acting **baking powder**

1 teaspoon **salt.**

*Combine*_____1½ cups finely chopped **dates** (7¼-oz. pkg.)

½ cup chopped **nuts** and ¼ cup of the sifted dry ingredients.

*Cream*_____⅔ cup **butter** (half shortening may be used); add gradually

1½ cups **sugar**, creaming well.

*Blend in*_____3 **egg yolks**, one at a time. Beat for 1 minute.

*Combine*_____1 cup **milk**

1 teaspoon **vanilla.** Add alternately with dry ingredients to creamed mixture, beginning and ending with dry ingredients. Blend thoroughly after each addition. (With electric mixer use low speed.)

*Add*_____floured nuts and dates.

*Beat*_____3 **egg whites** until stiff but not dry. Fold gently but thoroughly into batter.

*Pour*_____into well-greased and floured 9-inch tube pan. Cut through batter with spatula to break large air bubbles.

*Arrange*_____1 cup **milk chocolate candy kisses** over top of batter, pressing them down so that only tips show.

*Bake*_____in moderate oven (350°F.) 60 to 70 minutes. Cool a few minutes before removing from pan. Sprinkle with confectioners' sugar.

CHOCOLATE CANDY CAKE

Quick-Mix Method

This yellow cake has chopped nuts and chocolate candy bits right in the batter. A perfect frosting for this cake is the fluffy sea foam one on page 217.

Makes two 8-inch round layers

All ingredients must be at room temperature.

*Sift together*_____2 cups sifted **enriched flour**
3 teaspoons double-acting **baking powder**
1 teaspoon salt
¾ cup sugar.

*Add*_____½ cup **shortening**
¾ cup **milk**
¼ cup firmly packed **brown sugar**, sieved.

*Beat*_____for 2 minutes, 300 strokes, until batter is well blended. (With electric mixer blend at low speed, then beat at medium speed for 2 minutes.)

*Add*_____2 **eggs**, unbeaten
1 teaspoon **vanilla**.

*Beat*_____for 2 minutes.

*Pour*_____into two well-greased and floured 8-inch layer pans, at least 1¼ inches deep.

*Sprinkle*_____1 package **semi-sweet chocolate bits** (reserve 2 tablespoons for frosting) over top of batter, half on each layer.

*Bake*_____in moderate oven (350°F.) 30 to 40 min-

utes. Cool and frost with fluffy sea foam
frosting, page 217, folding in 2 tablespoons chocolate bits just before frosting cake.

COLONIAL RAISIN CAKE

Pillsbury Contest Winner by Mrs. C. H. Burghoff, Yalesville, Conn.

**You can bake this good, old-fashioned favorite in a round
tube pan or in a loaf pan, as you prefer. Frost with creamy
butter frosting—it will stay fresh a long time.**

Makes 9-inch tube cake*

All ingredients must be at room temperature.

*Sift together*_____2 cups sifted **enriched flour**
3 teaspoons double-acting **baking powder**
1 teaspoon **salt**
½ teaspoon **nutmeg.**

*Combine*_____⅔ cup **raisins** with 2 tablespoons of the
sifted dry ingredients.

*Cream*_____⅔ cup **shortening**; add gradually
1 cup **sugar,** creaming well.

*Blend in*_____3 **eggs,** one at a time.
Beat for 1 minute.

*Combine*_____⅔ cup **milk**
1 teaspoon **vanilla.** Add alternately with
dry ingredients to creamed mixture, beginning and ending with dry ingredients. Blend thoroughly after each addition. (With electric mixer use low
speed.)

*Fold in*_____floured raisins and
¼ cup chopped **citron,** if desired.

*Pour*_____into greased and floured 9-inch* tube

---

*If desired, cake may be baked in a 12x8x2-inch pan at 350°F. for
40 to 45 minutes. If glass baking pan is used, bake at 325°F.

pan. Cut through batter with spatula to break large air bubbles.

*Bake*_____in moderate oven (350°F.) 50 to 60 minutes. Cool a few minutes before removing from pan. Cool and frost with creamy butter frosting, page 210.

RUTH'S DOTTED SWISS CAKE
Pillsbury Contest Winner

Flecks of chocolate in the batter make this cake quite different and really luscious to eat. Frost with a creamy butter frosting.

Makes two 8 or 9-inch round layers

All ingredients must be at room temperature.

*Sift together*_____2 cups sifted **enriched flour**
3 teaspoons double-acting **baking powder**
1 teaspoon **salt.**

*Cream*_____½ cup **shortening**; add gradually
1¼ cups **sugar**, creaming well.

*Blend in*_____2 **eggs**, one at a time. Beat for 1 minute.

*Combine*_____1 cup **milk**
1 teaspoon **vanilla**
½ teaspoon **orange extract.** Add alternately with dry ingredients to creamed mixture, beginning and ending with dry ingredients. Blend thoroughly after each addition. (With electric mixer use low speed.)

*Blend in*_____2 squares (2 oz.) shaved **semi-sweet or sweet chocolate.**

*Pour*_____into two well-greased and floured 8-inch round layer pans, at least 1¼ inches deep, or two 9-inch layer pans.

*Bake*_____in moderate oven (350°F.) 30 to 40 minutes. Cool and frost with creamy butter frosting, page 210.

PINEAPPLE CAKE

Quick-Mix Method

This golden cake has pineapple juice blended right into the batter. A crushed pineapple filling and pineapple butter frosting make this cake a treat for the family or a party.

Makes two 8-inch round layers

All ingredients must be at room temperature.

Sift together	2 cups sifted **enriched flour**
	3 teaspoons double-acting **baking powder**
	1 teaspoon **salt**
	1 cup **sugar**.
Add	½ cup **shortening**
	¾ cup **pineapple juice**
	½ teaspoon grated **lemon rind**.
Beat	for 2 minutes, 300 strokes, until batter is well blended. (With electric mixer blend at low speed, then beat at medium speed for 2 minutes.)
Add	2 eggs, unbeaten
	½ teaspoon **vanilla**.
Beat	for 2 minutes.
Pour	into two well-greased and floured 8-inch layer pans, at least 1¼ inches deep.
Bake	in moderate oven (350°F.) 30 to 35 minutes. Cool; spread pineapple filling, page 222, between layers. Frost with pineapple butter icing, page 211.

ORANGE BLOSSOM CAKE

Quick-Mix Method

**Orange juice and rind add a fresh flavor to this 2-egg cake.
Frost it with a creamy butter icing.**

Makes two 8-inch round layers

All ingredients must be at room temperature.

Sift together............2 cups sifted enriched flour
3 teaspoons double-acting baking powder
1 teaspoon salt
1⅓ cups sugar.

Add............1 tablespoon grated orange rind
½ cup shortening
½ cup milk
⅓ cup orange juice.

Beat............for 2 minutes, 300 strokes, until batter is well blended. (With electric mixer blend at low speed, then beat at medium speed for 2 minutes.)

Add............2 eggs, unbeaten
½ teaspoon vanilla.

Beat............for 2 minutes.

Pour............into two well-greased and floured 8-inch layer pans, at least 1¼ inches deep.

Bake............in moderate oven (350°F.) 30 to 35 minutes. Cool and frost with creamy butter orange frosting, page 210.

Chocolate Cakes

AUNT CARRIE'S BONBON CAKE

THIRD PRIZE WINNER
Pillsbury's 1st Recipe Contest
by Mrs. Richard W. Sprague, San Marino, California

"This recipe came to me from a darling Southern gentlewoman who was one of the early pioneers in Arizona," says Mrs. Sprague. It has a milk-chocolate color and flavor.

Makes two 8-inch layers

All ingredients must be at room temperature.

*Sift together*___1¾ cups sifted **enriched flour**
2½ teaspoons **single-acting baking powder**
(or 2 teaspoons double-acting)
½ teaspoon **salt.**

*Combine*___2 squares (2 oz.) **chocolate**, finely-cut, and
5 tablespoons boiling **water.** Stir until smooth and of custard consistency.

*Cream*___½ cup **butter** (half shortening may be used); add gradually
1½ cups **sugar**, creaming well.

*Add*___cooled chocolate and
1 teaspoon **vanilla.**

*Blend in*___4 **egg yolks**, one at a time. Beat for 1 minute.

*Measure*___½ cup **milk.** Add alternately with dry ingredients to creamed mixture, beginning and ending with dry ingredients. Blend thoroughly after each addition. (With electric mixer use low speed.)

*Beat*___4 **egg whites** until stiff but not dry. Fold gently but thoroughly into batter.

Pour	into two well-greased and floured 8-inch layer pans, at least 1¼ inches deep.
Bake	in moderate oven (350°F.) 30 to 35 minutes. Cool layers, then fill with bonbon filling, page 222, and frost with fudge frosting, page 219.

DEVIL'S FOOD DELIGHT

Quick-Mix Method

This rich devil's food cake is always popular. And it's made the easy Quick-Mix way! Particularly good with a chocolate frosting. (The one on page 210 is quick and easy.)

Makes two 8-inch round layers*

All ingredients must be at room temperature.

Sift together	1⅔ cups sifted **enriched flour**
	1 teaspoon **soda**
	½ teaspoon double-acting **baking powder**
	1 teaspoon **salt**
	1⅓ cups sugar.
Add	½ cup shortening
	¾ cup **buttermilk** or sour milk.
Beat	for 2 minutes, 300 strokes, until batter is well blended. (With electric mixer blend at low speed, then beat at medium speed for 2 minutes.)
Add	¼ cup **buttermilk** or sour milk
	3 squares (3 oz.) **chocolate**, melted and cooled
	2 **eggs**, unbeaten
	1 teaspoon vanilla.
Beat	for 2 minutes.

*If desired, cake may be baked in 9x9x2 or 12x8x2-inch pan at 350° F. for 40 to 45 minutes.

Pour............................into two well-greased and floured 8-inch layer pans, at least 1¼ inches deep.*

Bake............................in moderate oven (350°F.) 30 to 35 minutes. Cool and frost with creamy butter chocolate frosting, page 210. Decorate with chopped walnuts.

---

*If desired, cake may be baked in 9x9x2 or 12x8x2-inch pan at 350° F. for 40 to 45 minutes.

CHOCOLATE MOCHA DOT CAKE

Quick-Mix Method

This rich chocolate cake has just a hint of coffee flavor. Our kitchen usually frosts it with fluffy frosting and decorates with chocolate bits for a "polka-dot" effect.

Makes two 8-inch round layers

All ingredients must be at room temperature.

Sift together......1¾ cups sifted **enriched flour**

½ teaspoon double-acting **baking powder**

1 teaspoon **soda**

1 teaspoon **salt**

1 teaspoon **cinnamon**

½ cup **cocoa**

1½ cups **sugar**.

Add............................½ cup **shortening**

½ cup **strong coffee**, cooled

⅓ cup **buttermilk** or sour milk.

Beat............................for 2 minutes, 300 strokes, until batter is well blended. (With electric mixer blend at low speed, then beat at medium speed for 2 minutes.)

Add............................⅓ cup **buttermilk** or sour milk

2 **eggs**, unbeaten

	1 teaspoon **vanilla**.
Beat	for 2 minutes.
Turn	into two well-greased and floured 8-inch layer pans, at least 1¼ inches deep.
Bake	in moderate oven (350°F.) 35 to 40 minutes. Cool and frost with mocha sea foam frosting, page 217. Decorate with chocolate bits.

BROWN SUGAR CHOCOLATE CAKE

Quick-Mix Method

There is brown sugar flavor and plenty of chocolate in this cake. It's made the easy Quick-Mix way and you can use up the extra egg whites by making a fluffy white frosting. Also, chocolate candy bits can be folded into the frosting to give a marbled look.

Makes two 8-inch square or two 9-inch round layers

All ingredients must be at room temperature.

Melt	2 squares (2 oz.) **chocolate**. Combine with ¼ cup **boiling water**. Stir until smooth and of custard consistency. Cool.
Sift together	2 cups sifted **enriched flour**
	1 teaspoon double-acting **baking** powder
	1 teaspoon **soda**
	1 teaspoon **salt**
	1 cup **sugar**.
Add	½ cup firmly packed **brown sugar**
	½ cup **shortening**
	⅔ cup **milk**.
Beat	for 2 minutes, 300 strokes, until batter is well blended. (With electric mixer blend at low speed, then beat at medium speed for 2 minutes.)

*Add*_____⅓ cup milk

cooled chocolate

1 egg

3 egg yolks (reserve whites for frosting)

1 teaspoon vanilla.

*Beat*_____for 2 minutes.

*Pour*_____into two well-greased and floured 8-inch square or 9-inch round layer pans.

*Bake*_____in moderate oven (350°F.) 30 to 40 minutes. Frost with fluffy white frosting, page 215.

COCOA LAYER CAKE

Pillsbury Contest Winner by Mrs. Peter Funcke, Cedar Rapids, Iowa

Mrs. Funcke made this cake "to order" for one of her children. And she frosts the cocoa-flavored layers with glamorous White Mountain frosting.

Makes two 8-inch round layers*

All ingredients must be at room temperature.

*Sift together*_____1¾ cups sifted enriched flour

1 teaspoon soda

½ teaspoon double-acting baking powder

1 teaspoon salt

¼ cup cocoa.

*Cream*_____½ cup shortening; add gradually

1 cup sugar, creaming well.

*Blend in*_____2 eggs, one at a time. Beat for 1 minute.

*Combine*_____½ cup evaporated milk

½ cup water

1 teaspoon vanilla. Add alternately with dry ingredients to creamed mixture, beginning and ending with dry ingredi-

*If desired, cake may be baked in two well-greased and floured 8-inch pie pans for 20 to 30 minutes. Frost and serve in wedges.

ents. Blend thoroughly after each addition. (With electric mixer use low
speed.)

Pour..................into two well-greased and floured 8-inch
round layer pans, at least 1¼ inches
deep.*

Bake..................in moderate oven (350°F.) 35 to 40 minutes. Cool and frost with White Moun-
tain frosting, page 218.

---

*If desired, cake may be baked in two well-greased and floured 8-inch
pie pans for 20 to 30 minutes. Frost and serve in wedges.

NEW ENGLAND FUDGE CAKE

Pillsbury Contest Winner by Mrs. Numa F. Pigeon, Springfield, Mass.

**This rich, moist chocolate fudge cake has chopped walnuts
inside. Frost it with a fluffy white frosting.**

Makes two 9-inch round layers

All ingredients must be at room temperature.

Sift together......1⅔ cups sifted enriched flour
2½ teaspoons double-acting baking powder
¼ teaspoon soda
1 teaspoon salt.

Cream..................⅔ cup shortening; add gradually
1½ cups sugar, creaming well.

Blend in..............4 egg yolks, one at a time. Beat for 1 minute.

Add......................3 squares (3 oz.) chocolate, melted and
cooled
1 cup chopped walnuts; mix well.

Combine..............1 cup milk
1 teaspoon vanilla. Add alternately with
dry ingredients to creamed mixture, beginning and ending with dry ingredi-

	ents. Blend thoroughly after each addition. (With electric mixer use low speed.)
Beat	4 egg whites until stiff but not dry. Fold gently but thoroughly into batter.
Pour	into two well-greased and floured 9-inch round layer pans.
Bake	in moderate oven (350°F.) 30 to 35 minutes. Cool and frost with fluffy white frosting, page 215.

DREAMBROSIA FUDGE CAKE

Pillsbury Contest Winner by Mrs. C. F. Lowman, Fountain City, Tenn.

There is shredded coconut in the batter of this moist chocolate fudge cake. Frost it with creamy butter frosting and top it with golden, toasted coconut.

Makes two 9-inch round layers

All ingredients must be at room temperature.

Sift together	2 cups sifted enriched flour
	3½ teaspoons single-acting baking powder (or 2½ teaspoons double-acting)
	½ teaspoon soda
	1 teaspoon salt.
Cream	½ cup butter (half shortening may be used); add gradually
	1¼ cups sugar, creaming well.
Blend in	3 egg yolks, one at a time
	3 squares (3 oz.) chocolate, melted and cooled. Beat for 1 minute.
Combine	1 cup milk
	1 teaspoon vanilla. Add alternately with dry ingredients to creamed mixture, beginning and ending with dry ingredi-

ents. Blend thoroughly after each addition. (With electric mixer use low speed.)

Fold in_____¾ cup moist shredded coconut.

Beat_____3 egg whites until stiff but not dry. Fold gently but thoroughly into batter.

Pour_____into two well-greased and floured 9-inch round layer pans.

Bake_____in moderate oven (350°F.) 30 to 40 minutes. Cool and frost with creamy butter frosting, page 210.

MISSION SUNDAY FUDGE CAKE

Pillsbury Contest Winner by Mrs. Albert C. Plagens, St. Paul, Minn.

A rich chocolate fudge loaf cake, with chopped nuts and shredded coconut in the batter. Frost with easy chocolate mallow frosting. Several pastors' wives in Minnesota double the recipe and bake this cake for "Mission Sunday" suppers.

Makes 8x8x2-inch cake*

All ingredients must be at room temperature.

Sift together_____1 cup sifted enriched flour
½ teaspoon soda
¼ teaspoon salt.

Cream_____½ cup butter (half shortening may be used); add gradually
1 cup firmly packed brown sugar, creaming well.

Blend in_____3 eggs, one at a time
1½ squares (1½ oz.) chocolate, melted and cooled. Beat for 1 minute.

Combine_____½ cup sour milk or buttermilk
1 teaspoon vanilla. Add alternately with

_____

*If desired, this recipe may be doubled and baked in a 14x10x2-inch pan for 1 hour.

dry ingredients to creamed mixture, beginning and ending with dry ingredients. Blend thoroughly after each addition. (With electric mixer use low speed.)

Fold in................¼ cup finely chopped **nuts**

½ cup shredded **coconut.**

Pour................into well-greased and floured 8x8x2-inch pan.

Bake................in slow oven (325°F.) 45 to 55 minutes. Cool and frost with chocolate mallow frosting, page 212.

APRICOT SURPRISE FUDGE CAKE

Pillsbury Contest Winner by Miss Florence Schoenleber, Lincoln, Neb.

Apricots are blended into chocolate fudge cake batter to make a really unusual combination of flavors.

Makes two 8-inch round layers

All ingredients must be at room temperature.

Sift together..........2 cups sifted **enriched flour**

2½ teaspoons double-acting **baking powder**

¼ teaspoon **soda**

½ teaspoon **salt.**

Cream................½ cup **butter** (half shortening may be used); add gradually

1¼ cups **sugar**, creaming well.

Blend in................2 **eggs**, one at a time

3 squares (3 oz.) **chocolate**, melted and cooled

1 teaspoon **vanilla.** Beat for 1 minute.

Measure................¾ cup **milk.** Add alternately with dry ingredients to creamed mixture, beginning and ending with dry ingredients. Blend thoroughly after each addition. (With electric mixer use low speed.)

Blend in .... ¾ cup cooked dried apricots, drained and coarsely cut.

Pour .... into two well-greased and floured 8-inch round layer cake pans, at least 1¼ inches deep.

Bake .... in moderate oven (350°F.) 35 to 40 minutes.

Beat .... ½ pint (1 cup) whipping cream. Sweeten to taste and spread between and on top of cooled layers. Decorate with additional bits of cooked apricots.

BUSY DAY CHOCOLATE CAKE

Pillsbury Contest Winner by Mrs. Stanley L. Smith, Kansas City, Mo.

Quick-Mix Method

"I found the original recipe, hand-written on the flyleaf of a cookbook," says Mrs. Smith. "The method of mixing is mine. This is my hurry-up cake. The time from lighting oven to serving is only one hour."

Makes 9x9x2-inch cake

All ingredients must be at room temperature.

Melt .... 2 squares (2 oz.) chocolate; cool.
Combine .... 1⅓ cups sifted enriched flour
1 cup sugar.
Add .... 1 teaspoon soda
½ teaspoon salt
¼ cup shortening
1 cup buttermilk or sour milk
1 egg

	1 teaspoon vanilla and cooled chocolate in large bowl.
Beat	with rotary beater for 3 minutes. (With electric mixer blend at low speed, then beat at medium speed for 3 minutes.)
Pour	into greased and floured 9x9x2-inch pan.
Bake	in moderate oven (350°F.) 40 to 45 minutes. Serve warm topped with whipped cream or frost as desired.

CHOCOLATE WISHING RING CAKE

Quick-Mix Method

This rich devil's food cake is baked in a ring mold pan. It's frosted with a quick cocoa butter icing. Bring it to the table filled with scoops of ice cream; a lovely, complete dessert.

Makes 9-inch ring cake*

All ingredients must be at room temperature.

Sift together	1⅓ cups sifted enriched flour 1 teaspoon double-acting baking powder 1 teaspoon salt ½ teaspoon soda 1¼ cups sugar.
Add	⅓ cup shortening ¾ cup buttermilk or sour milk.
Beat	for 2 minutes, 300 strokes, until batter is well blended. (With electric mixer blend at low speed, then beat at medium speed for 2 minutes.)
Add	2 eggs, unbeaten

*If desired, cake may be baked in two greased and floured 8-inch layer pans, at least 1¼ inches deep. Bake at 350°F. for 30 to 35 minutes.

2½ squares (2½ oz.) chocolate, melted and cooled

1 teaspoon vanilla.

Beat................for 2 minutes.

Pour................into well-greased and floured 9-inch ring mold, 3 inches deep, filling mold half full.

Bake................in moderate oven (375°F.) 30 to 35 minutes. Cool and frost with cocoa butter frosting, page 213. Before serving fill ring with scoops of ice cream.

RED DEVIL'S FOOD LOAF

For those who like a red chocolate cake, we recommend this recipe. It's inexpensive, easy, and the cake is mighty good eating.

Makes 12x8x2 or 10x10x2-inch cake

All ingredients must be at room temperature.

Sift together......1⅔ cups sifted enriched flour

½ teaspoon double-acting baking powder

1 teaspoon soda

1 teaspoon salt.

Cream................½ cup shortening; add gradually

1¼ cups sugar, creaming well.

Blend in................2 eggs, one at a time. Beat for 1 minute.

Add................2 squares (2 oz.) chocolate, melted and cooled.

Combine................1 cup milk and

1 teaspoon vanilla. Add alternately with dry ingredients to creamed mixture, beginning and ending with dry ingredients.

	Blend thoroughly after each addition. (With electric mixer use low speed.)
Pour	into well-greased and floured 12x8x2 or 10x10x2-inch pan.
Bake	in moderate oven (350°F.) 40 to 45 minutes. Cool. Frost with chocolate cream cheese frosting, page 213, and decorate with chopped nuts.

Spice and Ginger Cakes

SPICE CAKE

Quick-Mix Method

Spice cake is always popular. It's not too sweet, and it has just the right delicious tang. This spice cake is made our Quick-Mix way, and dressed up with banana frosting.

Makes two 8-inch round layers

All ingredients must be at room temperature.

Sift together	2 cups sifted enriched flour
	3 teaspoons double-acting baking powder
	1 teaspoon salt
	1 teaspoon cinnamon
	1 teaspoon allspice
	½ teaspoon cloves
	½ teaspoon nutmeg
	1 cup sugar.
Add	⅓ cup firmly packed brown sugar, sieved
	½ cup shortening
	¾ cup milk.

Beat	for 2 minutes, 300 strokes, until batter is well blended. (With electric mixer blend at low speed, then beat at medium speed for 2 minutes.)
Add	2 tablespoons **milk**
	2 **eggs**, unbeaten
	1 teaspoon **vanilla**.
Beat	for 2 minutes.
Pour	into two well-greased and floured 8-inch layer cake pans, at least 1¼ inches deep.
Bake	in moderate oven (350°F.) 30 to 35 minutes. Cool and frost with banana frosting, page 211.

AUNT LOU'S DIXIE SPICE CAKE

Pillsbury Contest Winner by Mrs. Lona Gibson, Latonia, Ky.

"This recipe has been in our family for over one hundred years," says Mrs. Gibson. **"It was brought from Pennsylvania by my great-grandmother."**

Makes two 9-inch round layers*

All ingredients must be at room temperature.

Sift together	2¾ cups sifted **enriched flour**
	1 teaspoon **soda**
	1 teaspoon **salt**
	½ teaspoon each: **nutmeg, allspice**.
Cream	1 cup **shortening**; add gradually
	½ cup **sugar**
	1½ cups firmly packed **brown sugar**, creaming well.
Blend in	3 **eggs**, one at a time. Beat for 1 minute.
Measure	1 cup **sour milk** or buttermilk. Add alter-

*If desired, cake may be baked in a 13x9x2-inch pan at 350°F. for 45 to 55 minutes.

Blend in................1 teaspoon vanilla

1 cup coarsely chopped black walnuts or English walnuts

Pour................into two, well-greased and floured 9-inch round layer cake pans, at least 1½ inches deep.

Bake................in moderate oven (350°F.) 35 to 45 minutes. Cool. Before serving, place cream filling between layers, page 221. Top with whipped cream.

LONDONDERRY SPICE CAKE

Pillsbury Contest Winner by Mrs. Rhoda Marquart, Beaverdam, Ohio

Spices and coffee give this cake an unusually delicious flavor. Raisins and brown sugar help keep it moist.

Makes 8x8x2-inch cake*

All ingredients must be at room temperature.

Sift together........1½ cups sifted enriched flour

1 teaspoon double-acting baking powder

1 teaspoon salt

½ teaspoon soda

½ teaspoon each: cinnamon, nutmeg, cloves.

Combine................½ cup cooked raisins with 2 tablespoons of the sifted dry ingredients.

Cream................½ cup butter (half shortening may be

---

*If desired, a large 13x9x2-inch cake may be made by doubling the ingredients and baking for 1 hour.

	used); add gradually
	½ cup sugar
	½ cup firmly packed **brown sugar**, creaming well.
Add	2 **eggs**, one at a time. Beat for 1 minute.
Measure	½ cup strong **coffee**, cooled. Add alternately with dry ingredients to creamed mixture, beginning and ending with dry ingredients. Blend thoroughly after each addition. (With electric mixer use low speed.)
Fold in	floured raisins.
Pour	into well-greased and floured 8x8x2-inch pan.
Bake	in moderate oven (350°F.) 45 to 50 minutes. Cool and frost with speedy caramel frosting, page 214, or serve cake warm with whipped cream.

MARDI GRAS SPICE CAKE

Pillsbury Contest Winners by Mrs. William Sonnenburg, Oak Lawn, Ill.

Quick-Mix Method

Cream and spice and everything nice—that's the secret of this festive dessert. Two layers are cut to make four, then filled and frosted with whipped cream.

Makes two 9-inch round layers*

All ingredients must be at room temperature.

Sift together — 2½ cups sifted **enriched flour**
2 teaspoons double-acting **baking powder**
1½ cups **sugar**
½ teaspoon **soda**
1 teaspoon **salt**

---

*If desired, cake may be baked in 12x8x2-inch pan for 40 to 50 minutes.

	1 teaspoon cinnamon
	½ teaspoon allspice
	½ teaspoon nutmeg.

Add............½ cup shortening
(half butter may be used)
1 cup milk
¼ cup dark molasses
1 teaspoon vanilla.

Beat............for 2 minutes, 300 strokes, until batter is well blended. (With electric mixer blend at low speed, then beat at medium speed for 2 minutes.)

Add............2 eggs; blend, then beat for 1 minute.

Pour............into two well-greased and floured 9-inch round layer pans.

Bake............in moderate oven (350°F.) 30 to 35 minutes. When layers are cool, cut crosswise to make four layers.

Beat............1 pint (2 cups) whipping cream until stiff. Sweeten to taste. Spread between layers; cover top and sides. Sprinkle chopped pecans over top. Chill cake in refrigerator until serving time.

SMÖRGÅSBORD SPICE CAKE

Pillsbury Contest Winner by Mrs. Ellis O. Carlson, Rockford, Ill.

The idea for this luscious spice cake came from Sweden many years ago. This recipe makes a glamorous "company" layer cake, topped with sea foam frosting. Or you can bake it as a practical and easy loaf cake.

Makes two 9-inch round layers*

All ingredients must be at room temperature.

---

*If desired, cake may be baked in a 12x8x2-inch pan at 350°F. for 40 to 50 minutes. If glass baking pan is used, bake at 325°F.

Sift together......2¼ cups sifted **enriched flour**

    2 teaspoons double-acting **baking powder**

    ½ teaspoon **soda**

    1 teaspoon **salt**

    1 teaspoon **cinnamon**

    ½ teaspoon **cloves**

    ½ teaspoon **ginger.**

Cream......½ cup **butter** (half shortening may be used); add gradually

    1 cup **sugar**

    ½ cup firmly packed **brown sugar**, creaming well.

Blend in......2 **eggs**, one at a time. Beat for 1 minute.

Combine......1 cup **top milk**

    1 teaspoon **vanilla**. Add alternately with dry ingredients to creamed mixture, beginning and ending with dry ingredients. Blend thoroughly after each addition. (With electric mixer use low speed.)

Pour......into two well-greased and floured 9-inch round layer pans.

Bake......in moderate oven (350°F.) 30 to 35 minutes. Cool and frost with sea foam frosting, page 217.

ENGLISH HONEY LOAF

Pillsbury Contest Winner by Mrs. Harry A. Winer, Kansas City, Mo.

"In my opinion," says Mrs. Winer, "one of the chief assets of this cake is that it can be baked days ahead of any holiday, relieving a hostess' mind for other duties that may be more pressing at the moment. This cake improves with age."

Makes 9x5x3-inch cake

All ingredients must be at room temperature.

Sift together......2 cups sifted **enriched flour**

1 teaspoon double-acting baking powder
¾ teaspoon **soda**
¾ teaspoon **salt**
¼ teaspoon **ginger**
½ teaspoon each: **cinnamon, cloves, allspice.**

Cream................. ⅓ cup **shortening**; add gradually
1 cup **sugar**, creaming well.

Blend in................ 2 **eggs**, one at a time. Beat for 1 minute.

Add................. ⅓ cup **honey**
1½ teaspoons grated **lemon rind**; mix until blended.

Measure................. ½ cup strong, cooled **coffee**. Add alternately with dry ingredients to creamed mixture, beginning and ending with dry ingredients. Blend thoroughly after each addition. (With electric mixer use low speed.)

Blend in................ ½ cup **raisins**
½ cup **chopped nuts.**

Pour................. into well-greased and floured 9x5x3-inch loaf pan. Cut through batter with spatula to break large air bubbles.

Bake................. in moderate oven (350°F.) 45 to 55 minutes. Cool thoroughly before cutting.

SAUCY APPLE CAKE

This brown sugar spice cake is filled with fruit and nuts. It's a moist cake that keeps well. Bake and store it in a loaf pan. Frost with a smooth butter icing.

Makes 9x9x2-inch cake

Sift together............ 2 cups sifted **enriched flour**

1½ teaspoons double-acting baking powder
½ teaspoon soda
1 teaspoon salt
1 teaspoon cinnamon
½ teaspoon nutmeg
½ teaspoon cloves

Blend............½ cup chopped nuts and
½ cup raisins with 1 tablespoon of the
sifted dry ingredients.

Cream............½ cup shortening; add gradually
½ cup sugar and
½ cup firmly packed brown sugar,
creaming well.

Blend in............2 eggs, unbeaten, one at a time. Beat for
1 minute.

Measure............1 cup applesauce. Add alternately with dry
ingredients to creamed mixture, begin-
ning and ending with dry ingredients.
Blend thoroughly after each addition.
(With electric mixer use low speed.)

Blend in............floured nuts and raisins. Mix thoroughly.

Pour............into well-greased and floured 9x9x2-inch
pan.

Bake............in moderate oven (350°F.) 45 to 50
minutes. Cool and frost with lemon
butter frosting, page 211.

GINGER CAKE

**This cake has been a favorite since grandmother's time. Top
with whipped cream for dessert.**

Makes 9x9x2-inch cake

Sift together............2 cups sifted enriched flour
½ teaspoon double-acting baking powder

	½ teaspoon soda
	½ teaspoon ginger
	1 teaspoon salt
	1 teaspoon cinnamon
	¼ teaspoon allspice
	¼ teaspoon cloves.

Cream..............½ cup shortening; add gradually

½ cup firmly packed brown sugar, creaming well.

Add..............2 eggs, one at a time. Beat for 1 minute.

Combine..............½ cup molasses and

1 cup boiling water; add alternately with dry ingredients to creamed mixture, beginning and ending with dry ingredients. Blend thoroughly after each addition. (With electric mixer use low speed.)

Pour..............into well-greased and floured 9x9x2-inch pan.

Bake..............in moderate oven (350°F.) 40 to 45 minutes.

SUPPERTIME GINGER CAKE

Pillsbury Contest Winner by Mrs. William T. Mooney, Petaluma, Calif.

Mellow molasses flavor and the tang of spices make this a truly luscious ginger cake. It's a cake that keeps well.

Makes 12x8x2-inch cake

All ingredients must be at room temperature.

Sift together..............2½ cups sifted enriched flour

1½ teaspoons double-acting baking powder

1 teaspoon soda

1 teaspoon salt

2 teaspoons cinnamon

1½ teaspoons ginger

½ teaspoon each: **nutmeg, cloves.**

Flour........................½ cup **raisins**

½ cup chopped **walnuts** with ¼ cup of the sifted dry ingredients.

Combine........................1 cup firmly packed **brown sugar**

⅔ cup dark **molasses**

2 **eggs** in large bowl. Beat well until thoroughly blended.

Add........................⅔ cup **shortening** and the sifted dry ingredients. Beat thoroughly.

Blend in........................1 cup boiling **water** gradually.

Fold in........................floured raisins and nuts.

Pour........................into greased and floured 12x8x2-inch pan.

Bake........................in moderate oven (350°F.) 45 to 50 minutes. Sprinkle with confectioners' sugar or top with creamy butter frosting, page 210.

GINGER TEA CAKE

Pillsbury Contest Winner by Mrs. A. R. Apple, Grosse Pointe Woods, Mich.

There's dark molasses for old-fashioned flavor and just a touch of spice in this ginger cake (and it's so easy to make).

Makes 8x8x2-inch cake*

Sift together.......1¼ cups sifted **enriched flour**

¼ cup **sugar**

1 teaspoon **soda**

½ teaspoon **salt**

½ teaspoon each: **ginger, cloves, cinnamon.**

Blend in........................¼ cup **shortening**

1 **egg**, unbeaten

*If desired, double recipe and bake in 13x9x2-inch pan for 35 to 40 minutes.

	½ cup dark molasses. Mix well.
Add	½ cup boiling water and blend thoroughly.
Pour	into greased and floured 8 x 8 x 2-inch pan.*
Bake	in moderate oven (350°F.) 30 to 35 minutes. Serve with whipped cream.

Variety Cakes

BURNT SUGAR CARAMEL CAKE

Quick-Mix Method

This old-fashioned favorite is made the modern Quick-Mix way. It's a rich cake that is especially good with caramel frosting.

Makes two 8-inch round layers

All ingredients must be at room temperature.

Melt	½ cup sugar in skillet over low heat until dark brown; stir constantly.
Add gradually	½ cup hot water, stirring until all of caramel is dissolved. Cool.
Pour	into measuring cup and add enough milk to make 1 cup.
Sift together	2 cups sifted enriched flour
	3 teaspoons double-acting baking powder
	1 teaspoon salt
	¾ cup sugar.
Add	½ cup shortening and the caramel-milk mixture.
Beat	for 2 minutes, 300 strokes, until batter is well blended. (With electric mixer blend at low speed, then beat at medium speed for 2 minutes.)

Add........................2 eggs, unbeaten
                   1 teaspoon vanilla.

Beat........................for 2 minutes.

Pour........................into two well-greased and floured 8-inch
                   layer pans, at least 1¼ inches deep.

Bake........................in moderate oven (350°F.) 30 to 35
                   minutes. Cool and frost with caramel
                   frosting, page 220.

MOCHA NUT MARBLE CAKE

Pillsbury Contest Winner by Mrs. Alfred Bennyworth, St. Louis, Mo.

Two distinctly different cakes in one! Almond-flavored white cake and mocha-flavored nut cake are mixed as separate batters, then marbled together.

Makes two 9-inch round layers

All ingredients must be at room temperature.

WHITE BATTER

Sift together........1½ cups sifted enriched flour
                   1½ teaspoons double-acting baking powder
                   ½ teaspoon salt
                   1 cup sugar.

Add........................½ cup shortening
                   ½ cup water
                   1 teaspoon almond extract.

Beat........................for 2 minutes, 300 strokes, until batter
                   is well blended. (With electric mixer
                   blend at low speed, then beat at medium
                   speed for 2 minutes.)

Add........................4 egg whites; beat for 2 minutes.

MOCHA NUT BATTER

Sift together........1½ cups sifted enriched flour
                   1½ teaspoons double-acting baking powder
                   ½ teaspoon salt.

Add _____1 cup firmly packed **brown sugar**, sieved
                    ½ cup **shortening**
                    ½ cup strong **coffee**, cooled
                    ½ teaspoon **lemon extract**.

Beat _____for 2 minutes, 300 strokes, until batter
                    is well blended.

Add _____4 **egg yolks**; beat for 2 minutes.

Fold in _____½ cup chopped **nuts**.

Spoon _____light and dark batters alternately into
                    two well-greased and floured 9-inch
                    round layer pans. Cut through batter
                    gently with spatula to break air bubbles,
                    then smooth surface.

Bake _____in moderate oven (350°F.) 35 to 40
                    minutes. Cool and frost with mocha
                    sea foam frosting, page 217.

BONNY BROWN SUGAR CAKE

Quick-Mix Method

Brown sugar gives this cake a tantalizing caramel flavor. It's
a Quick-Mix cake, fast and easy to make. Sea foam frosting
goes well with it.

Makes two 8-inch round layers

All ingredients must be at room temperature.

Sift together _____2 cups sifted **enriched flour**
                    3½ teaspoons double-acting **baking powder**
                    1 teaspoon **salt**
                    ½ cup **sugar**.

Add _____1 cup firmly packed **brown sugar**, sieved
                    ½ cup **shortening**
                    ¾ cup **milk**.

Beat .... for 2 minutes, 300 strokes, until batter is well blended. (With electric mixer blend at low speed, then beat at medium speed for 2 minutes.)

Add .... ¼ cup **milk**
2 **eggs**, unbeaten
1 teaspoon **vanilla**.

Beat .... for 2 minutes.

Pour .... into two well-greased and floured 8-inch layer pans, at least 1¼ inches deep.

Bake .... in moderate oven (350°F.) 30 to 35 minutes. Cool and frost with sea foam frosting, page 217.

MYSTERY MARBLE CAKE

Pillsbury Contest Winner by Mrs. J. F. Frewer, Savannah, Ga.

This cake has a particularly delicious blend of maple, choco-late and lemon flavors. It bakes in a tube pan and needs no icing.

Makes 9-inch tube cake

All ingredients must be at room temperature.

Sift together .... 2 cups sifted **enriched flour**
2 teaspoons double-acting **baking powder**
½ teaspoon **salt**.

Cream .... ⅔ cup **butter** (half shortening may be used); add gradually
2 cups **sugar**, creaming well.

Measure .... ¾ cup **milk**. Add alternately with dry in-gredients to creamed mixture, beginning and ending with dry ingredients. Blend thoroughly after each addition. (With electric mixer use low speed.)

Beat .... 6 **egg whites** until stiff but not dry. Fold gently but thoroughly into batter.

Place...................about 1 cup of batter in small bowl. Add
        1 tablespoon **cocoa** and
        ½ teaspoon **maple extract**. Mix well.

Blend................1 teaspoon **lemon extract** into remainder
        of light batter.

Pour...................½ inch of light batter into 9-inch greased
        tube pan; then dot with 3 teaspoons dark
        batter. Continue alternating light and
        dark batters.

Bake....................in moderate oven (350°F.) 50 to 60 min-
        utes. Cool 15 to 20 minutes before re-
        moving from pan.

MARBLE LAYER CAKE

Quick-Mix Method

**Here is our own marble cake—developed in our kitchen. Choco-
late and white batters are swirled throughout the cake to give
it a festive air. Try it with a fluffy white or your favorite fudge
frosting.**

Makes two 8-inch round layers

All ingredients must be at room temperature.

Sift together.......1¾ cups sifted **enriched flour**
        3 teaspoons double-acting **baking powder**
        1 teaspoon **salt**
        1¼ cups **sugar**.

Add.....................½ cup **shortening**
        ¾ cup **milk**.

Beat.....................for 2 minutes, 300 strokes, until batter
        is well blended. (With electric mixer
        blend at low speed, then beat at medium
        speed for 2 minutes.)

Add.....................2 **eggs**, unbeaten
        1 teaspoon **vanilla**
        ½ teaspoon **almond extract**.

Beat................................for 1 minute.
Divide..............................batter in half.
Combine.........................1 square (1 oz.) **chocolate**, melted
                                 ¼ teaspoon **soda**
                                 3 tablespoons **boiling water**; blend into
                                 one half of batter.
Spoon..............................white and chocolate batters alternately
                                 into two well-greased and floured 8-inch
                                 layer pans, at least 1¼ inches deep.
Bake................................in moderate oven (350° F.) 30 to 35
                                 minutes. Cool and frost as desired.

ORANGE MARBLE CAKE

Quick-Mix Method

**Orange and chocolate are among the most popular of flavors.
Here they are in a marble loaf cake, made by the Quick-Mix
method.**

Makes 9x9x2-inch cake

All ingredients must be at room temperature.

Sift together.......1¾ cups sifted **enriched flour**
                    2½ teaspoons double-acting **baking powder**
                    1 teaspoon **salt**
                    ¼ teaspoon **soda**
                    1¼ cups **sugar**.
Add...................½ cup **shortening**
                    ½ cup **milk**.
Beat..................for 2 minutes, 300 strokes, until batter
                    is well blended. (With electric mixer
                    blend at low speed, then beat at medium
                    speed for 2 minutes.)

Add................................¼ cup **milk**
2 **eggs**, unbeaten
1 teaspoon **almond extract**.

Beat................................for 2 minutes.

Divide...........................batter in half.

Add................................2 tablespoons grated **orange rind** to one half of batter.

Combine........................3 tablespoons **boiling water** and
1 square (1 oz.) **chocolate**, melted; blend into remaining half of batter.

Spoon...........................light and dark batters alternately into well-greased and floured 9x9x2-inch pan.

Bake..............................in moderate oven (350° F.) 45 to 50 minutes. Cool and frost with fluffy white frosting, page 215.

MOCHA LAYER CAKE

Quick-Mix Method

Coffee and brown sugar give this cake its distinctive flavor. Especially good frosted with mocha frosting.

Makes two 8-inch round layers

All ingredients must be at room temperature.

Sift together..............2 cups sifted **enriched flour**
3½ teaspoons double-acting **baking powder**
1 teaspoon **salt**
¾ cup **sugar**.

Add................................½ cup firmly packed **brown sugar**, sieved
½ cup **shortening**
½ cup **milk**.

Beat.................... for 2 minutes, 300 strokes, until batter is well blended. (With electric mixer blend at low speed, then beat at medium speed for 2 minutes.)

Add.................... ⅓ cup strong **coffee**, cooled
2 **eggs**, unbeaten
1 teaspoon **vanilla**.

Beat.................... for 2 minutes.

Pour.................... into two well-greased and floured 8-inch layer pans, at least 1¼ inches deep.

Bake.................... in moderate oven (350°F.) 30 to 35 minutes. Cool and frost with fluffy mocha sea foam frosting, page 217.

CARAMEL-NUT MERINGUE CAKE

Pillsbury Contest Winner by Mrs. G. A. Baird, Washington, D. C.

Here's a nut meringue torte that is something quite different. You'll like the easy, caramel meringue nut topping which is baked right on the cake.

Makes 9x9x2-inch cake

All ingredients must be at room temperature.

Sift together........ 1¾ cups sifted **enriched flour**
1 teaspoon double-acting **baking powder**
1 teaspoon **salt**.

Cream.................... ½ cup **shortening**; add gradually
1 cup **sugar**, creaming well.

Blend in.................... 2 **eggs** and
1 **egg yolk** (reserve white for meringue).
Beat 1 minute.

Combine............2 tablespoons milk

1 teaspoon vanilla. Add alternately with dry ingredients to creamed mixture, beginning and ending with dry ingredients. Blend thoroughly after each addition. (With electric mixer use low speed.)

Spread............in 9x9x2-inch pan lined with waxed paper that extends 1 inch beyond rim of pan.

Sprinkle with........½ cup chopped nuts.

MERINGUE

Beat............1 egg white until stiff but not dry.

Add............½ cup firmly packed brown sugar gradually, beating constantly until stiff.

Blend in

½ teaspoon vanilla.

Spread over nut-covered batter.

Bake............in slow oven (325°F.) 50 minutes.

WHIPPED CREAM LADY CAKE

Pillsbury Contest Winner by Mrs. William Berry, Kansas City, Mo.

There's no shortening in this simply prepared cake. Just blend the ingredients as directed into whipped cream and bake.

Makes two 8-inch round layers

Sift together............2 cups sifted enriched flour

3 teaspoons double-acting baking powder

½ teaspoon salt.

Pour............½ pint (1 cup) whipping cream into large mixing bowl. Beat until stiff.

Blend in............½ cup sugar; beat well.

Add............3 eggs, one at a time. Beat for 1 minute.

Blend in..............¾ cup sugar and
                      1 teaspoon vanilla; beat well.

Fold in..............dry ingredients gradually; mix thoroughly.

Pour..............into two well-greased and floured 8-inch round layer pans, at least 1¼ inches deep.

Bake..............in moderate oven (350°F.) 30 to 35 minutes. Cool and frost with tutti-frutti frosting, page 218.

MINCE PECAN CAKE

Pillsbury Contest Winner by Mrs. J. W. Hamilton, Altus, Okla.

Spicy mincemeat and chopped pecans give this cake a rich, mellow flavor. You can bake it in three majestic layers for a party or make up just half the recipe for a luscious family-size loaf cake.

Makes three 9-inch round layers*

All ingredients must be at room temperature.

Sift together........2½ cups sifted enriched flour
                      2 teaspoons double-acting baking powder
                      1 teaspoon soda
                      1 teaspoon salt.

Cream..............½ cup shortening; add gradually
                      1½ cups sugar, creaming well.

Blend in..............3 eggs, one at a time. Beat for 1 minute.

Combine..............1 cup milk
                      1 teaspoon vanilla. Add alternately with dry ingredients to creamed mixture, be-

*If desired, cake may be baked in 15x10x2-inch pan for 40 to 45 minutes. Or ingredients may be cut in half and cake baked in 8x8x2-inch pan for 40 to 50 minutes.

ginning and ending with dry ingredients. Blend thoroughly after each addition. (With electric mixer use low speed.)

Blend in.................½ cup chopped pecans
1½ cups prepared mincemeat.

Pour.....................into three well-greased and floured 9-inch round layer cake pans.

Bake.....................in moderate oven (350°F.) 30 to 35 minutes. Cool and frost with speedy caramel frosting, page 214.

ORANGE PRUNE CAKE

Quick-Mix Method

This moist, rich-flavored cake packs and carries well. And it stays fresh beautifully.

Makes 8x8x2-inch cake

All ingredients must be at room temperature.

Sift together.......1½ cups sifted enriched flour
1½ teaspoons double-acting baking powder
½ teaspoon soda
1 teaspoon salt
½ teaspoon cinnamon
1 cup sugar.

Add.....................⅓ cup shortening
⅔ cup thin sour cream
1 teaspoon vanilla.

Beat.....................for 2 minutes, 300 strokes, until batter is well blended. (With electric mixer blend at low speed, then beat at medium speed for 2 minutes.)

Add.....................2 eggs, unbeaten
⅔ cup cooked prunes, chopped.

Beat............................for 2 minutes.

Blend in....................½ cup chopped nuts.

Pour...........................into well-greased and floured 8x8x2-inch pan.

Bake...........................in moderate oven (350°F.) 50 to 60 minutes. Cool and frost with orange cream cheese frosting, page 213.

FESTIVE UPSIDE-DOWN CAKE

Pillsbury Contest Winner by Mrs. L. W. Willis, Portsmouth, Va.

Candied fruit and chopped nuts are scattered all the way through this high, upside-down fruit cake. It is made by the Quick-Mix method with pineapple juice for the liquid.

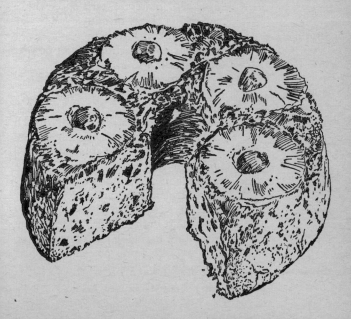

Makes 10-inch tube cake*

All ingredients must be at room temperature.

*Combine*_____½ cup sifted enriched flour
1½ cups mixed candied fruit, chopped
½ cup nuts, chopped.

*Prepare*_____10-inch tube pan (this must be the type with a stationary center tube) by generously greasing and flouring bottom and sides.*

*Spread*_____1 tablespoon soft butter over bottom of pan; sprinkle with
⅓ cup firmly packed brown sugar.

*Drain*_____1 No. 2 can sliced pineapple (reserve juice for cake) and place 5 pineapple slices on sugar. Fill center of each slice with a maraschino cherry or nut.

*Sift together*_____2 cups sifted enriched flour
3 teaspoons double-acting baking powder
1 teaspoon salt
1½ cups sugar.

*Add*_____½ cup shortening
¾ cup pineapple juice.

*Beat*_____for 2 minutes, 300 strokes, until batter is well blended. (With electric mixer blend at low speed, then beat at medium speed for 2 minutes.)

*Add*_____3 eggs, unbeaten; beat for 1 minute.

*Blend in*_____floured fruit and nuts; mix well.

*Pour*_____batter over pineapple slices.

*Bake*_____in moderate oven (350°F.) 70 to 80 minutes. Allow to cool in pan a few minutes. Turn upside down on serving plate. Serve with whipped cream or hard sauce.

---

*If desired, a 13x9x2-inch pan may also be used. Bake at 350°F. for 1 hour.

APRICOT TURNOVER CAKE

Pillsbury Contest Winner by Mrs. Joseph Arena, Forest Hills, N. Y.

Apricots make a deliciously different upside-down cake. And
the apricot juice is used for liquid in the cake itself.

Makes 8x8x2-inch cake

All ingredients must be at room temperature.

Melt........................¼ cup **butter** in 8x8x2-inch pan; sprinkle
with
½ cup firmly packed **brown sugar.**

Drain........................1 No. 2 can **apricot halves,** reserving juice
for cake. (Cooked, dried apricots may
also be used.) Arrange 16 halves in bottom of pan.

Sift together......1¼ cups sifted **enriched flour**
1½ teaspoons double-acting **baking powder**
¼ teaspoon **salt.**

Cream........................⅓ cup **shortening;** add gradually
½ cup **sugar,** creaming well.

Blend in........................1 **egg**
1 teaspoon **vanilla;** beat for 1 minute.

Measure........................½ cup **apricot juice.** Add alternately with
dry ingredients to creamed mixture, be-
ginning and ending with dry ingredients. Blend thoroughly after each addition. (With electric mixer use low
speed.) Pour over apricot halves.

Bake........................in moderate oven (350°F.) 40 to 45 minutes. Cool a few minutes. Turn out on
plate. Serve with cream.

CRANBERRY-TOPPED CAKE

Pillsbury Contest Winner by Mrs. Joseph Serafino, Muskegon, Mich.

There's no extra icing for this easy loaf! Cranberry sauce and
nuts bake right on the top of the batter.

Makes 8x8x2-inch cake

All ingredients must be at room temperature.

Combine	3 tablespoons sugar
	1 teaspoon grated lemon rind
	¼ teaspoon cinnamon
	⅓ cup chopped nuts.
Add	⅔ cup canned, jellied cranberry sauce that has been broken into pieces. Reserve for topping.
Sift together	2 cups sifted enriched flour
	2 teaspoons double-acting baking powder
	1 teaspoon salt.
Cream	⅓ cup shortening; add gradually
	1 cup sugar, creaming well.
Blend in	1 egg; beat for 1 minute.
Combine	¾ cup milk
	1 teaspoon lemon extract. Add alternately with dry ingredients to creamed mixture, beginning and ending with dry ingredients. Blend thoroughly after each addition. (With electric mixer use low speed.)
Pour	into well-greased and floured 8x8x2-inch pan. Spread cranberry topping over batter.
Bake	in moderate oven (350°F.) 45 to 50 min.

LIGHT FRUIT CAKE

This is a tasty and colorful *light* fruit cake to serve at holiday time. (Remember—your own homemade fruit cake makes a thoughtful gift.)

Makes 2¼ pound fruit cake

Sift together......1¼ cups sifted **enriched flour**
 ½ teaspoon double-acting **baking powder**
 1 teaspoon **salt**.

Cream.................½ cup **shortening**; add gradually
 ½ cup **sugar** and
 ½ cup firmly packed **brown sugar**, creaming well.

Add....................2 **eggs**, one at a time. Beat for 1 minute.

Blend in.............¼ cup thinly sliced **citron**
 ¼ cup sliced **candied orange peel**
 ¼ cup sliced **candied lemon peel**
 ¼ cup Sultana **raisins**
 1 cup **raisins**
 ½ cup chopped **candied cherries**
 ½ cup chopped **walnuts**.

Add....................dry and liquid ingredients alternately to creamed mixture, beginning and ending with dry ingredients. Blend thoroughly after each addition. (With electric mixer use low speed.)

Turn...................into well-greased and floured 9x4x3-inch pan which has been lined with greased heavy paper.

Bake...................in slow oven (300°F.) 1½ hours. Place pan of water on lower rack of oven during baking. This makes the cake more moist.

*Decorate*_____cake with blanched almonds and candied fruit after 1½ hours of baking. Return to oven and continue baking for 30 to 60 minutes.

*Wrap*_____cooled loaf in waxed paper or cloth. Store in a covered container in a cool place and let ripen a few weeks before using.

RICH DARK FRUIT CAKE

This rich, moist, spicy fruit cake is the traditional *dark* fruit cake. You can make it weeks ahead of time and store until needed.

Makes 2½ pound fruit cake

*Sift together*_____1½ cups sifted **enriched flour**
½ teaspoon double-acting **baking powder**
¼ teaspoon **soda**
1 teaspoon **salt**
1 teaspoon **cinnamon**
¼ teaspoon **nutmeg**
¼ teaspoon **cloves.**

*Cream*_____½ cup **shortening**; add gradually
½ cup firmly packed **brown sugar**, creaming well.

*Add*_____2 **eggs**, one at a time. Beat for 1 minute.

*Blend in*_____¼ cup thinly sliced **citron**
¼ cup sliced **candied orange peel**
¼ cup sliced **candied lemon peel**
1 cup **raisins**
½ cup diced **candied cherries**
½ cup chopped **nuts.**

*Combine*_____¼ cup **molasses**
¼ cup **water** or **fruit juice.**

Add............................dry and liquid ingredients alternately to creamed mixture, beginning and ending with dry ingredients. Blend thoroughly after each addition. (With electric mixer use low speed.)

Turn...........................into well-greased and floured 9x4x3-inch pan which has been lined with greased heavy paper.

Bake...........................in slow oven (300°F.) 1½ hours. Place pan of water on lower rack of oven during baking. This makes the cake more moist.

Decorate....................cake with blanched almonds and candied fruit after 1½ hours of baking. Return to oven and continue baking for 1 hour.

Wrap..........................cooled loaf in waxed paper or cloth. Store in a covered container in a cool place and let ripen a few weeks before using.

Cupcakes

FEATHER CUPCAKES

Quick-Mix Method

In this recipe you get both white and chocolate tea cakes from one mixing. Light, delicate, delicious.

Makes about 15 white and 15 chocolate cupcakes

All ingredients must be at room temperature.

Sift together.......2½ cups sifted enriched flour
             4 teaspoons double-acting baking powder
             1½ teaspoons salt
             1¾ cups sugar.

*Add*_____¾ cup shortening
1 cup milk.

*Beat*_____for 2 minutes, 300 strokes, until batter
is well blended. (With electric mixer
blend at low speed, then beat at medium
speed for 2 minutes.)

*Add*_____1½ teaspoons vanilla
¼ cup milk
3 eggs, unbeaten.

*Beat*_____for 2 minutes.

*Fill*_____well-greased and floured muffin pans ½
full with half of the batter.

*Blend*_____2 squares (2 oz.) chocolate, melted and
cooled, into remainder of batter. Fill
additional muffin pans.

*Bake*_____in moderate oven (375°F.) 15 to 20 minutes. Cool and frost as desired.

PINEAPPLE TEA CAKES

Pillsbury Contest Winner by Mrs. William Kretchman, Atkinson, Neb.

**These cupcakes have pineapple and chocolate bits folded into
them. Incidentally, they pack and carry well in lunch boxes.
These cakes stay fresh for days.**

Makes 18 medium cupcakes

All ingredients must be at room temperature.

*Sift together*_____2 cups sifted enriched flour
1 teaspoon double-acting baking powder
½ teaspoon soda
1 teaspoon salt.

*Cream*_____½ cup shortening; add gradually
½ cup sugar and
½ cup firmly packed brown sugar, creaming well.

Blend in................2 **eggs**, one at a time. Beat for 1 minute.

Add................½ cup sweetened, **crushed pineapple** (pulp and juice).

Measure................½ cup **water**; add alternately with dry ingredients to creamed mixture, beginning and ending with dry ingredients. Blend thoroughly after each addition. (With electric mixer use low speed.)

Add................1 teaspoon **vanilla**

1 6-oz. package semi-sweet **chocolate bits**.

Divide................batter into medium-sized cupcake pans, well greased or lined with paper baking cups. Fill ⅓ to ½ full.

Bake................in moderate oven (350°F.) 20 to 25 minutes. Cool and frost with pineapple butter frosting, page 211.

Sponge Cakes

A TRUE SPONGE CAKE *contains no baking powder. Its lightness is due to the beating of the egg whites and yolks and the technique of blending ingredients.*

How to Make a Perfect Sponge Cake

Mixing Eggs—Have eggs at room temperature as they will then produce a higher and more tender sponge cake.

—Whites: The whites should be beaten until they flow very slowly in the bowl. The points formed when the beater is raised should not stand up at the tips but should fold over to form rounded peaks.

A wire whisk or a rotary or electric
beater may be used for beating the whites.
Usually a higher cake is obtained by
using a whisk. If an electric mixer is
used, test the consistency of the whites
frequently to avoid overbeating.

If the whites are not beaten enough,
the cake will be low in volume, tough and
compact. If they are overbeaten, the cake
will be low in volume and have a coarse
texture.

—Yolks: The egg yolks should be beaten until
they are very thick and lemon colored.
This is more easily done using a small
bowl and a rotary or electric mixer,
since 5 to 10 minutes of beating are usually required.

Folding—The beaten whites, yolks and other ingredients
should be combined with the least possible handling.
Fold the sifted dry ingredients gently into the egg
whites with a down, lifting, folding-over stroke. The
ingredients should be thoroughly combined without
losing any of the enclosed air.

Pan Preparation—The batter should be poured into an
ungreased tube pan—ungreased for a higher cake. Cut
gently through the batter with a spatula to remove
large air pockets.

Baking—Bake at a low to moderate temperature (300° to
350°F.) for time specified in recipe. A low baking temperature is generally used. Sponge type cakes baked
at a higher temperature for a shorter time are more
moist, with a browner crust. An oven with an accurate
heat control is essential.

Cooling—A sponge cake is very delicate when taken from
the oven and will shrink unless it is inverted in the

pan and allowed to cool thoroughly. There should be about 1 inch of space between the table and the cake to allow air to circulate. When cooled, carefully release cake from pan by inserting spatula with straight motions down and up between cake and pan. Continue all around the cake and center tube, then gently tap pan to release cake.

JONQUIL SPONGE CAKE

BEST OF CLASS WINNER
Pillsbury's 1st Recipe Contest

by Mrs. Estella Worley, Los Angeles, Calif.

There's an airy lightness about this cake and a tender melt-in-your-mouth delicacy. Mrs. Worley adds lemon to give it a fresh, distinctive flavor.

Makes 10-inch tube cake

All ingredients must be at room temperature.

*Combine*_____1½ cups **sugar**

½ cup **water** in saucepan. Place over low heat and stir until dissolved. Then boil gently until mixture spins a 2-inch thread (230°-234°F.).

*Beat*_____8 **egg yolks** until thick and lemon colored.

*Pour*_____hot syrup over yolks, beating constantly.

*Add gradually*__1½ cups sifted **enriched flour** and

1 teaspoon **salt**. Beat for 2 minutes. (With electric mixer blend at lowest speed, then beat at medium speed for 2 minutes.)

*Beat*_____8 **egg whites** until foamy. Sprinkle

1 teaspoon **cream of tartar** over whites and continue beating until very stiff, but not dry. Fold into egg yolk mixture.

Blend in............1 teaspoon vanilla
                   1 tablespoon **lemon juice**
                   1 teaspoon grated **lemon rind**.

Pour............into ungreased 10-inch tube pan. Cut gently through batter with spatula to break large air pockets.

Bake............in moderate oven (350°F.) 40 to 45 minutes. Cool in inverted pan about 1 hour.

CINDERELLA SPONGE CAKE

Once you know how to make a good sponge cake you have the basis for literally dozens of luscious desserts, with berry, fruit or ice cream toppings.

Makes 9-inch tube cake

Eggs should be at room temperature.

Combine............½ cup **sugar**
                   1 tablespoon **water**
                   5 **egg yolks** (⅓ to ½ cup).

Beat............until thick and lemon colored. (With electric mixer use high speed for 7 to 10 minutes.)

Blend in............1½ teaspoons grated **lemon rind**
                   2 tablespoons **lemon juice**.

Beat............5 **egg whites** (¾ cup) and
                   ½ teaspoon **salt** until foamy.

Add............½ teaspoon **cream of tartar** and continue beating until very stiff but not dry.

Fold in............½ cup **sugar**, a tablespoon at a time.

Combine............yolk and white mixtures carefully but thoroughly.

Fold in............¾ cup sifted **enriched flour**, two tablespoons at a time.

Pour	into ungreased 9-inch tube pan. Cut through batter gently with spatula to break large air pockets.
Bake	in slow oven (325°F.) 60 to 70 minutes until light brown. Cool in inverted pan 1 hour.

BUTTERCUP SPONGE CAKE

Pillsbury Contest Winner by Mrs. Sylvan Eisenstein, Doniphan, Mo.

This old-fashioned sponge cake is made in a way that is quite out of the ordinary. You can top it with fruit or cut it into wedges and add your favorite frosting.

Makes 10-inch tube cake

All ingredients must be at room temperature.

Combine	1½ cups sugar
	½ cup water in saucepan. Place over low heat and stir until dissolved. Then boil gently until mixture spins a 2-inch thread (230°-234°F.).
Beat	7 egg whites until foamy. Add
	1 teaspoon cream of tartar and continue beating until egg whites are just stiff enough to stand in peaks.
Pour	hot syrup over egg whites slowly, beating constantly. Continue beating for 2 minutes. Cool slightly.
Beat	7 egg yolks until light. Add
	1 teaspoon almond extract and continue beating until very thick and lemon colored.
Fold	egg yolks gently but thoroughly into egg white mixture.

Sift in............1 cup sifted **enriched flour** and
1 teaspoon salt, folding gently into batter.

Pour............into ungreased 10-inch tube pan. Cut
through batter with spatula to break
large air pockets.

Bake............in slow oven (325°F.) 50 to 60 minutes.
Cool in inverted pan about 1 hour. Serve
cake with sweetened berries, fruit or ice
cream. Or cut cake into small wedges;
frost wedges with varicolored confectioners' sugar frostings and decorate
with cherries, nuts or coconut.

OLD-TIME BUTTER SPONGE CAKE

Pillsbury Contest Winner by Mrs. Thomas W. Wolfe, Hagerstown, Md.

**Extra egg yolks in the refrigerator? Then try this dainty butter
sponge cake. Serve it plain or with fresh fruits.**

Makes 10-inch tube cake

All ingredients must be at room temperature.

Sift together......2¼ cups sifted **enriched flour**
2 teaspoons double-acting **baking powder**
1 teaspoon salt.

Beat............11 **egg yolks** until thick and lemon colored.
Add gradually
2 cups **sugar**, beating thoroughly.

Combine............1 cup scalded **milk**
1 teaspoon vanilla
½ teaspoon **lemon extract**. Add gradually
to beaten egg yolks, beating well after
each addition.

Fold in gradually......sifted dry ingredients.

Add............½ cup melted **butter**, blending well.

Pour............................into ungreased 10-inch tube pan. Cut through batter with spatula to break large air pockets.

Bake............................in moderate oven (350°F.) 50 to 60 minutes. Cool in inverted pan about 1 hour.

MOTHER'S SPONGE CAKE

Pillsbury Contest Winner by Miss Margaret M. Sullivan, Newport, N. H.

This hot-milk sponge cake is an old-time favorite. Tender, moist, delicious and so economical and easy. Serve it with fresh fruits and ice cream.

Makes 8x8x2-inch cake

Sift together............1 cup sifted **enriched flour**

1 teaspoon double-acting **baking powder**

¼ teaspoon **salt**.

Beat............................2 **eggs** thoroughly until thick and light (7 to 10 minutes).

Add gradually.......1 cup **sugar**, beating constantly.

Fold in........................sifted dry ingredients, carefully but quickly.

Add............................1 teaspoon **vanilla** and

½ cup hot, scalded **milk** all at once. Fold in thoroughly, blending as quickly as possible.

Pour............................into 8x8x2-inch pan.

Bake............................in moderate oven (350°F.) 30 to 35 min.

Angel Food Cakes

THE MAIN DIFFERENCE *between an angel food and a sponge cake is that an angel food contains only egg whites.*

How to Make a Perfect Angel Food Cake

Sifting—Sift the cake flour before measuring, then sift the flour and half of the sugar together several times. This mixes the sugar thoroughly with the flour and separates the flour particles—it also incorporates air, making the mixture feathery-light. A very fine granulated sugar makes a finer-textured angel food.

Beating—The egg whites are beaten as for sponge cake. Half of the sugar is then folded in. Sprinkle sugar, a tablespoon at a time, over the beaten whites and fold gently until the sugar is completely dissolved.

Combining—Sift the dry ingredients, a small amount at a time, over the egg whites and continue the folding process until all the ingredients are combined. Bake and cool as for sponge cake.

ANGEL FOOD CAKE

Treat it lightly, keep an eye on the recipe . . . and this angel
food turns out beautifully!

Makes 10-inch tube cake

Sift together
two times.............. 1 cup sifted cake flour
 ¾ cup sifted sugar.
Beat....................1¼ cups egg whites with
 ¼ teaspoon salt until foamy.
Sprinkle.............1¼ teaspoons cream of tartar over egg

whites and continue beating until stiff but not dry.

Fold in............¾ cup **sugar**, a small amount at a time, until all sugar has been added.

Add............1 teaspoon **vanilla**

¼ teaspoon **almond extract**.

Sift in............dry ingredients gradually, folding in carefully.

Turn............into ungreased tube pan.

Bake............in slow oven (325°F.) 60 to 70 minutes.

Cool............in inverted cake pan about 1 hour.

Serve............unfrosted or frost as desired.

CHOCOLATE ANGEL FOOD CAKE

PREPARE Angel Food Cake, substituting cocoa for ¼ cup flour. Sift the cocoa with the flour and sugar.

Chiffon Cake

ROYAL VELVET CHIFFON CAKE

This light and tender cake is made with salad oil. It's a cake that stays fresh and delicious. It can be served in many different ways.

Makes 9 or 10-inch tube cake

Sift together......1½ cups sifted **enriched flour**

1¾ teaspoons double-acting **baking powder**

1 teaspoon **salt**

1 cup **sugar**.

Add............⅓ cup **salad oil**

⅔ cup **liquid** (juice from 2 medium **oranges** plus water)

2 tablespoons grated **orange rind**

5 **egg yolks**, unbeaten.

Beat _____ until smooth.

Beat _____ 5 egg whites with

¼ teaspoon **cream of tartar** until egg whites are stiff but not dry.

Add _____ ¼ cup **sugar** gradually; beat to a very stiff meringue. Do not underbeat.

Fold _____ egg yolk mixture carefully into egg whites until completely blended.

Pour _____ into ungreased 9-inch or 10-inch tube pan.

Bake _____ in slow oven (325°F.) 65 to 70 minutes for 9-inch pan, 55 to 60 minutes for 10-inch pan.

Cool _____ in inverted pan about 1 hour. Frost with confectioners' sugar icing, boiled frosting or top with fresh fruit, ice cream or whipped cream.

Wedding Cake

WEDDING CAKE

The loveliest of all—the bride's wedding cake! This cake must be particularly elegant, tender and delicate. (You'll find special wedding cake hints on the following pages.)

Serves 75
Makes 12, 9, and 6-inch tiers

BAKE EACH TIER *in layers to give more level tiers and lighter textured cake. These directions are for layered tiers (two layers for each tier). Make the cake as close to the wedding day as plans permit. It is well to set aside two days for making the cake so it may be baked and frosted on one day and decorated the next.*

BAKE two 12-inch layers at 350°F. for 40 to 50 minutes.
BAKE two 9-inch layers at 350°F. for 25 to 35 minutes.
BAKE two 6-inch layers at 350°F. for 30 to 40 minutes.
PREPARE pans by greasing and flouring the bottoms.

Sift together............3 cups sifted **cake flour**
3½ teaspoons double-acting **baking powder**
1 teaspoon **salt**.

Cream....................⅔ cup **shortening**; add gradually
1½ cups **sugar**, creaming well.

Combine............1¼ cups **milk**
1½ teaspoons **vanilla**.

Add........................dry and liquid ingredients alternately to creamed mixture, beginning and ending with dry ingredients. Blend thoroughly. (With electric mixer use low speed.)

Beat....................⅔ cup **egg whites** until stiff but not dry.

Add gradually......¼ cup **sugar**, beating constantly until stiff.

Fold........................egg white mixture carefully into batter.

Measure...................batter by cupfuls into well-greased and floured pans. This amount of batter (7 cups) makes one of the following combinations:

A. one 12-inch layer—measure 5½ cups of batter

one 6-inch layer—measure 1½ cups of batter

Bake one 12-inch and one 6-inch layer at the same time.

B. two 9-inch layers—measure 3½ cups of batter for each.

These proportions of batter should fill pans no more than half full.

Bake........................12-inch layers in preheated moderate oven (350°F.) 40 to 50 minutes.

9-inch layers in preheated moderate oven
(350°F.) 25 to 35 minutes.
6-inch layers in preheated moderate oven
(350°F.) 30 to 40 minutes.
Cool and frost.

TO MAKE this cake in the home size oven it will be necessary
to make and bake three batches of batter and to bake A. twice
and B. once. For best results it is preferable to mix fresh batter
for each baking so it may be baked as soon as it is mixed.

It is advisable to frost entire cake with a thin coating of
wedding cake frosting the same day as it is baked to retain
freshness and to set crumbs. If tiers are baked on successive
days, frost layers as soon as they are cooled.

Wedding Cake Frosting

Cream............1½ cups vegetable **shortening** or uncolored
margarine (if desired, part butter may be
used for flavor but frosting will be
creamy in color).

Add............¾ cup (6) unbeaten **egg whites**.

Blend in
gradually............3 lbs. (about 10½ cups) sifted **confectioners' sugar**. Stir until well blended. (If
electric mixer is used, beat at low speed
to avoid air bubbles.)

Add............2 tablespoons **vanilla** and
3 tablespoons **glycerine** for gloss. For a
very white frosting add one drop of blue
food coloring to 2 tablespoons of frosting. To avoid getting too much blue
color, gradually combine with rest of
frosting. If necessary, frosting may be
thinned to spreading consistency with
cream, 1 tablespoon at a time.

To Frost Cake—Brush crumbs from sides of cake layers. Place first 12-inch layer either on heavy cardboard disk to facilitate handling when finished or directly on large cake plate. Frost top and add second 12-inch layer. Frost just enough to set any remaining crumbs and to coat tier. Center a 9-inch layer on 12-inch tier, frost, and top with second 9-inch layer. Frost and add top tier in same manner. Now the undercoat has been applied to cake and cake is ready for final frosting.

Refrost entire cake with wedding cake frosting starting either with top or bottom tier. This may be done the same day or the following day. Keep frosting as smooth as possible. A spatula dipped in hot water helps to smooth rough places.

Decorate with ornamental frosting immediately or on the following day.

Ornamental Frosting

Beat............3 egg whites until stiff.

Add............1½ cups sifted confectioners' sugar. With mixer, beat at low speed until smooth (about 10 minutes).

Cream............⅓ cup vegetable shortening (keeps frosting soft) and
¾ cup sifted confectioners' sugar.

Combine............the two mixtures.

Add............1 tablespoon glycerine (for gloss)
½ teaspoon almond flavoring or 1 teaspoon vanilla.

Blend in............1½ cups sifted confectioners' sugar. Beat until frosting holds its shape.

To Decorate Cake—Decorate frosted cake with cake decorator or paper cones. Make as many frosting cones as there will be tints of frostings. Fashion cones of heavy waxed paper, double thickness of light waxed paper, parchment or any glazed paper cut in a triangle 19x15x12-inches. Fold into cone and roll down point at wide end until top is level. This will prevent cone's unfolding.

1. To tint frosting—separate it into as many bowls as colors of frosting are desired. Add food coloring sparingly by drops.

2. For a number of designs—dots, lines, stems, forget-me-nots, daisy, and lily of the valley—the cone may be used with no metal tip. Merely cut off the very tip—enlarge to give desired flow. For leaf design cut tip in V shape. To use with metal tip, cut off tip of cone and drop in metal tip. Basic tips include the plain, leaf, rosette and border ones.

3. Fill cone no more than two-thirds full. Leave enough free cone above frosting so it may be folded over securely and force frosting thru bottom tip. Bring back and front of cone together at top and fold down in ¼-inch layers to frosting.

4. Frost cake as desired, exerting pressure from top of cone. As frosting is used in cone, fold top over further to keep fold just above frosting.

5. Keep all frosting and cones not in use under a damp towel to keep moist. When a cone does dry at the tip, squeeze out a little frosting before going on with the design.

6. Plan design before beginning to decorate cake and lightly mark off areas for such designs as scallops with a toothpick.

7. Practice on waxed paper before beginning to decorate

cake to determine consistency. Too soft frosting spreads, does not give clear cut design and is reluctant to break off. Too stiff frosting is difficult to squeeze and tends to break and crack.

Frostings

A BEAUTIFUL FROSTING *does so much for a cake! It helps keep a cake moist and fresh. And it gives you a chance to add your own individual touch to your cake . . . in the way you form your frosting into hollows and ridges . . . in the way you decorate it (with nuts, fruit or coconut—any number of ways) —and in the particular frosting you choose for your cake.*

There are many different kinds of frostings, of course. And each kind has its own special advantage.

Fluffy white cooked frosting is perhaps the most elegant of all. It is easy to manage, and easily coaxed into deep ripples and swirls.

Rich, creamy fudge frosting, too, dresses up a cake beautifully.

Smooth, creamy butter frosting is a wise choice if you are in a hurry and want a simple, failure-proof frosting—or if you want a frosting that keeps fresh for days, and packs and carries well. (This is a frosting that sticks to the cake itself, you know —and not to the waxed paper that you put over it.)

And here are some frosting secrets. Cooking temperature is very important when you are making any kind of cooked frosting. Use a candy thermometer, if you have one, or learn to know the correct stages of "doneness." Work quickly when using a fudge-type frosting. If your frosting begins to harden before you are finished, you can add a small amount of cream or milk to it, a teaspoon at a time, to bring it back to a consistency that is easy to spread.

But first, before you begin frosting, you might notice our special cake-frosting hints. We think they'll make cake-frosting easier and more fun for you.

Brushing crumbs from sides of cake.

How to Frost a Cake

ALWAYS cool cake thoroughly before frosting. Brush the loose crumbs from sides of cake. To keep cake plate clean while frosting, place 4 strips of waxed paper under edges of cake to form a square. When cake is frosted, waxed paper can be slipped out easily. Place first layer top-side down; spread frosting or filling completely to edge. Allow to set slightly before adding second cake layer. (If you use a confectioners' sugar frosting, you may make the filling thicker to prevent the layers from slipping. Then the rest of the mixture may be thinned to the desired spreading consistency for top and sides of cake.)

Place top layer on filling, bottom-side down. Frost sides by applying frosting with a spatula, using free, easy strokes. Spread with an upward stroke leaving a ridge of frosting around top of cake. Keep sides straight.

Spread frosting on top, making swirls with spatula or back of spoon. Avoid smooth, flat sides or top. The frosting should give the cake height and make it as good to look at as it is to eat.

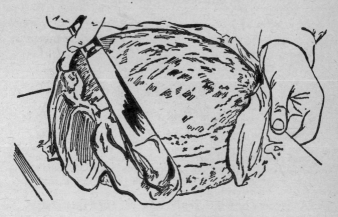

Fig. 1—Frost sides with upward stroke.

Fig. 2—Cake should look pretty.

Uncooked Frostings

ANY FLAVOR *of frosting you like can be made this sure and easy way.. Nuts, shredded coconut, fruit or marshmallows may be added to make a change.*

CREAMY BUTTER FROSTING

In Eight Flavors

Here's a basic butter cream frosting and seven ways to vary
its flavor. Amounts of butter, salt, sugar and vanilla remain
the same. Variety is yours when you vary the liquid and flavoring. For extra richness, add either an egg yolk or egg white to
creamed butter and use a little less cream.

Frosts 8 or 9-inch round layer cake or 15x10x2 or
13x9x2-inch oblong cake
Half recipe frosts 12x8x2, 11x7x2,
9x9x2 or 8x8x2-inch cake

Cream..................¼ cup **butter** or shortening
¼ teaspoon **salt.**
Blend in..................3 cups sifted **confectioners' sugar** alternately with
4 to 6 tablespoons scalded **cream.**
Add..................1 teaspoon **vanilla.**
Beat until creamy.

CHOCOLATE BUTTER FROSTING

PREPARE Creamy Butter Frosting, adding 1½ squares (1½ oz.)
melted chocolate with vanilla. Thin frosting with additional
cream if necessary.

ORANGE BUTTER FROSTING

PREPARE Creamy Butter Frosting, creaming 1 teaspoon grated
orange rind with butter and salt. Blend in 3 tablespoons orange
juice and about 2 tablespoons cream alternately with sugar.

LEMON BUTTER FROSTING

PREPARE Creamy Butter Frosting, creaming 1 teaspoon grated lemon rind with butter and salt. Substitute 2 teaspoons lemon juice for 1 tablespoon cream.

SPICE BUTTER FROSTING

PREPARE Creamy Butter Frosting, creaming ⅛ teaspoon cloves and ⅛ teaspoon nutmeg with butter and salt.

BANANA BUTTER FROSTING

BLEND together ⅓ cup mashed, ripe banana (1 medium) and ½ teaspoon lemon juice. Substitute banana for cream in Creamy Butter Frosting recipe.

BROWNED BUTTER FROSTING

PREPARE Creamy Butter Frosting, browning the butter in saucepan before blending with sugar. Increase cream to 8 or 9 tablespoons.

NUT FROSTING

PREPARE Creamy Butter Frosting, blending ½ cup chopped nuts into frosting.

PINEAPPLE BUTTER ICING

Frosts 8 or 9-inch round layer cake

Half recipe frosts 18 cupcakes or 12x8x2 or 9x9x2-inch cake

Combine............¼ cup melted **butter** and
                    1 cup sifted **confectioners' sugar**; mix well.
Blend in............6 tablespoons **crushed pineapple** (pulp and juice) alternately with
                    2 cups sifted **confectioners' sugar**; mix until well blended. Thin with small amount of hot water if necessary.

SPEEDY FUDGE FROSTING

Frosts 8 or 9-inch round layer cake
Half recipe frosts 9x9x2 or 8x8x2-inch cake

Melt..................2 squares (2 oz.) chocolate.
Scald..................⅓ cup cream or top milk with
3 tablespoons butter. Remove from heat.
Add..................3 cups sifted confectioners' sugar, all at once. Then add
⅛ teaspoon salt
1 teaspoon vanilla.
Blend in..................melted chocolate and beat until thick enough to spread. Thin with small amount of cream if necessary.

CHOCOLATE MALLOW FROSTING

Frosts 9x9x2 or 8x8x2-inch cake

Melt..................1 square (1 oz.) chocolate and
2 tablespoons butter over hot water.
Add..................chocolate mixture to
1½ cups sifted confectioners' sugar.
Blend in..................1 teaspoon vanilla and
2 to 3 tablespoons cream until of proper spreading consistency.
Add..................6 marshmallows, cut in eighths.

CHOCOLATE CREAM CHEESE FROSTING

Frosts 8 or 9-inch round layer cake
Half recipe frosts 12x8x2 or 9x9x2-inch cake

Soften _____ 1 package (3 oz.) **cream cheese** by adding
3 tablespoons **milk**, a tablespoon at a time.

Add _____ 2½ to 3 cups sifted **confectioners' sugar** gradually, blending well after each addition.

Blend in _____ 2 squares (2 oz.) **chocolate**, melted, and
⅛ teaspoon **salt**. Beat until smooth.

ORANGE CREAM CHEESE FROSTING

Frosts 12x8x2 or 9x9x2-inch cake

Cream _____ 1 tablespoon **butter**
1 package (3 oz.) **cream cheese**
2 teaspoons grated **orange rind**
⅛ teaspoon **salt**.

Add _____ 2 cups sifted **confectioners' sugar** gradually, beating well.

COCOA BUTTER FROSTING

Frosts 9-inch ring cake or 13x9x2-inch cake

Sift together _____ 2½ cups sifted **confectioners' sugar**
¼ cup **cocoa**
⅛ teaspoon **salt**.

Cream _____ ⅓ cup **butter**. Blend in
3 tablespoons hot **cream** alternately with sugar-cocoa mixture.

Add _____ 1 **egg yolk**
1 teaspoon **vanilla**. Blend thoroughly.

SPEEDY CARAMEL FROSTING

*Frosts 8 or 9-inch layer cake or 15x10x2 or 13x9x2-inch
oblong cake

Half recipe frosts 9x9x2 or 8x8x2-inch cake

Melt.................½ cup **butter** (half shortening may be
used) in large saucepan.

Blend in.............1 cup firmly packed **brown sugar**
¼ teaspoon **salt.** Cook over low heat 2 minutes, stirring constantly.

Add.................¼ cup **milk** and continue stirring until mixture comes to a boil. Remove from heat.

Blend in............2½ cups sifted **confectioners' sugar** gradually.

Add.................½ teaspoon **vanilla** and mix well. Thin with
small amount of cream if necessary.

*For 9-inch three layer cake, follow Speedy Caramel Frosting recipe,
using ¾ cup butter, 1½ cups brown sugar, ¼ teaspoon salt, ⅓ cup
milk, 3½ cups (1 lb.) sifted confectioners' sugar and ½ teaspoon vanilla.

ORNAMENTAL FROSTING

Cream...............2 tablespoons **butter.** Blend in
2 cups sifted **confectioners' sugar,** mixing
well.

Add.................2 to 4 tablespoons hot **cream** a little at a time,
½ teaspoon **vanilla.**

Blend...............until frosting is consistency to force
through a decorating tube. If desired,
frosting may be tinted different colors by
adding a few drops of vegetable coloring.

LAZY-DAISY FROSTING

The easiest of all frostings are the "baked-on" kind. This frosting requires only a few minutes under the broiler. Excellent for hurry-up baking!

Frosts 15x10x2 or 13x9x2-inch oblong cake

Half recipe frosts 9x9x2 or 8x8x2-inch cake

*Combine*_____ ¼ cup **butter**, melted
½ cup firmly packed **brown sugar**
¾ cup shredded **coconut** or **nuts**
3 tablespoons **cream**.

*Spread*_____on warm cake; place under broiler until slightly brown.

Cooked Frostings

PERHAPS *the prettiest, the richest, the most festive frostings are the type that require cooking. You'll find the following recipes are quite easily prepared.*

FLUFFY WHITE FROSTING

Two Egg White Recipe

Frosts 8 or 9-inch layer cake, 15x10x2 or 13x9x2-inch oblong cake

*Combine*_____2 **egg whites**
¾ cup **sugar**
⅓ cup **light corn syrup**
2 tablespoons **water**
¼ teaspoon **salt**

	¼ teaspoon **cream of tartar** in top of double boiler.
*Cook*_____	over rapidly boiling water, beating with rotary beater or electric mixer until mixture stands in peaks. Remove from heat.
*Add*_____	1 teaspoon vanilla; continue beating until thick enough to spread.

One Egg White Recipe

Frosts 12x8x2 or 9x9x2-inch cake, or top and sides of 8 or 9-inch layer cake

COMBINE 1 egg white, ⅔ cup sugar, ¼ cup light corn syrup, 2 tablespoons water, ⅛ teaspoon cream of tartar and ⅛ teaspoon salt in top of double boiler. Proceed as directed in Two Egg White Recipe.

Three Egg White Recipe

Frosts three-layer 9-inch cake

COMBINE 3 egg whites, 1 cup sugar, ¾ cup light corn syrup, 3 tablespoons water, ¼ teaspoon cream of tartar and ¼ teaspoon salt in top of double boiler. Proceed as directed in Two Egg White Recipe, adding 1½ teaspoons vanilla.

CHERRY FROSTING

PREPARE Two Egg White Fluffy White Frosting, substituting 2 tablespoons maraschino cherry juice for water. If desired, fold in ½ cup chopped nuts or cherries.

LADY BALTIMORE FROSTING

PREPARE Two Egg White Fluffy White Frosting. Add ½ cup chopped candied cherries, ⅓ cup chopped figs, ⅓ cup raisins and ¼ cup chopped pecans to ⅓ of frosting and place between layers. Frost top and sides of cake with balance of frosting. Decorate with chopped fruit.

PEPPERMINT FROSTING
PREPARE Two Egg White Fluffy White Frosting, folding in ½ cup crushed peppermint candy or 2 drops peppermint flavoring just before frosting cake.

NUT FROSTING
PREPARE Two Egg White Fluffy White Frosting, folding in ½ cup chopped nuts just before frosting cake.

SEA FOAM FROSTING
PREPARE Two Egg White Fluffy White Frosting, substituting ¾ cup brown sugar for granulated sugar.

MOCHA SEA FOAM FROSTING
PREPARE Two Egg White Fluffy White Frosting, substituting ¾ cup brown sugar for granulated sugar and 2 tablespoons strong coffee for water.

ALMOND FROSTING
PREPARE Two Egg White Fluffy White Frosting, decreasing vanilla to ½ teaspoon and adding ½ teaspoon almond extract.

FLUFFY MARBLE FROSTING
PREPARE Two Egg White Fluffy White Frosting, folding in 2 tablespoons semi-sweet chocolate bits just before frosting cake.

FLUFFY CHOCOLATE FROSTING
PREPARE Two Egg White Fluffy White Frosting, folding in 2 squares (2 oz.) melted chocolate just before frosting cake. Do not beat frosting after adding chocolate.

SEVEN-MINUTE FROSTING

Frosts 8 or 9-inch layer cake

*Combine*_____2 egg whites
1½ cups sugar

⅓ cup cold water
1 tablespoon light corn syrup
¼ teaspoon cream of tartar
⅛ teaspoon salt in top of double boiler.

Cook................over rapidly boiling water, beating with
rotary beater or electric mixer until mix-
ture stands in peaks. Remove from heat.

Add................1 teaspoon vanilla; continue beating until
thick enough to spread.

WHITE MOUNTAIN FROSTING

Frosts 8 or 9-inch layer cake
Half recipe frosts 12x8x2 or 9x9x2-inch cake

Cook................2 cups sugar
1 tablespoon light corn syrup
¾ cup water
⅛ teaspoon salt over low heat, stirring until
sugar is dissolved.

Cover................saucepan for 2 to 3 minutes to dissolve
sugar crystals on sides of pan. Uncover
and continue cooking until a little syrup
dropped in cold water forms a firm soft
ball (236°F.). Remove from heat.

Beat................2 egg whites until stiff but not dry. Add
hot syrup very slowly to beaten egg
whites, beating constantly.

Blend in................1 teaspoon vanilla. Beat until frosting is of
desired consistency.

TUTTI-FRUTTI FROSTING

PREPARE White Mountain Frosting, blending in ½ cup
chopped, candied pineapple and ½ cup chopped, candied cherries just before frosting cake.

PECAN FONDANT FROSTING

Frosts 13x9x2-inch cake

Cook.................3 cups sugar

½ cup light corn syrup

¾ cup water over low heat, stirring until sugar dissolves.

Cover.................saucepan 2 to 3 minutes to dissolve sugar crystals on sides of pan. Uncover, continue cooking until a little · syrup dropped in cold water forms a firm ball (244° to 248°F.). Remove from heat.

Beat.................2 egg whites in large mixer bowl until foamy. Add

1 teaspoon vanilla

⅛ teaspoon almond extract

½ teaspoon salt. Beat until stiff but not dry.

Pour.................hot syrup slowly over egg whites, beating constantly. Continue beating until frosting stands in peaks and loses gloss, about 10 minutes.

Add.................¼ cup chopped pecans. Thin with cream if necessary. Spread quickly on cooled cake.

FUDGE FROSTING

*Frosts 8 or 9-inch layer cake

Combine.................2 cups sugar

¾ cup top milk or thin cream

---

*For larger cake follow Fudge Frosting recipe, using 3 cups sugar, 1 cup top milk, ¼ teaspoon salt, 3 squares chocolate, 3 tablespoons light corn syrup, 3 tablespoons butter and 1 teaspoon vanilla.

2 squares (2 oz.) chocolate
2 tablespoons light corn syrup
⅛ teaspoon salt in saucepan.

Cook............over low heat and stir until dissolved. Cook until a little syrup dropped in cold water forms a very soft ball (230° to 234°F.); stir occasionally to prevent scorching. Remove from heat.

Add............2 tablespoons **butter**. Cool to lukewarm (110°F.).

Add............1 teaspoon **vanilla** and beat until thick and creamy. Thin with a small amount of cream if necessary.

CARAMEL FROSTING

Frosts 8 or 9-inch layer cake

Combine............1 cup firmly packed **brown sugar**
1 cup **sugar**
⅔ cup **heavy cream** in saucepan. Heat slowly, stirring until dissolved.

Cook............until a little syrup dropped in cold water forms a soft ball (232° to 234°F.). Remove from heat and cool to lukewarm (110°F.).

Add............½ teaspoon **vanilla**
⅛ teaspoon **salt**. Beat until thick. Thin with cream, a teaspoon at a time, if necessary.

Fillings

PLACE *a luscious, smooth, pretty filling between two layers of cake . . . and you add a really special touch to your cakes. Here are several filling ideas.*

CREAM FILLING

Fills two 8 or 9-inch layers

Heat................... 1 cup milk. Add
        2 tablespoons butter.

Combine............. ⅓ cup enriched flour
        ¼ teaspoon salt
        ⅓ cup sugar.

Add................... ½ cup cold milk and stir until smooth. Add to hot milk; stir constantly until thick.

Blend in............. 2 slightly beaten egg yolks, to which a little of the hot mixture has been added. Cook about 2 minutes, stirring constantly. Cover; cool.

Add................... 1 teaspoon vanilla.

LEMON FILLING

Fills two 8 or 9-inch layers

Blend together..... ¼ cup cornstarch
        ¼ teaspoon salt
        ⅔ cup sugar.

Add................... 1 cup water and mix well. Cook over direct heat until thick, stirring constantly.

Beat................... 1 egg yolk slightly. Add a little of hot mixture, then return to mixture in saucepan.

Cook................over low heat about 2 minutes, stirring constantly. Remove from heat.

Add................3 tablespoons lemon juice
1 tablespoon grated lemon rind. Cool.

LIME FILLING

PREPARE Lemon Filling, substituting 3 tablespoons lime juice and 1 tablespoon grated lime rind for lemon juice and rind. Add 2 drops green coloring.

PINEAPPLE FILLING

Fills two 8 or 9-inch layers

*Blend together*__¼ cup cornstarch
½ cup sugar.

*Add gradually*__¾ cup hot water. Cook until thick and clear, stirring constantly.

Add................1 cup crushed pineapple
2 teaspoons lemon juice. Cool.

BONBON FILLING

Fills two 8 or 9-inch layers

Combine................1 cup sugar
6 tablespoons water
1½ teaspoons light corn syrup
⅛ teaspoon salt in saucepan. Cook over low heat, stirring until sugar dissolves.

Cover................saucepan and cook 2 to 3 minutes. Uncover; continue cooking until a little syrup dropped in cold water forms a soft ball (236° F.). Remove from heat.

Beat................1 egg white until stiff. Add hot syrup slowly, beating constantly.

Blend in................½ teaspoon vanilla. Beat until filling is of desired consistency.

CHAPTER SIX

Cookies

NOTHING *can quite take the place of cookies. They're favorites with children and grown-ups. They satisfy in-between-meal appetites as nothing else can. They can be eaten any time, any way . . . they go as well with milk or coffee as they do with ice cream, custard or sauces.*

And they're easy to make. In fact, if you're just learning how to cook, make one of your first projects—cookies! You can't fail. Simply follow our special cooky-making hints.

How to Make Perfect Cookies

Rolled Cookies—A pastry cloth for rolling out cooky dough will keep the dough from sticking and from picking up extra flour (which makes cookies dry and hard). The thinner the dough is rolled the crisper the cookies will be. Roll gently with a light touch. Bake on cooky sheet —ungreased for cookies high in fat, greased for cookies with little or no shortening. If cooky sheet is not available, a pan with sides may be turned upside down and cookies baked on the bottom of the pan.

A pastry wheel may be used for cutting rectangular, diamond or triangle shaped cookies. It is a speedy method and makes rerolling of dough unnecessary.

Drop Cookies—Chilling drop cooky dough keeps it from spreading and flattening. Drop from a teaspoon, using another spoon to push dough onto cooky sheet. Allow ample space between cookies as the dough will tend to spread.

Refrigerator Cookies—Mold refrigerator cooky dough with the hands into a roll as big around as the size of cookies desired. Wrap in waxed paper or aluminum foil—or mold in a small loaf pan. Chill dough for several hours until it is firm enough to slice. Slice into cookies of desired thickness with a thin-bladed, sharp knife. Dough may be stored in refrigerator several days and cookies baked as needed.

Pressed Cookies—If the cooky dough and cooky sheet are cold, the cookies will be easier to mold and will hold their shape better. Follow the directions which accompany the cooky press. Force the dough through the press by pressing the plunger. Lift the press when the cooky is formed on the sheet. Vary shape of cookies by using different plates. A pastry tube may be used if a press is not available.

How to Store Cookies—Cool cookies thoroughly before storing. Store soft cookies in a tightly covered container. A slice of apple, orange or bread helps keep cookies moist. Crisp cookies should be stored in a loosely covered container.

STARLIGHT MINT SURPRISE COOKIES

SECOND PRIZE WINNER
Pillsbury's 1st Recipe Contest
by Miss Laura Rott, Naperville, Ill.

Looks just like a plain filled cooky with a walnut topping. But what a luscious surprise when you take a bite!

Makes 4½ dozen cookies

Sift together............3 cups sifted **enriched flour**
　　　　　　　1 teaspoon **soda**
　　　　　　　½ teaspoon **salt**.

Cream	1 cup **butter** (half shortening may be used); add gradually
	1 cup **sugar**
	½ cup firmly packed **brown sugar**, creaming well.
Blend in	2 **eggs**, unbeaten
	2 tablespoons **water**
	1 teaspoon **vanilla**; beat well.
Add	dry ingredients; mix thoroughly. Cover and refrigerate at least 2 hours.
Open	1 package (9 oz.) solid **chocolate mint candy wafers**. Enclose each wafer in about 1 tablespoon of chilled dough.
Place	on greased baking sheet about 2 inches apart.
Top	each with **a walnut half**.
Bake	in moderate oven (375°F.) 10 to 12 min.

Drop Cookies

DROP COOKIES

Notice how many ways these cookies can be varied! This is
a simple, basic recipe you'll want to stir up often.

Makes about 3½ dozen cookies

Sift together	2 cups sifted **enriched flour**
	1 teaspoon double-acting **baking powder**
	¾ teaspoon **salt**.
Cream	⅔ cup **shortening**; add gradually
	1 cup **sugar**. Cream until light and fluffy.
Add	1 **egg**, beat well.
Blend in	half of the dry ingredients.
Add	⅓ cup **milk**

	1 teaspoon **vanilla** and combine thoroughly.
Blend in	remaining dry ingredients.
Drop	by level tablespoonfuls onto greased cooky sheet, allowing room for spreading.
Bake	in moderately hot oven (400°F.) 12 to 15 minutes. Do not stack or store until cold.

CHOCOLATE NUT DROP COOKIES

PREPARE Drop Cookies, adding 2 squares (2 oz.) chocolate, melted and cooled, and ½ cup chopped nuts before adding dry ingredients.

HERMITS

PREPARE Drop Cookies, sifting 1 teaspoon cinnamon and ¼ teaspoon nutmeg with dry ingredients. Add ½ cup raisins and ½ cup chopped nuts after adding dry ingredients.

ORANGE CRISPS

PREPARE Drop Cookies, adding 4 teaspoons grated orange rind to shortening.

GUMDROP COOKIES

PREPARE Drop Cookies, adding ¾ cup gumdrops, finely cut, and ½ cup chopped nuts after dry ingredients.

CHOCOLATE CHIP COOKIES

PREPARE Drop Cookies, decreasing sugar to ½ cup and adding ½ cup firmly-packed brown sugar. Blend in one 7 or 8-oz. package semi-sweet chocolate bits and ½ cup chopped nuts after adding dry ingredients.

LEMON DROPS

PREPARE Drop Cookies, adding 2 teaspoons grated lemon rind to shortening.

PEANUT BUTTER COOKIES

PREPARE Drop Cookies, decreasing shortening to ½ cup and adding ½ cup peanut butter.

FIVE-WAY HOLIDAY COOKIES

Now you can make five varieties of cookies from just one mixing! And no beating eggs. No rolling. No cutting. You'll find
that all five kinds keep well and pack well.

Makes 7 dozen medium cookies

Combine..............thoroughly in large bowl
1⅓ cups soft **shortening** (half butter may be
used)
2 cups **sugar**.

Add..............2 **eggs**, unbeaten
¼ cup **cream**
2 teaspoons **vanilla**.

Sift together..............4 cups sifted **enriched flour**
2 teaspoons double-acting **baking powder**
1½ teaspoons **salt**. Add to blended mixture;
mix well.

Divide..............dough into five parts. Place portions,
one at a time, in second bowl. Flavor
each portion by adding ingredients as
directed below. Drop by tablespoonfuls
onto greased cooky sheets. Flatten
slightly with spatula.

COCONUT

Add..............½ cup shredded **coconut**. Dip tops of cookies in egg yolk or white and top with
plain or tinted coconut.

ORANGE-PECAN

Blend in..............1 tablespoon grated **orange rind** and
¼ cup chopped **pecans**. Top with half
pecan.

CHOCOLATE

*Add*_____1 square (1 oz.) **chocolate**, melted and cooled

1 tablespoon **cream**

¼ cup chopped **nuts**.

PLAIN

Decorate with **colored sugar, candied fruit** or **nuts**.

FRUIT

*Add*_____½ cup diced **candied fruit** or ⅓ cup mincemeat.

*Bake*_____in moderately hot oven (400°F.) 8 to 10 minutes. Cool and store in tight containers.

FAVORITE MOLASSES COOKIES

This recipe makes the kind of fat, spicy cookies grandmother used to keep in the cooky jar.

Makes 4 dozen cookies

*Sift together*____2¼ cups sifted **enriched flour**

1 teaspoon **salt**

½ teaspoon **soda**

½ teaspoon **ginger**

½ teaspoon **cinnamon**.

*Cream*_____⅔ cup **shortening** with

1 teaspoon grated **lemon rind** and

½ cup **sugar**.

*Blend in*_____1 **egg**

½ cup light **molasses**.

*Add*_____dry ingredients gradually; mix well.

*Drop*_____by tablespoonfuls onto greased cooky sheet, allowing room for spreading.

*Bake*_____in moderate oven (375°F.) 12 minutes.

CARAMEL PECAN COOKIES

There's brown sugar flavor in these cookies and pecan halves
on top.

Makes 4½ dozen cookies

Sift together........1½ cups sifted **enriched flour**
                      ½ teaspoon **salt.**
Cream..................½ cup **shortening**; add gradually
                      ½ cup firmly packed **brown sugar** and
                      ½ cup light **corn syrup**. Cream until light
                         and fluffy.
Blend in..............1 **egg**
                      1 teaspoon **vanilla.**
Add.......................dry ingredients gradually; mix until well
                         blended.
Drop.....................by teaspoonfuls onto greased cooky
                         sheet. Press each cooky flat with fork.
Place...................a pecan half on top of each cooky.
Bake....................in moderately hot oven (400°F.) 8 to 10
                         minutes. Do not stack or store until cold.

OLD-FASHIONED OATMEAL COOKIES

Here is an easy recipe for real, old-time oatmeal cookies.
Make them plain—or add raisins and nuts, if you like.

Makes 4½ dozen cookies

Sift together........1¾ cups sifted **enriched flour**
                      ½ teaspoon **soda**
                      1 teaspoon **salt**
                      ½ teaspoon **cinnamon**
                      ¼ teaspoon **cloves.**
Cream..................¾ cup **shortening**; add gradually
                      ½ cup **sugar**

	1 cup firmly packed **brown sugar**, creaming well.
Blend in	1 **egg**; beat well.
Combine	½ cup **buttermilk** or **sour milk**
	¼ cup **light corn syrup**
	1 teaspoon **vanilla**.
Add	dry and liquid ingredients alternately to creamed mixture, beginning and ending with dry ingredients.
Blend in	2 cups **rolled oats**
	1 cup chopped **nuts**
	1 cup **raisins**.
Drop	by rounded tablespoonfuls onto greased cooky sheet, allowing room for spreading.
Bake	in moderate oven (375°F.) 12 to 15 minutes. Do not stack or store until cold.

CHOCOLATE-FILLED TEA COOKIES

Pillsbury Contest Winner

Drop cookies are sandwiched together with chocolate filling.

Makes about 5 dozen small cookies

Sift together	1¾ cups sifted **enriched flour**
	1½ teaspoons double-acting **baking powder**
	1 teaspoon **salt**.
Cream	⅓ cup **butter** or shortening. Add gradually
	¾ cup **sugar**, creaming until light and fluffy.
Blend in	3 **eggs**, one at a time. Beat one minute.
Add	2 tablespoons **milk**
	1 teaspoon **vanilla**.
Blend in	dry ingredients gradually. Mix well.
Drop	by level teaspoonfuls onto greased cooky sheet.

Bake................in moderate oven (350°F.) 8 to 10 minutes.

Spread................chocolate filling (or your favorite fudge frosting) between two cookies. Place bottoms of cookies together, sandwich style.

CHOCOLATE FILLING

COMBINE 1½ cups sifted confectioners' sugar, 3 tablespoons cocoa and ⅛ teaspoon salt. Cream 3 tablespoons butter. Blend in 3 tablespoons hot cream alternately with dry ingredients. Add ½ teaspoon vanilla and beat well. Thin with additional cream if necessary. Spread filling between cookies.

HALLOWEEN COOKIES

Drop the dough for these spicy molasses cookies from a spoon or roll them out and cut them into holiday shapes. (You might decorate them, too, with tinted icing.)

Makes 2 dozen large cookies

Sift together................2 cups sifted **enriched flour**
½ teaspoon double-acting **baking powder**
½ teaspoon each: **soda, salt, cinnamon**
¼ teaspoon each: **nutmeg, cloves.**

Add................½ cup firmly packed **brown sugar**
⅓ cup **shortening**
1 **egg**
¼ cup **buttermilk** or sour milk
⅓ cup **molasses.**

Beat................for 2 minutes until well blended and smooth.

Drop................by tablespoonfuls onto greased cooky sheet, allowing room for spreading. Flatten slightly.

Bake................in moderately hot oven (400°F.) 8 to 10 minutes.

Decorate................with creamy butter icing. A cone made from heavy paper may be used as a decorating tube.

ROLLED HALLOWEEN COOKIES

PREPARE Halloween Cookies, adding ⅓ to ½ cup additional flour until dough is stiff enough to roll. Use cardboard patterns and a sharp, pointed knife to cut Halloween, Christmas or other holiday shapes.

CREAMY BUTTER ICING

CREAM 2 tablespoons butter. Blend in gradually 2 cups sifted confectioners' sugar. Add 2 tablespoons hot cream, a little at a time, until of spreading consistency. Add ½ teaspoon vanilla. If desired, frosting may be colored to suit the holiday.

MOTHER'S MINT MIST COOKIES

Pillsbury Contest Winner by Mrs. Murray S. Goodfellow, Hanover, Pa.

These delicate peppermint drops are delicious with tea or coffee. And note—this recipe makes 5 dozen cookies.

Makes 5 dozen cookies

*Sift together*_____2 cups sifted **enriched flour**
½ teaspoon **soda**
¼ teaspoon **cream of tartar.**

*Cream*_____½ cup **butter** (half shortening may be used)
1 cup sugar; blend until light and fluffy.

*Blend in*_____1 **egg**
½ teaspoon **vanilla**
¼ teaspoon **peppermint flavoring.** Mix well.

*Add*_____½ cup **buttermilk** or sour milk alternately with dry ingredients to creamed mixture, blending well after each addition. The dough will be quite soft.

*Drop*_____by level tablespoonfuls onto well-greased cooky sheet. Grease bottom of small glass; dip into sugar and press cooky flat.

*Bake*_____in moderately hot oven (375°F.) 8 to 10 minutes or until delicately brown. Cool on wire rack. Do not stack or store until cool.

PEPPERMINT CREAM-TOPPED PUFFS

Pillsbury Contest Winner by Mrs. Richard Milton Dietz, Lancaster, Pa.

Delicate sponge puffs . . . topped with whipped cream and crushed peppermint candy. A different kind of cooky dessert.

Makes 4 dozen puffs

*Sift together*____ ½ cup sifted enriched flour
½ teaspoon salt.

*Beat*_____ 2 egg whites until stiff. Blend in
½ cup sifted confectioners' sugar and beat until mixture stands in peaks.

*Beat*_____ 2 eggs and
2 egg yolks in large bowl until thick and lemon colored. Fold in beaten egg whites.

*Blend in*_____ sifted dry ingredients and
1 teaspoon vanilla.

*Drop*_____ by level tablespoonfuls onto cooky sheet covered with ungreased wrapping paper. The batter will be very thin.

*Bake*_____ in moderate oven (350°F.) 8 to 10 minutes. Remove from paper immediately.

Before serving:

*Whip*_____ 1 pint (2 cups) whipping cream. Fold in
1 cup crushed peppermint stick candy. Arrange puffs in clusters of three. Top with peppermint whipped cream. If desired, decorate with maraschino cherries. Makes about 16 servings.

Rolled Cookies

OLD-FASHIONED SUGAR COOKIES

These old favorites are rich and tender, and you can decorate them if you wish. Blend your favorite herb into the basic dough for unusual flavor.

Makes 5 dozen cookies

Sift together——1½ cups sifted enriched flour
 ½ teaspoon double-acting baking powder
 ½ teaspoon salt
 ½ teaspoon soda
 ½ cup sugar.

Cut in——————½ cup shortening until mixture resembles coarse meal.

Blend in—————1 egg
 2 tablespoons milk
 1 teaspoon vanilla.

Roll out—————on floured board to $\frac{1}{16}$-inch thickness. Cut with 2½-inch cutter. Place on ungreased cooky sheet.

Bake——————in moderately hot oven (400°F.) 6 to 8 minutes.

TASTY HERB TREATS

PREPARE Old-Fashioned Sugar Cookies, decreasing vanilla to ½ teaspoon. Blend in 1½ teaspoons of one of the following herbs: caraway, cardamom seed, dill or aniseed.

SWEDISH COOKIES

Roll these cookies, twist them, or press them. Any way you shape them, they turn out to be among the most delicate of all cookies. (This is a good recipe to keep in mind, when you want to use up extra egg yolks.)

Makes about 5½ dozen cookies

Cook————————6 egg yolks. (Separate yolks from whites; drop yolks from saucer one at a time into hot, salted water. Simmer until hard cooked.)

Sift together————2 cups sifted enriched flour
½ teaspoon salt.

Cream————————¾ cup shortening; add gradually
¾ cup sugar, beating until light and fluffy.

Add————————————cooked egg yolks which have been put through a wire sieve and
½ teaspoon lemon extract.

Blend————————3 tablespoons cream and dry ingredients alternately into creamed mixture, beating well after each addition.

Roll————————————dough to ⅛-inch thickness and cut into desired cooky shapes. Place on greased cooky sheet. Decorate with colored sugar, candied fruit, nuts or coconut. If desired, this dough may be used in a cooky press. Cookies may also be shaped into knots by gently rolling a rounded teaspoon of dough on a lightly-floured canvas or board until about 6 inches in length and tying in a loose knot.

Bake————————————in moderate oven (375°F.) until edges become delicately browned—6 to 8 minutes for rolled or pressed cookies, 10 to 12 minutes for knots.

FILLED COOKIES

These are plump, man-sized cookies. Fill them with raisin or date filling.

Makes 18 to 24 cookies

Sift together——1¾ cups sifted **enriched flour**
½ teaspoon double-acting **baking powder**
½ teaspoon **salt**
½ teaspoon **soda**
½ cup **sugar.**

Cut in————½ cup **shortening** until mixture resembles coarse meal.

Blend in————1 **egg**
2 tablespoons **milk**
1 teaspoon **vanilla.**

Mix————until well blended and smooth.

Roll out————on floured board to ⅛-inch thickness. Cut into rounds with 2½-inch cutter.

Place————a tablespoon of raisin or date filling in center of half the rounds; top with remaining rounds.

Seal————edges together with fork; prick top.

Bake————in moderately hot oven (400°F.) 10 minutes.

RAISIN OR DATE FILLING

COMBINE 1½ cups chopped dates or raisins, ½ cup sugar and ½ cup water in saucepan. Cook for 15 minutes or until thickened, stirring constantly. Remove from heat. Blend in ½ teaspoon lemon rind, 1 tablespoon lemon juice and ¼ cup chopped nuts. Fill cookies as directed.

DATE PINWHEEL COOKIES

Spice and a swirl of date filling make this cooky good to eat and good to look at.

Makes about 5 dozen small cookies

Sift together	2 cups sifted enriched flour
	½ teaspoon double-acting baking powder
	½ teaspoon salt
	¼ teaspoon cinnamon
	¼ teaspoon cloves.
Cream	½ cup shortening; add gradually
	1 cup firmly packed brown sugar, creaming well.
Blend in	1 egg
	1 teaspoon vanilla.
Add	dry ingredients gradually and mix well.
Roll out	on lightly-floured board to about ¼-inch thickness, keeping a rectangular shape.
Spread	dough with date filling.
Roll	as for jelly roll. Wrap in waxed paper and chill for several hours.
Cut	slices ¼-inch thick. Place on greased cooky sheet.
Bake	in moderate oven (375°F.) 10 to 12 minutes. Do not stack or store until cold.

DATE FILLING

COMBINE one 8-oz. package dates or figs, finely chopped, ½ cup sugar and ½ cup water in saucepan. Cook over direct heat, stirring constantly until thick. Cool thoroughly. Add ½ cup chopped nuts. Spread mixture on cooky dough as directed.

Refrigerator Cookies

REFRIGERATOR COOKIES

You can mix up these cookies at your leisure and chill the dough in your refrigerator. Then when you want fresh-baked cookies, cut and bake in a jiffy. (Notice the different kinds of cookies you can make from this basic recipe!)

Makes about 6 dozen cookies

*Sift together*_____2 cups sifted **enriched flour**
               1 teaspoon double-acting **baking powder**
               ½ teaspoon salt.

*Cream*_____⅔ cup **shortening** with
               ½ cup firmly packed **brown sugar** and
               ½ cup granulated **sugar**.

*Add*_____1 **egg**
               1 teaspoon **vanilla**. Beat until light.

*Blend in*_____dry ingredients.

*Divide*_____mixture into two equal parts. Place on waxed paper and shape into rolls, 1½ inches in diameter. Wrap in waxed paper. Chill thoroughly several hours.

*Cut*_____in slices about ⅛-inch thick and place on ungreased cooky sheets.

*Bake*_____in hot oven (425°F.) 5 to 7 minutes. Do not stack or store until cold.

LEMON NUT REFRIGERATOR COOKIES

PREPARE Refrigerator Cookies, omitting vanilla. Add 1 tablespoon lemon juice and 1 tablespoon lemon rind. Blend in ½ cup chopped nuts before adding dry ingredients.

CHOCOLATE NUT REFRIGERATOR COOKIES

PREPARE Refrigerator Cookies, adding 2 squares (2 oz.) chocolate, melted and cooled, and ½ cup chopped nuts before adding dry ingredients.

SPICE REFRIGERATOR COOKIES

PREPARE Refrigerator Cookies, sifting 1 teaspoon cinnamon and ¼ teaspoon nutmeg with dry ingredients.

ORANGE REFRIGERATOR COOKIES

PREPARE Refrigerator Cookies, adding 4 teaspoons grated orange rind to shortening.

COCONUT REFRIGERATOR COOKIES

PREPARE Refrigerator Cookies, adding ¾ cup grated coconut before adding dry ingredients.

BRAZIL NUT REFRIGERATOR SLICES

Pillsbury Contest Winner by Mrs. Leroy Wettstein, New Holstein, Wis.

There's a single slice of Brazil nut right in the center of each cooky. The cookies themselves are flavored with coconut and molasses. Keep the dough in the refrigerator—slice and bake as needed.

Makes about 7 dozen cookies

*Sift together*_____2¼ cups sifted **enriched flour**
                     ½ teaspoon **soda.**
*Cream*_____½ cup **butter** (half shortening may be used). Add gradually
                     1 cup **sugar,** creaming well.
*Blend in*_____2 **eggs**
                     1 tablespoon **molasses**
                     ½ cup shredded **coconut.** Mix well.
*Add*_____sifted dry ingredients. Blend thoroughly.
*Divide*_____dough into two equal parts. Place on waxed paper and shape into long rolls, 1½ inches in diameter.

Place	Brazil nuts (about ¼ lb., shelled) end to end in a single row lengthwise on top of each roll. Press nuts into dough until they form a core in the center of each roll. Reshape top of roll.
Chill	rolls in refrigerator at least 3 hours or overnight.
Cut	in slices about ⅛-inch thick with a sharp knife (use a sawing motion). Place on well-greased cooky sheet.
Bake	in moderate oven (350°F.) 10 to 12 minutes.

HERB CHEESE CANAPÉS

Pillsbury Contest Winner by Mrs. Melvin P. Spalding, Pleasantville, N. Y.

"These wafers are good with soup, delicious served with salad, and as a simple finish to a meal, just enjoyed with a cup of coffee," says Mrs. Spalding. Store the dough in your refrigerator and bake as needed.

Makes about 5 dozen wafers

Sift together	1 cup sifted **enriched flour** ¼ teaspoon **celery seed** ⅛ teaspoon **pepper.**
Cream	½ cup **butter** (half shortening may be used) in large bowl.
Blend in	cream cheese spread (one 5-oz. jar) smoky cheese spread (one 5-oz. jar). Cream thoroughly.
Add	sifted dry ingredients to creamed mixture. Mix well.
Chill	dough in refrigerator 1 hour.
Place	on waxed paper and shape into a round roll 2 inches in diameter. Wrap in waxed paper.

Chill	thoroughly in refrigerator at least 4 hours or overnight.
Cut	into slices about ⅛-inch thick and place on ungreased cooky sheets.
Bake	in hot oven (450°F.) 8 to 10 minutes. Serve warm. Dough may be kept in refrigerator and baked as needed.

Bars

SEA FOAM NUT SQUARES

BEST OF CLASS WINNER
Pillsbury's 1st Recipe Contest
by Mrs. E. R. Wagoner, Bryan, Texas

If you like panocha fudge you'll love these nut squares.

Makes about 4 dozen squares

Sift together	2 cups sifted **enriched flour**
	1 teaspoon double-acting **baking powder**
	½ teaspoon **salt**
	⅛ teaspoon soda.
Cream	½ cup **shortening**; add gradually
	¼ cup sugar
	½ cup firmly packed **brown sugar** and cream until light and fluffy.
Add	2 **egg yolks**
	2 tablespoons cold **water**. Mix well; add
	½ teaspoon **vanilla**.
Measure	¼ cup **milk**; add alternately with dry ingredients to creamed mixture. Blend well.
Spread	in greased and floured 15x10-inch pan or in two 9x9x2-inch pans.

*Beat*_____2 egg whites until stiff but not dry. Add
                      1½ cups firmly packed **brown sugar** a little at
                      a time, beating well after each addition.

*Spread*_____over cooky dough and sprinkle with
                      1 cup chopped **nuts**.

*Bake*_____in slow oven (325°F.) 25 to 30 minutes.
                      Cut into bars or squares while still warm.

CHOCOLATE NUT SQUARES

You can make these cookies thin and crisp, or fat and chewy.
They're especially rich in chocolate and nuts.

Makes 24 squares

*Blend together*_____2 eggs, slightly beaten
                      1 cup **sugar**
                      ½ teaspoon **salt**
                      1 teaspoon **vanilla**.

*Add*_____2 squares (2 oz.) **chocolate**, melted and
                      cooled
                      ½ cup melted **shortening**.

*Add gradually*_____½ cup sifted **enriched flour**; mix until well
                      blended.

*Pour*_____into greased, shallow 15x10-inch pan.
                      For brownie-type cooky, use a 12x8 or
                      10x10-inch pan.

*Sprinkle with*_____½ cup chopped **nuts**.

*Bake*_____in moderate oven (350°F.) 25 to 30 min-
                      utes. Cut into 2½-inch squares while still
                      warm.

SAUCEPAN BROWNIES

Here's an unusual method of making good, chewy brownies.
You melt chocolate, then mix the brownies in the same pan.
No other bowls necessary. Bake and cut in thick squares.
They're quick, easy and so good.

Makes about 16 brownies

Melt............⅓ cup **shortening** and
2 squares (2 oz.) **chocolate** in saucepan over very low heat, stirring constantly. Cool.

Blend in............1 cup **sugar**
1 teaspoon **vanilla**.

Add............2 **eggs**, one at a time, beating well after each.

Sift together......¾ cup sifted **enriched flour**
¼ teaspoon **salt**.

Add............½ cup chopped **nuts** to flour mixture.

Blend............dry ingredients into chocolate mixture; beat well. Pour into greased and floured 8x8x2-inch pan.

Bake............in moderate oven (350°F.) 35 to 40 minutes. Cut into squares while still warm.

DREAM BARS

These bars have a rich brown sugar base, and a meringue topping with chopped nuts and coconut.

Makes about 4 dozen bars

Combine............2½ cups sifted **enriched flour**
1 cup firmly packed **brown sugar**
½ teaspoon **salt**.

Cut in————————1 cup shortening until mixture resembles coarse meal.

Press————————mixture firmly into ungreased 15x10-inch pan or in two 9x9x2-inch pans.

Bake————————in moderate oven (350°F.) 10 minutes. Remove from oven and cover with topping.

Topping

Sift together———½ cup sifted enriched flour
1 teaspoon double-acting baking powder
½ teaspoon salt.

Beat————————6 egg whites until stiff.

Add gradually———2 cups firmly packed brown sugar, sieved, and beat until mixture stands in peaks.

Add————————2 teaspoons vanilla.

Fold in————————the sifted dry ingredients.

Blend in————————1½ cups chopped nuts and
2 cups shredded coconut. Spread over baked mixture.

Bake————————in moderate oven (350°F.) 25 to 30 minutes. Cut into bars while still warm. Leave in pan until cool.

MINNESOTA HARVEST BARS

Pillsbury Contest Winner by Miss Aquina G. Shea, Glyndon, Minn.

Dates, nuts, spices and a hint of pumpkin give these bars a very special flavor. Serve as a cooky or top with whipped cream for an easy dessert.

Makes about 12 bars

Combine————————½ cup dates, chopped
½ cup walnuts, chopped
2 tablespoons flour.

Sift together	½ cup sifted **enriched flour**
	½ teaspoon double-acting **baking powder**
	¼ teaspoon **soda**
	½ teaspoon **salt**
	½ teaspoon each: **cinnamon, nutmeg, ginger.**
Melt	¼ cup **shortening** in 2-quart saucepan over low flame.
Add	1 cup firmly packed **brown sugar** and stir until well blended. Remove from heat.
Blend in	⅔ cup canned **pumpkin** and mix thoroughly.
Add	2 **eggs**, one at a time, beating well. Add ½ teaspoon **vanilla.**
Blend in	sifted dry ingredients and mix thoroughly.
Add	floured **dates** and **nuts.**
Pour	into well-greased 9x9x2-inch pan.
Bake	in moderate oven (350°F.) 30 to 35 minutes. Cool. Cut into bars. Sprinkle with confectioners' sugar.

SPICY COCONUT BARS

Pillsbury Contest Winner by Mrs. Albert P. Kimball, New York, N. Y.

"This recipe", says Mrs. Kimball, "was given to me by a New Hampshire farm woman who said it was her grandmother's favorite cooky, which she made for all church socials."

Makes 36 bars

Sift together	2 cups sifted **enriched flour**
	1 teaspoon double-acting **baking powder**
	¼ teaspoon **soda**
	1 teaspoon **salt**
	1 teaspoon **cinnamon**
	½ teaspoon **nutmeg.**

Cream............½ cup **shortening**. Add gradually

1 cup firmly packed **brown sugar** and cream thoroughly.

Add............1 **egg**, unbeaten

¾ cup **pumpkin**, cooked or canned

2 tablespoons **molasses**

1 teaspoon **vanilla**.

Blend in............sifted dry ingredients. Mix well.

Spread............in greased 15x10-inch shallow pan or two 8x8-inch square pans.

Beat............1 **egg** until thick. Gradually add

½ cup firmly packed **brown sugar** and continue beating until stiff.

Blend in............¾ cup toasted **coconut**. Spread over dough.

Bake............in moderate oven (350°F.) 25 to 30 minutes. Cut into bars when cool.

FIRESIDE FRUIT BARS

Pillsbury Contest Winner by Miss Jenifer Trace, Wilmington, Del.

These chewy bars are filled with nuts and candied fruit. Spices add dash; orange juice and rind add flavor.

Makes about 2½ dozen bars

Sift together............2 cups sifted **enriched flour**

½ teaspoon **soda**

½ teaspoon **salt**

½ teaspoon **cinnamon**

¼ teaspoon **nutmeg**.

Cream............⅔ cup **shortening**. Add gradually

½ cup **sugar** and cream until light and fluffy.

Blend in............1 teaspoon grated **orange rind**.

Combine............½ cup undiluted **evaporated milk**
      ¼ cup **orange juice.**

Add............dry ingredients alternately with liquid, beginning and ending with dry ingredients.

Blend in............⅔ cup chopped, mixed **candied fruit**
      ¼ cup chopped **nuts.**

Spread............in greased and floured 15x10-inch shallow pan.

Bake............in moderate oven (350°F.) 15 to 20 minutes. Cool. Frost with orange frosting. Cut into bars with sharp knife.

ORANGE FROSTING

COMBINE 3 cups sifted confectioners' sugar and ½ teaspoon grated orange rind. Blend in 2 tablespoons orange juice and 2 to 3 tablespoons evaporated milk. Beat until smooth. Spread on cooled bars.

DATE-NUT BARS

These cooky bars are filled with dates and nuts. Chewy and delicious.

Makes 40 bars

Sift together............1 cup sifted **enriched flour**
      1 teaspoon double-acting **baking powder**
      ¼ teaspoon **salt.**

Add............1½ cups chopped **dates**
      1 cup chopped **nuts.**

Beat............3 **eggs** until foamy.

Add gradually............1 cup firmly packed **brown sugar,** beating well after each addition.

Add............1 teaspoon **vanilla.**

Fold in............dry ingredients, dates and nuts. Beat well.

*Spread*_____evenly in well-greased 12x8x2-inch pan.

*Bake*_____in moderate oven (350°F.) 20 to 25 minutes. Cut into 2½x1-inch bars while still warm. Roll in confectioners' sugar.

CINNAMON CRUNCHES

These crisp, chewy cookies have just the right amount of sweetness—just the right amount of spice.

Makes about 24 bars

*Sift together*_____1 cup sifted **enriched flour**
¼ teaspoon **salt**
¼ teaspoon **cinnamon.**

*Cream*_____⅓ cup **shortening**; add gradually
½ cup **sugar.** Cream well.

*Blend in*_____1 **egg yolk**
2 tablespoons **milk**
¼ teaspoon **vanilla.**

*Add*_____dry ingredients gradually and mix well.

*Spread*_____mixture in ungreased 11x7-inch pan.

*Beat*_____1 **egg white** slightly. Spread over surface of dough.

*Combine*_____3 tablespoons **sugar**
¼ teaspoon **cinnamon**
¼ cup chopped **nuts.** Sprinkle evenly over top.

*Bake*_____in moderate oven (350°F.) 30 minutes. Cut into bars or squares while still warm.

HOOSIER PEANUT BARS

Pillsbury Contest Winner by Mrs. Edgar L. Bleeke, Fort Wayne, Ind.

Brown-sugar bars with a layer of semi-sweet chocolate and a meringue topping sprinkled with chopped peanuts.

Makes about 24 bars

Sift together............2 cups sifted enriched flour
　　　　　　　　　2 teaspoons double-acting baking powder
　　　　　　　　　1 teaspoon soda
　　　　　　　　　½ teaspoon salt.

*Cream*_____½ cup shortening. Add gradually
　　　　　　　　　½ cup sugar
　　　　　　　　　½ cup firmly packed brown sugar. Mix well.

Blend in..............2 egg yolks
　　　　　　　　　1 teaspoon vanilla.

*Add*_____3 tablespoons cold water alternately with sifted dry ingredients. The dough will be very stiff.

*Press*_____dough into two greased and floured 8x8x2-inch pans.*

Sprinkle..............1 package semi-sweet chocolate bits (6 or 7 oz.) over dough and press in gently.

*Beat*_____2 egg whites until foamy. Gradually add
　　　　　　　　　1 cup firmly packed brown sugar and beat until stiff. Spread over chocolate bits.

*Top with*_____¾ cup chopped salted peanuts.

*Bake*_____in slow oven (325°F.) 30 to 35 minutes. Cut into bars or squares while still warm.

_____

*If desired, bake in a 15x10-inch jelly roll pan.

MARSHMALLOW FUDGE BARS

Pillsbury Contest Winner by Mrs. Elmer Ellis Mooring, Dallas, Tex.

These extra-rich, candy-like squares are especially good served with ice cream. The chocolate pecan bars are topped with marshmallow halves, then a fudge frosting goes on top.

Makes 16 bars

*Sift together*_____¾ cup sifted enriched flour
¼ teaspoon double-acting baking powder
¼ teaspoon salt
2 tablespoons cocoa.

*Cream*_____½ cup shortening. Add gradually
¾ cup sugar; cream until light and fluffy.

*Blend in*_____2 eggs, one at a time, beating well after each addition.

*Add*_____sifted dry ingredients to creamed mixture and mix well.

*Blend in*_____1 teaspoon vanilla
½ cup chopped pecans.

*Spread*_____in greased and floured 12x8-inch pan.

*Bake*_____in moderate oven (350°F.) 25 to 30 minutes.

*Cover*_____top of baked bars with 12 soft marshmallows cut in half. Return to oven for 3 minutes or until marshmallows are soft.

*Spread*_____marshmallows evenly. Cool; cover with easy chocolate frosting.

EASY CHOCOLATE FROSTING

COMBINE ½ cup firmly packed brown sugar, ¼ cup water and 2 squares chocolate in saucepan. Let come to a boil and cook for 3 minutes. Add 3 tablespoons butter and 1 teaspoon vanilla. Cool. Blend in 1½ cups sifted confectioners' sugar. If necessary, thin with a small amount of cream. Spread over marshmallow topping. Cut into bars.

Special Occasion Cookies

PARTY PRESS COOKIES

We developed this cooky dough especially for use in your cooky press. This dough is easy to work with and the cookies shape beautifully. Especially nice for teas, showers . . . whenever you want a dainty cooky that's rich and buttery.

Makes 6 to 7 dozen tiny cookies

*Sift together*____1½ cups sifted enriched flour
½ teaspoon salt.

*Cream*_____½ cup shortening thoroughly (part butter may be used for flavor). Add gradually ½ cup sugar; mix well.

*Blend in*_____1 egg
½ teaspoon vanilla
½ teaspoon almond extract. Mix thoroughly.

*Add*_____half of dry ingredients. Mix well. Add remaining dry ingredients and beat until well blended.

*Press*_____dough through a cooky press onto ungreased baking sheets. Do not fill cooky press more than ½ to ⅔ full. If desired, cookies may be decorated with candied cherries, citron, nuts or colored sugar.

*Bake*_____in moderately hot oven (400°F.) 8 to 10 minutes until delicately browned. Do not stack or store until cold.

SPICE STICKS

PREPARE Party Press Cookies, sifting 1¼ teaspoons cinnamon, ½ teaspoon cloves, ¾ teaspoon nutmeg and ¼ teaspoon allspice with dry ingredients. Press dough through cooky press, shaping into 2x1-inch "sticks."

ORANGE OR LEMON CRESCENTS

PREPARE Party Press Cookies, creaming 2 teaspoons grated lemon rind or orange rind with shortening. Proceed as directed, shaping dough into crescents.

NUT TWISTS

PREPARE Party Press Cookies, adding ½ cup finely chopped nuts before blending in dry ingredients. Shape dough into figure eights.

COCONUT WREATHS

PREPARE Party Press Cookies, adding ½ cup finely chopped, moist coconut before blending in dry ingredients. Shape dough into circles. Decorate with bits of candied cherry and citron.

PRALINE BUTTER NUGGETS

Pillsbury Contest Winner by Mrs. John Maxwell, Fort Smith, Ark.

Blend bits of pecan candy into this extra-rich butter-cooky dough. Roll into balls to bake and then dip in powdered sugar. An especially tasty cooky.

Makes 2 dozen cookies

Melt	¼ cup sugar in heavy skillet over low heat until golden brown in color.
Add	¼ cup pecan halves. Pour on greased waxed paper. Cool. Chop fine when hard.
Sift together	1½ cups sifted enriched flour
	½ teaspoon salt.
Add	¼ cup firmly packed brown sugar.
Cream	⅓ cup butter and
	⅓ cup shortening.
Blend in	sifted dry ingredients.
Add	1 teaspoon vanilla and the chopped pecan-sugar candy.

Roll_____dough into round balls with hands, using about 1 level tablespoon dough for each ball. Place on ungreased baking sheet.

Bake_____in slow oven (300°F.) 25 to 30 minutes. Roll hot cookies in confectioners' sugar.

SPRINGERLE

This traditional German cooky is a favorite during the holidays. It's flavored with anise and imprinted with a pretty design. These cookies become softer when stored in a tightly covered cooky jar.

Makes about 5 dozen cookies

Sift together____3¾ cups sifted enriched flour
½ teaspoon salt.

Beat_____4 eggs until thick and lemon colored. Add gradually
2 cups sugar, beating constantly. Continue beating for 15 minutes.

Fold_____dry ingredients into egg mixture.

Roll_____dough to about ⅓-inch thickness on lightly-floured board, keeping rectangular shape.

Press_____springerle board well into dough. Or use a rolling pin on which springerle forms are marked.

Cut_____cookies apart with a sharp knife. Place on ungreased baking sheet sprinkled with anise seed.

Cover_____dough with towel and allow to dry out overnight.

Bake_____in moderate oven (375°F.) 5 minutes, then reduce heat to 300°F. and continue baking for 25 minutes.

HOLIDAY NUGGETS

These dainty cookies hold their delicate flavor and stay fresh for days. A favorite cooky for holidays or any time.

Makes 3½ dozen small cookies

Sift together............2 cups sifted **enriched flour**
½ teaspoon **salt**.

*Cream
thoroughly*............¾ cup **shortening**
¼ cup **butter** or margarine
½ cup sifted **confectioners' sugar.**

Blend in............1 tablespoon **vanilla**
1 teaspoon **almond extract**
½ cup chopped **nuts.**

Add............dry ingredients gradually; mix until dough is smooth and well blended.

Shape............into small balls using 1 tablespoon of dough for each cooky. Place on ungreased baking sheet and flatten slightly.

Bake............in slow oven (325°F.) 20 to 25 minutes.

Roll............warm cookies in confectioners' sugar. For color, mix confectioners' sugar with colored crystallized sugar.

BUTTERSCOTCH CRISPS

This is a good-sized recipe for crisp, tender butterscotch cookies. Easy too—and quick to make.

Makes 4 dozen cookies

*Sift together*_____2 cups sifted **enriched flour**
½ teaspoon salt.

*Cream*_____¾ cup **shortening**; add gradually
1 cup firmly packed **brown sugar**; beat until light and fluffy.

*Add*_____1 egg
½ cup chopped **nuts**
1 teaspoon **vanilla**; beat well.

*Add*_____dry ingredients; mix well.

*Shape*_____into small round balls and place on ungreased cooky sheet. Flatten with fork.

*Bake*_____in moderately hot oven (400°F.) 8 to 10 minutes.

GINGERSNAPS

These are dark ginger cookies, full of spice and flavor.

Makes 6 dozen cookies

*Sift together*_____2½ cups sifted **enriched flour**
1 tablespoon **cocoa**
½ teaspoon salt
1½ teaspoons **ginger**
1½ teaspoons **soda**.

*Cream*_____½ cup **shortening** with
1 cup **sugar**.

*Add*_____3 tablespoons **light molasses**
⅓ cup **corn syrup**.

Blend in............1 egg
1½ teaspoons vinegar
1½ teaspoons vanilla.
Add gradually..........half of the dry ingredients. Mix until well blended.
Blend in............1½ teaspoons hot water. Add remaining dry ingredients.
Chill..............thoroughly several hours.
Roll..............dough into small balls using 1 rounded teaspoon of dough for each cooky. Place on ungreased cooky sheet.
Bake..............in moderate oven (375°F.) 12 to 15 min.

CARAMEL NUT DROPS

These brown sugar cookies are molded into tiny balls and rolled in chopped nuts.

Makes 3 dozen cookies

Sift together..........2 cups sifted enriched flour
2 teaspoons double-acting baking powder
½ teaspoon salt.
Cream............¾ cup shortening with
½ cup firmly packed brown sugar.
Blend in............1 egg yolk
½ teaspoon vanilla.
Add..............dry ingredients to creamed mixture; mix until well blended.
Shape............dough into small balls, about the size of a walnut.
Dip into............1 egg white, unbeaten, then in
½ cup finely chopped nuts. Place on greased cooky sheet.
Bake..............in moderate oven (350°F.) 15 to 20 min.

PFEFFERNUSSE

Here's a spicy, brown sugar cooky from Germany. Especially popular during the holiday season. The longer you keep them, the softer they become. (Their flavor improves, too.)

Makes about 4½ dozen cookies

*Sift together*___4½ cups sifted enriched flour
¼ teaspoon soda
1 teaspoon each: cloves, nutmeg, salt
⅛ teaspoon cinnamon
¼ teaspoon black pepper.

*Add*_____2 teaspoons anise seed.

*Combine*_____4 eggs, slightly beaten
2 cups firmly packed brown sugar. Add to dry ingredients and mix well. If desired, dough may be chilled.

*Shape*_____dough with well-floured hands into balls the size of walnuts. Place on greased baking sheets.

*Cover*_____cookies with a towel. Let stand at room temperature overnight.

*Bake*_____in moderate oven (350°F.) 20 to 25 minutes. Shake warm cookies, a few at a time, in paper bag containing confectioners' sugar. When cold, store in tightly covered jar.

SANDBAKELSE

(Swedish Butter Tarts)

These Swedish butter tarts are a Christmas favorite. Serve them with or without a filling. They're tender, buttery and very rich.

Makes 7 dozen sandbakelse

Cream
*thoroughly*_____2 cups **butter**. Add gradually
⠀⠀⠀⠀⠀⠀⠀⠀⠀⠀2 cups **sugar**, creaming until light.
*Blend in*_____1 **egg**, unbeaten
⠀⠀⠀⠀⠀⠀⠀⠀⠀⠀1 teaspoon **almond extract**
⠀⠀⠀⠀⠀⠀⠀⠀⠀⠀½ teaspoon **salt**.
*Add gradually*_____6 cups sifted **enriched flour**; mix well after each addition.
*Press*_____small amount of dough evenly into bottoms and sides of shallow 3-inch tart shells or fluted cupcake pans. (The crispness of the baked product depends upon the thinness of this layer of dough.)
*Bake*_____in hot oven (450°F.) 8 to 10 minutes. Cool slightly. To remove, turn pans upside down and tap gently, so that cookies will drop out. They should retain the shape of the mold. Sandbakelse may be served plain as a cooky or served as a dessert with whipped cream filling. Or they may be prepared with a baked coconut-caramel filling.

Whipped Cream Filling

(Makes enough filling for about 2 dozen sandbakelse)

FOLD ½ cup jam into 1 cup whipped cream. Fill baked sandbakelse and serve at once.

Coconut-Caramel Filling

(Makes enough filling for about 2 dozen sandbakelse)

COMBINE 2 tablespoons flour, ¼ teaspoon double-acting baking powder, ¼ teaspoon salt. Beat 2 eggs thoroughly. Mix together ¾ cup firmly packed brown sugar, 1 cup chopped almonds, 1 cup shredded coconut and fold into beaten eggs. Add dry ingredients and mix thoroughly. Place 1 tablespoon filling in each unbaked sandbakel shell. Bake as directed for sandbakelse.

KRUM KAKA

(Swedish Cone Cookies)

Here is a real Scandinavian delicacy. These thin, crisp buttery-rich cookies are baked on top of the range in a special Korno Krum Kaka or Wafer Iron. To keep them crisp, store without filling in a dry place, uncovered.

Makes about 4 dozen 5-inch cookies

Beat................3 eggs thoroughly. Add gradually
1 cup sugar.

Blend in............1 cup milk
1 cup melted butter; mix well.

Add................1 teaspoon vanilla or cardamom.

Blend in............2 cups sifted enriched flour. Mix thoroughly.

Drop................batter, one tablespoon at a time, on hot krum kaka wafer iron and close iron at once.

Bake................for about 1½ minutes, turning constantly until cooky is delicately browned.

Remove............cooky from iron. Let stand for a few seconds and with aid of a fork, roll cooky into cone. Cool completely before storing.

FATTIGMANSKAKOR

(Swedish Poor Man's Cookies)

These Scandinavian "poor man's cookies" are especially popular during the Christmas holidays. They're fried in deep fat—
delicious served with coffee as a light dessert.

Makes 3 dozen cookies

*Beat*_____3 egg yolks until light. Add
3 tablespoons sugar
3 tablespoons heavy cream; beat well.

*Blend in*_____¼ teaspoon crushed cardamom or 1 teaspoon brandy.

*Add*_____1¼ to 1½ cups sifted enriched flour; mix well to
make a smooth dough.

*Roll out*_____dough to about $\frac{1}{16}$-inch thickness. Cut in
strips about 1½ inches wide. Cut diag-
onally at 4-inch intervals. Make 2-inch
slit crosswise in center, and slip one end
through slit.

*Fry*_____in hot deep fat (350°F.) until delicately
browned, about 1½ minutes. Drain on
unglazed paper. Cool and sprinkle with
confectioners' sugar, if desired.

SPRITZ

Fragile, crisp and delicate! These dainty cookies are shaped
easily with a cooky press. In many homes, Christmas wouldn't
be complete without them.

Makes 6 dozen cookies

*Cream*_____1 cup butter; add gradually
½ cup sugar, creaming until light and
fluffy.

Add_____1 egg
                    ¾ teaspoon **salt**
                    ¾ teaspoon **almond extract** (lemon or rum
                        may be substituted). Beat well.
Blend in_____2½ cups sifted **enriched flour** gradually; mix
                        thoroughly.
Place_____dough in cooky press and press into vari-
                        ous sizes and shapes onto greased cooky
                        sheet. Keep cookies quite small and
                        dainty. Cookies may be decorated with
                        bits of candied cherries and citron.
Bake_____in hot oven (400°F.) about 8 minutes.
                        Do not stack or store until cold.

FRENCH LACE COOKIES

These rolled, cone-shaped cookies look like bits of dainty,
crocheted lace . . . and they taste like crisp candy. Serve with
ice cream or as an unusual snack with tea or coffee.

Makes about 5 dozen cookies

Combine_____1 cup sifted **enriched flour**
                    1 cup finely chopped **nuts.**
Pour_____½ cup **corn syrup,** light or dark, into sauce-
                        pan.
Add_____¼ cup **butter**
                    ¼ cup **shortening**
                    ⅔ cup firmly packed **brown sugar.**
Place_____over direct heat and bring to boiling
                        point. Remove immediately from heat.
Blend in_____flour and nuts gradually.
Drop_____by rounded teaspoonfuls on greased
                        cooky sheet. Place 3 inches apart to allow
                        room for spreading.

| Bake | in slow oven (325°F.) 8 to 10 minutes until light brown. Cool 1 minute. Remove carefully from baking sheet with spatula. If desired, cookies may be rolled into cone shape while still warm. Cool on wire rack. |

Cooky Drops

PINEAPPLE CHERRY DROPS

Pillsbury Contest Winner by Mrs. Robert Bennetts, Davison, Mich.

A bit of cooked rice, crushed pineapple and candied cherries make these cookies quite unusual. They keep fresh a long time.

Makes about 5½ dozen cookies

Sift together	2 cups sifted **enriched flour** 2 teaspoons double-acting **baking powder** ½ teaspoon **salt**.
Combine	¼ cup chopped **candied cherries** with 2 tablespoons of the sifted dry ingredients.
Cream	½ cup **shortening**; add gradually 1 cup firmly packed **brown sugar** and cream until light and fluffy.
Add	2 **eggs**, unbeaten. Mix well.
Blend	¼ cup drained, **crushed pineapple** and 1 teaspoon **vanilla** into creamed mixture.
Add	sifted dry ingredients. Mix well.
Fold in	¼ cup cooked **rice**, mashed or sieved, and the floured cherries.
Drop	by level tablespoonfuls onto greased cooky sheet.
Bake	in moderate oven (375°F.) 8 to 10 min.

CHAPTER SEVEN

Desserts

WHETHER you are planning party refreshments or the finishing touch for a meal, desserts offer you a spectacular way to show off your artistry and skill.

Your dessert need not be elaborate. It may be the easiest one in the book. But if it suits the occasion . . . if it suits the rest of your menu, it is perfect.

With a rich and filling main course, for instance, you would probably choose something light—lemon pudding or apple crisp. But if you were serving a simple meal (with a fresh salad, perhaps, and soup) you might want to go all-out, and bring on the strawberry shortcake or your own homemade cream-filled eclairs.

You will find both simple and elaborate desserts in this chapter. We think you'll want to try your hand at them.

MOUNT VERNON DESSERT

BEST OF CLASS WINNER
Pillsbury's 1st Recipe Contest
by Mrs. Harry W. O'Donnell, Crandon, Wisconsin

**Grandmother's old-fashioned upside-down cake gone modern!
For Mrs. O'Donnell makes it the Quick-Mix way.**

Makes 12x8x2-inch cake

All ingredients must be at room temperature.

Prepare .... 12x8x2-inch pan by greasing well with butter. Sprinkle

  ½ cup firmly packed **brown sugar** over bottom of pan. Add

  1 No. 2 can drained **pie cherries**. Reserve juice for sauce.

Sift together ..... 1¾ cups sifted **enriched flour**

  2 teaspoons double-acting **baking powder**

  ½ teaspoon **salt**

  1 cup **sugar**.

Add .... ⅓ cup **shortening**

  ¾ cup **milk**

  1 teaspoon **vanilla**.

Beat .... for 1½ minutes, about 250 strokes, until batter is well blended. (If electric mixer is used, blend at low speed, then beat at medium speed for 1½ minutes.)

Add .... 1 **egg**, unbeaten

Beat .... for 1½ minutes.

Pour .... over cherries in pan.

Bake .... in moderate oven (350°F.) 35 to 45 minutes. (If glass baking pan is used, bake at 325°F.)

CHERRY SAUCE

COMBINE ½ cup sugar, 2 tablespoons cornstarch and 1½ cups juice (juice from cherries plus water). Cook until thickened, stirring constantly. Remove from heat; add ⅛ teaspoon almond extract and few drops red coloring, if desired. Serve warm over warm cake.

PINEAPPLE UPSIDE-DOWN CAKE

This dessert can be made in just a few minutes. You will find you can vary this basic cake and use peaches or apricots as the "upside-down."

Makes 8x8x2-inch cake

All ingredients must be at room temperature.

*Prepare*_____8x8x2-inch pan by greasing well with butter. Spread with
¼ cup firmly packed brown sugar and
2 tablespoons melted butter.

*Arrange*_____4 pineapple slices in bottom of pan.

*Sift together*____1¼ cups sifted enriched flour
2 teaspoons double-acting baking powder
½ teaspoon salt
¾ cup sugar.

*Add*_____¼ cup shortening
1 egg, unbeaten
½ cup milk
1 teaspoon vanilla.

*Beat*_____for 3 minutes, 150 strokes per minute, until batter is well blended. (With electric mixer blend at low speed, then beat at medium speed for 3 minutes.)

*Pour*_____batter over fruit.

*Bake*_____in moderate oven (350°F.) 35 to 40 minutes.

*Turn*_____upside down on serving plate. Serve with whipped cream.

APRICOT UPSIDE-DOWN CAKE

PREPARE Pineapple Upside-Down Cake, substituting 16 canned or cooked dried apricot halves for pineapple.

PEACH UPSIDE-DOWN CAKE

PREPARE Pineapple Upside-Down Cake, substituting 1 pint drained peach slices or about 9 peach halves for pineapple.

JELLY ROLL

Sponge cake baked in a shallow pan, spread with your favorite jelly or fresh strawberry filling.

Serves 8

Sift together——— ⅔ cup sifted **enriched** flour
⅜ teaspoon double-acting **baking** powder
¼ teaspoon **salt.**

Beat——————4 eggs until thick and lemon colored.

Add gradually—— ¾ cup sugar, a tablespoon at a time, beating thoroughly after each addition.

Blend in—————1 teaspoon vanilla.

Sift———————dry ingredients over egg mixture gradually, folding in carefully but thoroughly.

Spread—————batter evenly in 15x10-inch jelly roll pan which has been greased and lined with waxed paper.

Bake———————in moderately hot oven (400°F.) 12 to 15 minutes.

Turn———————warm cake out on tea towel which has been heavily sprinkled with confectioners' sugar; remove paper and trim crisp edges of cake.

Roll———————warm cake in towel. Cool on rack, seam side down. Unroll and spread with a favorite jelly. Reroll.

STRAWBERRY ROLL

PREPARE Jelly Roll, substituting strawberry filling for jelly.
Strawberry Filling: Whip ¾ cup cream until stiff. Fold in
¼ cup sifted confectioners' sugar and 1 cup sliced, fresh or
frozen strawberries. Spread on cooled cake. Store in refrigerator until serving time.

CHOCOLATE ROLL

This chocolate roll, with swirls of rich cream filling, is a delicious dessert.

Serves 8

Sift together——½ cup sifted **enriched flour**
⅓ cup cocoa
1½ teaspoons double-acting **baking powder**
½ teaspoon **salt**
¼ teaspoon soda.

Combine————3 eggs
3 tablespoons water
1 teaspoon vanilla; beat until thick and
lemon colored.

Add gradually——¾ cup sugar, a tablespoon at a time, beating
thoroughly after each addition.

Sift————————dry ingredients over egg mixture gradually, folding in carefully but thoroughly.

Spread——————batter evenly in 15x10-inch jelly roll pan
which has been greased and lined with
waxed paper.

Bake————————in moderate oven (350°F.) 30 minutes.

Turn————————cake onto tea towel which has been
heavily sprinkled with confectioners'
sugar; remove paper and trim crisp edges
of cake.

*Roll*_____warm cake in towel as for jelly roll. Cool on rack, seam side down. Unroll and spread with vanilla filling. Reroll. Store in refrigerator until serving time. Slice and serve with whipped cream.

VANILLA FILLING

COMBINE ⅔ cup sifted enriched flour, ⅔ cup sugar and ½ teaspoon salt in top of double boiler. Add gradually 2 cups scalded milk, stirring constantly. Cook over boiling water until thickened, stirring constantly. Continue cooking about 15 minutes longer, stirring occasionally. Beat 1 egg slightly and stir in a little of the hot mixture. Blend into mixture in double boiler and cook 2 minutes, stirring constantly. Remove from over hot water. Add 1 tablespoon butter and 1 teaspoon vanilla. Cool; spread on cake.

CHOCOLATE FLUFF ROLL

Pillsbury Contest Winner by Mrs. Carmel Fredine, Minneapolis, Minn.

This beautiful roll is made by wrapping delicate sponge cake in mint-flavored chocolate whipped cream.

Serves 8

*Sift together*_____⅔ cup sifted **enriched flour**
1 teaspoon double-acting **baking powder**
½ teaspoon **salt.**

*Beat*_____4 **egg whites** until they form soft mounds.

*Add*_____½ cup **sugar,** 2 tablespoons at a time, beating until very stiff.

*Beat*_____4 **egg yolks** until thick and lemon colored.

*Add gradually*____¼ cup **sugar**
2 tablespoons **water**
1 teaspoon **vanilla.** Beat well.

*Fold*_____egg yolk mixture carefully into egg whites.

*Sift*_____dry ingredients over egg mixture and fold in carefully.

*Spread*_____batter evenly in 15x10-inch jelly roll pan, greased and lined with waxed paper that extends beyond rim of pan.

*Bake*_____in moderate oven (375°F.) 12 to 15 minutes.

*Turn*_____cake onto tea towel which has been heavily sprinkled with confectioners' sugar or cocoa. Remove paper and trim the edges.

*Roll*_____warm cake in towel. Cool on rack, seam side down. Unroll and spread with half of chocolate mint cream. Reroll.

*Frost*_____with balance of chocolate mint cream. Chill thoroughly before serving.

CHOCOLATE MINT CREAM

COMBINE ½ cup sugar, ¼ cup cocoa, ⅛ teaspoon salt, ½ teaspoon vanilla and ¼ teaspoon peppermint extract. Blend in 1½ cups whipping cream. Refrigerate for at least 3 hours. Beat with rotary beater until stiff. Use as filling and frosting for roll.

CHOCOLATE CANDY STICK CREAM

FOLLOW recipe for chocolate mint cream, increasing vanilla to 1 teaspoon and omitting peppermint extract. Fold ½ cup finely-crushed peppermint stick candy into whipped cream.

BOSTON CREAM PIE

In spite of its name, this elegant dessert really belongs to the cake and dessert family. The layers are light, and the filling is smooth and plentiful.

Makes two 8-inch layers

Sift together———1 cup sifted **enriched flour**
1 teaspoon double-acting **baking powder**
½ teaspoon **salt.**

Combine———3 **egg yolks**
⅓ cup **water**
1 teaspoon grated **lemon rind**
½ teaspoon **vanilla**; beat thoroughly.

Add gradually——1 cup **sugar**, beating well after each addition, and
2 tablespoons **lemon juice.**

Fold———————dry ingredients into egg mixture gradually, blending carefully but thoroughly.

Beat—————————3 **egg whites** until stiff but not dry; fold into batter.

Pour————————into two 8-inch round layer cake pans which have been greased and lined with waxed paper.

Bake————————in slow oven (325°F.) 35 to 40 minutes. Cool, fill with cream filling and frost with creamy chocolate frosting.

CREAM FILLING

HEAT 1 cup milk and add 2 tablespoons butter. Combine ⅓ cup enriched flour, ¼ teaspoon salt and ⅓ cup sugar. Add ½ cup cold milk to dry ingredients and stir until smooth; then add to hot milk in saucepan, stirring constantly until thick. Blend in 2 slightly beaten egg yolks, to which a little of the hot mixture has been added. Cook about 2 minutes. Cool. Add 1 teaspoon vanilla and spread filling between layers of cake.

CREAMY CHOCOLATE FROSTING

MELT ½ square (½ oz.) chocolate in ¼ cup milk in saucepan over low heat. Combine 1 tablespoon flour, ¼ cup sugar and ⅛ teaspoon salt. Add to milk mixture; stir constantly until thick and smooth. Remove from heat. Add 1 teaspoon butter and ½ teaspoon vanilla. Spread on top of cake while still warm.

PEACH BOSTON CREAM DESSERT

PREPARE Boston Cream Pie and Cream Filling as directed above. Spread fresh or canned peach slices or halves over filling between layers. Top dessert with whipped cream and additional peaches.

DATE-NUT TORTE

This is an easy dessert. Chopped dates and nuts are folded into a cake-like batter, and mounds of meringue are baked on top.

Makes 9-inch round cake or 8x8x2-inch square cake

*Sift together*_____1 cup sifted enriched flour
1 ½ teaspoons double-acting baking powder
½ teaspoon salt.

*Cream*_____½ cup shortening with
1 teaspoon vanilla; add gradually
½ cup sugar, creaming well.

*Beat thoroughly*____2 eggs
2 egg yolks (reserve whites for meringue)
2 tablespoons water

*Add*_____eggs and dry ingredients alternately to creamed mixture, beginning and ending with dry ingredients. Blend thoroughly after each addition. (With electric mixer use low speed.)

*Blend in*_____½ cup chopped dates
1 cup chopped walnuts.

Pour................................into greased and floured 9-inch round spring-form pan (2¾ inches deep) or 8x8x2-inch pan lined with waxed paper.

Beat................................2 egg whites until foamy.

Add................................⅛ teaspoon salt and
⅛ teaspoon cream of tartar; beat until egg whites form slight mounds when beater is raised.

Add gradually........½ cup sugar; beat until meringue stands in peaks. Spread meringue over cake batter.

Bake................................in slow oven (325°F.) 1 hour.

PEACH MERINGUE DESSERT

This dessert features a meringue topping and cake batter baked together. Add peaches and whipped cream, if you like, or serve the cake plain. It's good, too, topped with frozen strawberries or ice cream.

Makes 9x9x2-inch cake

All ingredients must be at room temperature.

MERINGUE
(Prepare before mixing cake.)

Beat................................3 egg whites and
⅛ teaspoon salt with rotary beater until foamy.*

Add................................½ teaspoon cream of tartar and beat until stiff and dry.

Beat in................................¾ cup sugar, 2 tablespoons at a time, until mixture stands in very stiff peaks. Last half of sugar may be folded in.

Add................................1 teaspoon vanilla.

---

*Meringue may be mixed with electric mixer. Use large mixer bowl; beat at high speed until mixture is very stiff.

CAKE

(Measure ingredients before making meringue.)

*Sift together*_____1 cup sifted enriched flour

1½ teaspoons double-acting baking powder

½ teaspoon salt

½ cup sugar.

*Add*_____3 egg yolks, unbeaten

½ cup top milk

¼ cup shortening

1 teaspoon vanilla.

*Beat*_____for 2 minutes, 300 strokes, until batter is well blended.*

*Pour*_____into 9x9x2-inch pan lined with waxed paper that extends 1 inch beyond rim of pan.

*Spread*_____meringue over batter. With back of spoon shape furrows in meringue to hold peach slices.

*Bake*_____in slow oven (325°F.) 50 minutes. Remove from pan and cool.

*Place*_____fresh or canned peach slices in furrows. Serve with whipped cream and peach slices. Note: This cake is also delicious served with sweetened, crushed berries or ice cream.

_____

*To mix cake, use small mixer bowl and blend at low speed; then beat at medium speed for 2 minutes.

GINGER CAKE APPLE FLUFF

Pillsbury Contest Winner by Mrs. George Alfred Keep, Oswego, Ore.

Applesauce is blended into whipped cream to make a special topping for this spicy homemade ginger cake.

Makes 8x8x2-inch cake

*Sift together*_____2 cups sifted enriched flour

1 teaspoon double-acting baking powder

1 teaspoon **salt**

½ teaspoon **soda**

1 teaspoon **cinnamon**

1½ teaspoons **ginger.**

*Melt*_____½ cup **shortening** in

⅔ cup **boiling water.**

*Beat*_____1 **egg** until frothy. Add

½ cup **sugar** gradually; beat until thick and lemon colored.

*Add*_____½ cup light **molasses** and the shortening-water mixture.

*Blend in*_____sifted dry ingredients and beat until smooth.

*Pour*_____into well-greased and floured 8x8x2-inch pan.

*Bake*_____in moderate oven (350°F.) 40 to 45 minutes. Cool and serve with apple fluff.

APPLE FLUFF

BEAT ½ pint (1 cup) whipping cream until stiff. Fold in ½ cup sifted confectioners' sugar, 2 tablespoons lemon juice and 1 cup sweetened, thick applesauce. Chill thoroughly; or place in refrigerator tray and partially freeze. Serve on top of ginger cake.

CHEESE CAKE

There's fluffy cottage cheese filling on a crisp cooky-like crust. Fresh lemon adds flavor. This is a favorite rich dessert to top off a simple meal.

Makes 9-inch square cake

*Sift together*____1½ cups sifted **enriched flour**

½ teaspoon double-acting **baking powder**

½ teaspoon **salt**

⅓ cup **sugar.**

Cut in _____ ⅓ cup **butter** or margarine until particles resemble small peas. (Reserve ½ cup of mixture for topping.)

Beat _____ 1 **egg**; sprinkle over flour mixture, tossing lightly with fork until blended.

Press _____ into bottom and sides of 9x9x2-inch pan.

Cream _____ ¼ cup **butter** or margarine; add gradually 1 cup **sugar**, creaming well.

Blend in _____ 4 **egg yolks**, one at a time. Beat for 1 minute.

Add _____ 1 tablespoon **lemon juice**
1 teaspoon grated **lemon rind**; mix well.

Blend in _____ 2⅔ cups (1½ lbs.) **cottage cheese**, sieved
½ cup **cream**
¼ cup sifted **enriched flour**
½ teaspoon **salt**.

Beat _____ 4 **egg whites** until stiff but not dry. Fold gently but thoroughly into cheese mixture.

Turn _____ into pastry-lined pan and sprinkle with the reserved ½ cup flour-butter mixture.

Bake _____ in slow oven (325°F.) 80 to 90 minutes. Cool and serve.

Steamed Puddings

STEAMED PUDDING *is an old-fashioned dessert which is still popular today—especially at holiday time. You'll find this dessert easy to make, if you follow these tips on steaming.*

How to Make a Perfect Steamed Pudding

Preparation—Fill greased cans, jelly glasses, or molds ⅔ full and cover tightly. Double-thick waxed paper fastened with a rubber band or aluminum foil works very well.

Steaming—Place the molds on a rack in the steamer and add boiling water to about half the depth of the mold. (A steamer may be improvised by placing a cake rack in the bottom of a kettle which has a tight-fitting cover.) Have enough boiling water to last through the steaming period as it is advisable not to lift the cover. The water should be kept at the boiling point.

Serving—Remove the covers as soon as the puddings are done and let stand a few minutes before unmolding. They may be kept warm in the oven until serving time.

For flaming pudding, pour rum or brandy over the pudding and light it just before serving.

Hard sauce flavored with brandy or rum or a creamy butter sauce is delicious served with steamed pudding.

Storing—Steamed pudding stores well wrapped in waxed paper. Reheat in steamer or in top of double boiler over boiling water.

STEAMED PUDDING

There is a wonderful spicy fragrance to this rich, old-fashioned pudding. (At holiday time, serve it flaming, if you like!)

Serves 8 to 10

Sift together——1½ cups sifted enriched flour

3 teaspoons double-acting baking powder

½ teaspoon salt

1 teaspoon cinnamon

1 teaspoon allspice

¼ teaspoon cloves.

Add——————½ cup ground suet

½ cup chopped nuts

½ cup raisins

½ cup chopped dates; mix thoroughly until well blended.

Combine................1 cup firmly packed **brown sugar**
                            ½ cup **fruit juice**
                            1 **egg**, well beaten
Add......................liquid to dry ingredients; mix well.
Pour....................batter into greased and floured 1-quart
                            mold or round cans. Cover tightly.
Place...................mold on rack in steamer. Add boiling
                            water to half the depth of mold. Cover.
                            Keep water at boiling point.
Steam..................for 1½ hours. Let stand a few minutes
                            before unmolding. Serve warm with
                            hard sauce.

HARD SAUCE

CREAM ½ cup butter until light. Add 2 cups sifted confectioners' sugar gradually, creaming well. Add 1 teaspoon vanilla and ⅛ teaspoon salt; beat until smooth and fluffy.

SNO CAPS

These individual steamed puddings are particularly delicate. You can top them with chocolate fudge sauce, caramel with pecans, or your favorite fruit sauce.

Makes 6 cakes

Sift together..........1 cup sifted **enriched flour**
                            2 teaspoons double-acting **baking powder**
                            ½ teaspoon **salt**
                            ½ cup **sugar**.
Add......................¼ cup **shortening**
                            ⅓ cup **milk**.
Beat....................for 2 minutes, 300 strokes, until batter is
                            well blended. (With electric mixer blend
                            at low speed, then beat at medium speed
                            for 2 minutes.)

Add	3 egg whites, unbeaten
	1 teaspoon vanilla.
Beat	for 2 minutes.
Fill	well-greased custard cups about one half full. Cover tightly with aluminum foil or a double thickness of waxed paper tied securely.
Place	custard cups on rack in steamer. Add boiling water to one inch depth. Cover. Keep water at boiling point.
Steam	30 to 35 minutes. Remove from cups. Cool. Sprinkle with confectioners' sugar and serve in one of the following ways.

Serving Suggestions

Chocolate Fudge Sauce and Mint Ice Cream: Melt 1 package semi-sweet chocolate bits over boiling water. Add 3 tablespoons boiling water and blend well. Add 4 tablespoons top milk and stir until smooth. Place each cake on a slice of peppermint ice cream and top with chocolate fudge sauce.

Pineapple-Mint Sauce: Combine 1 tablespoon cornstarch and ¼ cup sugar. Add 1 cup pineapple juice, 1 cup crushed pineapple and a few mint leaves. Cook over direct heat until clear, stirring constantly. Remove from heat. Serve on cake and decorate with sugared mint leaf.

Caramel-Nut Sauce: Combine 2 tablespoons cornstarch and 1 cup firmly packed brown sugar. Add 1 cup water. Cook over direct heat until thick and clear, stirring constantly. Remove from heat and add ½ cup pecans and 2 tablespoons butter. Place each cake on a slice of vanilla ice cream and top with caramel-nut sauce.

Berry Topping: Top cakes with fresh or frozen berries, crushed and sweetened, and top with whipped cream.

FRUIT SHORTCAKE

Rich, flaky biscuit dough is cut into rounds or made into one large cake. Serve it . . . topped with fresh or frozen straw-berries, raspberries, peaches—any fruit you choose—and whipped cream.

Serves 6

*Sift together*_____2 cups sifted enriched flour
3 teaspoons double-acting baking powder
1 teaspoon salt
2 tablespoons sugar.

*Cut in*_____½ cup shortening until mixture resembles coarse meal.

*Combine*_____6 tablespoons milk
1 egg, well beaten.

*Add*_____liquid to dry ingredients and mix only until all flour is dampened. Knead gently on floured board or pastry cloth for a few seconds.

*Roll*_____dough to ½-inch thickness; cut into six 3-inch rounds. Brush lightly with melted butter.

*Place*_____on ungreased baking sheet.

*Bake*_____in hot oven (450°F.) 12 minutes.

*Place*_____crushed and sweetened berries or fruit between split shortcake rounds. Top with whipped cream and whole fruit or berries. One quart of fruit is adequate for six servings.

FAMILY SHORTCAKE

PREPARE Fruit Shortcake, rolling or patting dough into two 8-inch rounds. Fit one round into greased 8-inch layer cake pan.

Brush with butter and top with other round of dough. Bake at 450°F. for 12 to 15 minutes. Cool slightly and place on serving dish. Remove top layer. Cover bottom layer with crushed and sweetened berries or fruit. Replace other layer and top with whipped cream and whole fruit.

STRAWBERRY SUNSHINE DESSERT

Pillsbury Contest Winner by Miss Elizabeth Lightcap, Washington, D. C.

Golden bits of pineapple are baked upside-down fashion with rich biscuit shortcake. Serve topped with a fluff of whipped cream and strawberries.

Serves 6

*Spread*_____1¼ cups drained, crushed pineapple (No. 2 can) in 8-inch casserole or cake pan.

*Combine*_____1 tablespoon flour
⅓ cup sugar. Sprinkle over pineapple.

*Sift together*_____1 cup sifted enriched flour
1½ teaspoons double-acting baking powder
½ teaspoon salt
2 tablespoons sugar.

*Cut in*_____¼ cup butter until mixture resembles coarse meal.

*Add*_____⅓ cup milk and mix to a soft dough.

*Spread*_____dough over pineapple mixture.

*Bake*_____in hot oven (425°F.) 15 to 20 minutes. Turn upside down on plate. Serve warm or cold with strawberry cream topping.

STRAWBERRY CREAM TOPPING

WHIP 1 cup heavy cream. Fold in 1 cup sliced, sweetened strawberries. Serve on top of dessert. Decorate with additional whole strawberries.

PINEAPPLE HALO DESSERT

Pillsbury Contest Winner by Mrs. Arnold Creager, Pleasantville, Ind.

Tuck golden slices of pineapple between circles of flaky, pine-
apple-flavored biscuit dough for this unusual dessert. There's a
different, fluffy topping of strawberries.

Serves 6

Sift together......2¼ cups sifted enriched flour
                  3 teaspoons double-acting baking powder
                  ½ teaspoon salt
                  ⅓ cup sugar.

*Cut in*_____⅓ cup shortening until mixture resembles
                  coarse meal.

*Blend together*_____1 egg, slightly beaten
                  3 tablespoons milk
                  ⅓ cup pineapple juice (No. 2 can sliced
                  pineapple).

*Add*_____liquid all at once to dry ingredients, mix-
                  ing well.

*Roll*_____out dough on floured board or pastry
                  cloth to about ⅛-inch thickness.

*Cut*_____into 12 rounds about 3½ inches in di-
                  ameter or 1 inch wider than pineapple
                  slice. Then cut a small hole in the center
                  of each round, doughnut-fashion.

*Place*_____a slice of pineapple on each of six rounds
                  of dough. Top with remaining rounds.
                  Seal inner and outer edges. Brush with
                  melted butter. Place on ungreased baking
                  sheet.

*Bake*_____in hot oven (450°F.) 12 to 15 minutes.
                  Serve with strawberry-whip topping.

STRAWBERRY-WHIP TOPPING

BEAT 1 cup (½ pint) whipping cream until stiff; sweeten to taste. Fold in 2 cups sweetened, sliced strawberries.

ALASKAN CRANBERRY COBBLER

Pillsbury Contest Winner by Mrs. Ethel Hansen, Anchorage, Alaska

Economy, ease and old-fashioned goodness are all wrapped up in this cobbler dessert. Bright red cranberry sauce gives it a most intriguing tartness.

Serves 8

Sift together .... 2¼ cups sifted enriched flour
2 teaspoons double-acting baking powder
½ teaspoon salt
¼ cup sugar.

Combine _____ 1 cup milk
2 tablespoons melted butter; add to dry ingredients all at once, stirring quickly to form a soft dough.

Pour _____ ¼ cup melted butter or margarine in 2-quart casserole.

Spread _____ half of dough in casserole.

Pour _____ 2 cups hot cranberry sauce over dough.

Drop _____ remaining dough by tablespoonfuls on cranberry sauce.

Combine _____ 2 tablespoons sugar
¼ teaspoon cinnamon; sprinkle over cobbler.

Bake _____ in moderate oven (350°F.) 35 to 40 minutes or until brown. Serve warm with cream.

FRUIT PINWHEELS

Your favorite fruit is rolled up, jelly-roll fashion, inside a flaky, tender biscuit, to make an easy, thrifty dessert. Serve with additional fruit or with cream.

Serves 6

PINWHEEL DOUGH

*Sift together*____1½ cups sifted enriched flour,
2½ teaspoons double-acting baking powder
½ teaspoon salt
2 tablespoons sugar.

*Cut in*_____⅓ cup butter or shortening until mixture resembles coarse meal.

*Add*_____½ cup milk; mix only until all flour is dampened. Knead gently on floured board or pastry cloth for a few seconds. Roll to 10x9-inch rectangle.

*Spread with*_____1 tablespoon soft butter
2 tablespoons sugar
½ teaspoon cinnamon
1½ to 2 cups drained fruit (see suggestions below).

*Roll*_____as for jelly roll; cut into six slices.

*Pour*_____fruit sauce in 8x8x2-inch pan. Place pinwheels on sauce.

*Bake*_____in hot oven (425°F.) 20 to 25 minutes. Serve warm or cold with cream.

FRUIT SAUCES

(Prepare before making Pinwheel Dough.)

DRAIN juice from desired fruit. Use fruit in rolled pinwheels; thicken and flavor juice for sauce as directed below.

CHERRY

COMBINE 2 tablespoons flour and ⅔ cup sugar. Add 1 cup

liquid (juice from No. 2 can cherries plus water) and cook until thick, stirring constantly. Add 2 tablespoons butter, 1 teaspoon lemon juice and 1 teaspoon grated lemon rind.

BLUEBERRY

COMBINE 2 tablespoons flour, ¼ cup brown sugar, ¼ cup sugar and ¼ teaspoon nutmeg. Add 1 cup liquid (juice from No. 1 tall can of blueberries plus water) and cook until thick, stirring constantly. Add 2 tablespoons butter, 1 tablespoon lemon juice and 1 teaspoon grated lemon rind.

PEACH

COMBINE 2 tablespoons flour and 2 tablespoons sugar. Add 1 cup juice from No. 2½ can sliced peaches and cook until thick, stirring constantly. Add 2 tablespoons butter, 2 tablespoons orange juice and 1 teaspoon grated orange rind.

APRICOT

COMBINE 2 tablespoons flour and 2 tablespoons brown sugar. Add 1 cup juice from No. 2½ can apricots and cook until thick, stirring constantly. Add 2 tablespoons butter, 1 tablespoon lemon juice and 1 teaspoon grated lemon rind.

HASTY COBBLER DESSERT

PREPARE dough as for Fruit Pinwheels, adding 1 beaten egg to milk. Place all of fruit and sauce in 8x8x2-inch pan. Divide dough in six portions and drop on top of fruit. Bake and serve as for Pinwheels.

OLD-FASHIONED APPLE TURNOVERS

Here is apple pie that you can eat with your fingers! To make these tarts, you simply fold the pastry around apple slices.

Makes 10 turnovers

*Sift together*_____3 cups sifted **enriched flour**
1 teaspoon **salt.**

*Cut in*_____1 cup **shortening** until particles are the size of small peas.

*Sprinkle*_____9 to 10 tablespoons cold **water** over mixture until dough is moist enough to hold together.

*Roll out*_____on lightly-floured board or pastry cloth to about ⅛-inch thickness. Cut into ten 5-inch squares.

*Combine*_____⅔ cup sugar
1 teaspoon **cinnamon**
¼ teaspoon **cloves**
¼ teaspoon **nutmeg.**

*Divide*_____4 cups sliced apples equally among pastry squares. Sprinkle with sugar mixture. Dot with **butter.** Moisten edges of pastry and fold over to form a triangle.

*Seal*_____edges with fork and cut small slits in top to allow escape of steam. Brush tops lightly with cream or top milk and sprinkle with sugar.

*Bake*_____in hot oven (425°F.) 30 to 35 minutes. Serve with orange sauce.

ORANGE SAUCE

COMBINE 3 tablespoons flour and ½ cup sugar. Add 1 cup orange juice, 1½ tablespoons lemon juice and 2 tablespoons

butter. Mix thoroughly. Cook over low heat, stirring constantly
until mixture begins to boil. Remove from heat.

GOLDEN PEAR TARTLETS

Pillsbury Contest Winner by Mrs. Sigmund Broda, Bronx, N. Y.

A pear and a dab of jelly are tucked inside each tartlet. (And
you'll find the crisp pastry has a distinctive nut-like flavor.)

Makes 6 tarts

*Sift together*____1½ cups sifted **enriched flour**
½ teaspoon double-acting **baking powder**
1 teaspoon **salt**
1 tablespoon **sugar.**

*Add*_____⅓ cup **wheat bran.**

*Cut in*_____⅔ cup **shortening** until particles are the size
of small peas.

*Sprinkle*_____3 to 4 tablespoons **water** gradually over mixture, tossing with fork until dough is
moist enough to hold together. Form
into a ball.

*Roll*_____dough on lightly-floured board or pastry
cloth to about an 18x10-inch rectangle.
Cut into six equal rectangles.

*Place*_____a canned **pear half**, well drained, on each
of the pastry rectangles. Place a teaspoon
of **tart jelly** in hollow of each pear.
Sprinkle each pear with ½ teaspoon
sugar.

*Fold*_____half of pastry over pear; moisten edges
and seal well.

*Place*_____tarts, flat side down, on ungreased
baking sheet.

*Bake*_____in hot oven (450°F.) 18 to 20 minutes.
Serve warm with plain or whipped
cream.

Cream Puffs and Eclairs

CREAM PUFFS *and eclairs are glamorous desserts and are surprisingly easy to make. Cream puffs and eclairs differ only in shape—cream puffs are round, eclairs long.*

How to Make Perfect Cream Puffs and Eclairs

Cooking—Add dry ingredients all at once to boiling water and shortening. Cook over direct heat, stirring constantly until the mixture forms a smooth compact ball, leaving the sides of the pan clean. Cool slightly and beat in eggs one at a time.

Baking—Drop dough by spoonfuls onto greased baking sheet. A pastry bag is helpful for shaping eclairs. Allow ample space for puffs to expand during baking. Cream puffs and eclairs may be made from the size of a walnut to the size of a large egg. When cool, slice across top or make a small cut in one side of puff for filling.

Filling—Cream puffs lend themselves to a variety of fillings. Whipped cream is generally used although custard or chocolate cream, and ice cream fillings are also delicious. A chocolate or caramel sauce topping adds a party air to these pastries. Eclairs are generally frosted with chocolate icing.

Small cream puffs—filled with shrimp, chicken salad or cheese combinations—make attractive bite-size hors d'oeuvres or salad accompaniments.

CREAM PUFFS

We think you'll find these cream puffs easy to make. And
sometime, for a special party, serve the tidbit puffs.

Makes 18 cream puffs

*Melt*_____½ cup shortening in
1 cup boiling water.

*Sift together*_____1 cup sifted enriched flour
½ teaspoon salt; add to liquid ingredients,
all at once, stirring constantly. Cook
until mixture leaves sides of pan in a
smooth compact ball. Remove from heat;
cool for about 1 minute.

*Add*_____4 eggs, one at a time, beating vigorously
after each addition until mixture is
smooth again.

*Drop*_____by rounded tablespoonfuls 1½ inches
apart on greased baking sheet.

*Bake*_____in hot oven (450°F.) 10 minutes, then at
400°F. for 25 minutes. Fill cooled puffs
with ice cream, whipped cream, or the
following cream filling.

CREAM FILLING

COMBINE ⅓ cup enriched flour, ½ cup sugar and ⅛ teaspoon
salt in top of double boiler. Blend in 2 cups milk gradually.
Cook over boiling water until thickened, stirring constantly.
Blend a little hot filling into 3 slightly beaten egg yolks, then
return to hot mixture. Cook about 2 minutes longer, stirring
constantly. Remove from heat. Add 2 tablespoons butter and
1 teaspoon vanilla. Cover; cool. Fold in 1 cup whipped cream.

Tidbit Puffs

PREPARE *Cream Puff batter, but make puffs very tiny (½ to 1 teaspoon batter for each). Bake at 450°F. for 7 to 8 minutes, then at 400°F. for 12 to 15 minutes. These are nice for parties and special occasions.*

ECLAIRS

Prepare————————Cream Puff batter and place in pastry bag.

Force————————batter through plain round end onto greased baking sheet. Make eclairs ½ to 1 inch wide and 3 to 4 inches long.

Bake————————in hot oven (450°F.) 10 minutes, then at 400°F. for 25 minutes. Fill with cream filling. Frost top with cocoa butter frosting, page 213.

Meringue Shells

MERINGUE SHELLS *are prepared in much the same way that pie meringue is prepared. However, meringue shells contain more sugar and are beaten for a longer time, to a stiffer consistency.*

How to Make Perfect Meringue Shells

Mixing—Beat the egg whites until foamy. Add the sugar gradually and beat until the meringue stands in stiff, sharp peaks. Lemon juice gives body to the meringues and helps make them tender.

Shaping—Shape meringues into nest or cup shapes on unglazed paper on cooky sheet with spoon or pastry tube.

Baking—Bake in a very slow oven until meringues are thoroughly dried out. They should not brown but should
be a creamy color on top.

Serving—Remove shells from paper with wet knife. Cool
and fill with fruit, ice cream or whipped cream.

MERINGUE SHELLS

These crisp, dainty meringue shells require only three ingredients. Serve them with your favorite fruit sauce or ice cream.

Makes about 12 medium shells

*Beat*_____4 egg whites until foamy.

*Add gradually*____1 cup sugar, a tablespoon at a time, beating
thoroughly after each addition. Continue
beating until meringue forms sharp
peaks when beater is raised.

*Add*_____1 tablespoon lemon juice and continue
beating until meringue again forms
sharp peaks.

*Shape*_____into nests or rounds with spoon or pastry
bag on unglazed paper or greased baking
sheet. Allow ample space between meringues.

*Bake*_____in a very slow oven (250°F.) 1 hour and
20 minutes until the shells are thoroughly dried and the tops are cream
colored.

*Remove*_____from paper carefully as soon as baked.
Cool completely before serving.

*Fill*_____shells with sweetened fruit, ice cream or
flavored whipped cream. Top with
whipped cream, sauce or fruit.

CINNAMON APPLE DUMPLING DESSERT

Pillsbury Contest Winner by Mrs. Edward Gallagher, San Francisco, Calif.

These sweet, rich dessert dumplings are spiced and delicately tinted with red cinnamon candies, then they're steamed in a skillet like regular dinner dumplings. Serve them with cream for dessert.

Serves 8

Blend .... 2 tablespoons melted **butter** and
¼ cup sifted **enriched flour** in 10-inch skillet or shallow pan that has a tight cover.

Add gradually ...... 2 cups **apple juice**, blending until smooth,
½ cup **sugar**. Cook until thickened, stirring constantly.

Add .... 1 tablespoon **red cinnamon candies**
3 medium-sized **apples**, sliced, unpeeled. Heat to boiling point.

Sift together .... 1½ cups sifted **enriched flour**
2 teaspoons double-acting **baking powder**
¼ teaspoon **salt**
¼ cup **sugar**
½ teaspoon **nutmeg**.

Cut in .... 2 tablespoons **shortening** until mixture resembles coarse meal.

Add .... ⅔ cup **milk** and mix only until all flour is dampened.

Dip .... tablespoon into cold water. Then drop dough from spoon onto hot apples and syrup.

Simmer .... uncovered for 10 minutes. Then cover tightly and simmer 10 minutes more. Serve warm with cream.

GLAZED APPLE DUMPLINGS

Pillsbury Contest Winner by Miss Blanche Joyner, Franklin, Va.

These extra-good apple dumplings have a touch of cheese in
them . . . and marshmallow brown-sugar sauce on top.

Makes 10 dumplings

*Sift together*____2½ cups sifted enriched flour
2 teaspoons double-acting baking powder
1 teaspoon salt.

*Add*_____3 tablespoons grated cheese.

*Cut in*_____6 tablespoons shortening with pastry
blender until mixture resembles coarse
meal.

*Add gradually*____1 cup thin cream and mix lightly with fork.
Mold into a ball.

*Roll*_____dough to about ⅛-inch thickness. Cut
into ten 6-inch rounds.

*Pare*_____3 apples and slice thin. Place apple slices
on each round of dough. Sprinkle each
round with a tablespoon of sugar and ⅛
teaspoon nutmeg.

*Moisten*_____edges of dough; bring edges together
and seal at top. Place in 15x10x2-inch
pan.

*Pour*_____½ cup milk and
¼ cup water over dumplings.

*Bake*_____in moderate oven (375°F.) 40 to 45 minutes. Serve warm with brown-sugar
sauce.

BROWN-SUGAR SAUCE

BLEND 1 cup sugar and 1 cup firmly packed brown sugar in
saucepan. Add 1 tablespoon cornstarch and 1 cup water. Cook
over low heat until smooth and slightly thickened. Add 6

marshmallows, 3 tablespoons butter and cook slowly until dissolved, stirring constantly. Cool slightly, then add 2 teaspoons vanilla. Serve warm over warm dumplings.

APPLE CRISP

One of the easiest desserts we know—good to eat, too. Tender
apples with a crispy crumb crust.

Serves 6

Prepare	8x8x2 or 10x6x2-inch pan by greasing well with butter.
Arrange	5 cups sliced apples (4 to 5 apples) in bottom of pan.
Pour	¼ cup water and 1 tablespoon lemon juice over apples.
Blend together	1 cup sugar ½ cup sifted enriched flour ¼ cup butter or margarine 1 teaspoon cinnamon. Sprinkle over apples.
Bake	in moderate oven (375°F.) 45 minutes. Serve warm with cream.

APPLE CANDY CRISP

Pillsbury Contest Winner by Mrs. Casimir Stubbie, Fort Worth, Tex.

Crushed peanut brittle makes this apple crisp different and
especially delicious. (A quick and easy dessert.)

Serves 4 to 6

Prepare	8x8x2 or 10x6x2-inch pan by greasing well with butter.
Arrange	6 cups sliced apples (5 to 6 apples) in bottom of pan.

Sprinkle with	¼ cup sugar
	½ teaspoon salt
	1 tablespoon lemon juice.
Sift together	¾ cup sifted enriched flour
	½ cup sugar
	1 teaspoon cinnamon.
Blend in	¼ cup melted butter; mix until crumbly. Add
	¼ pound finely crushed peanut brittle.
Pack	over apples in pan and add
	¼ cup water.
Bake	in moderately hot oven (400°F.) 30 to 40 minutes. Serve warm with cream.

LEMON PUDDING

A cool refreshingly light dessert—perfect after a hearty dinner.

Serves 6

Sift together	¼ cup sifted enriched flour
	1 cup sugar
	¼ teaspoon salt.
Blend together	3 egg yolks, well beaten
	¼ cup lemon juice
	1½ cups milk
	1 tablespoon grated lemon rind.
Combine	liquid with dry ingredients; beat until smooth and well blended.
Beat	3 egg whites until stiff. Fold into batter.
Pour	into greased 8x8x2-inch pan. Place in another pan filled with hot water.
Bake	in moderate oven (325°F.) 45 minutes. Serve warm or cold.

CHOCOLATE LUSH

It's all that the name implies—really luscious! Chocolate cake
and syrup are baked together to make this easy dessert.

Serves 8

Sift together............1 cup sifted **enriched flour**
2 teaspoons double-acting **baking powder**
½ teaspoon **salt**
¾ cup **sugar**
2 tablespoons **cocoa**.

Combine............2 tablespoons melted **shortening**
½ cup **milk**
1 teaspoon **vanilla**
½ cup chopped **nuts**; add to dry ingredients.

Mix............until well blended. Spread in ungreased
8x8x2-inch pan.

Combine............¾ cup firmly packed **brown sugar**
4 tablespoons **cocoa**
1¾ cups hot **water**; pour over top of batter.

Bake............in moderate oven (350°F.) 45 minutes.
Cut into squares and serve warm or cold.

Top............the inverted squares with chocolate
"lush" from bottom of pan.

CARAMEL SOUR CREAM PUDDING

Cake batter and a rich, brown sugar cream sauce are baked together. The result is a rich, caramel-flavored pudding.

Serves 6

Sift together............1 cup sifted enriched flour
2 teaspoons double-acting baking powder
½ teaspoon salt.

Cream....................2 tablespoons sugar and
2 tablespoons shortening until light and fluffy.

Beat.......................1 egg yolk thoroughly; add to creamed mixture.

Add........................⅓ cup milk alternately with sifted dry ingredients to creamed mixture, beginning and ending with dry ingredients. Blend thoroughly after each addition. (With electric mixer use low speed.)

Pour.......................into well-greased 8-inch round casserole.

Combine.................1 tablespoon flour and
1 cup firmly packed brown sugar.

Blend together........1 cup sour cream
½ cup sour milk
¼ teaspoon soda. Add to brown sugar mixture. Pour over batter.

Bake.......................in moderate oven (350°F.) 40 minutes. Serve warm with whipped cream.

PEACH COTTAGE PUDDING

Old-fashioned and good! This easy one-egg cake can be served with spicy peach sauce—or any of your favorite toppings.

Makes 8x8x2-inch cake

All ingredients must be at room temperature.

*Sift together*____1⅛ cups sifted enriched flour
2 teaspoons double-acting baking powder
½ teaspoon salt
¾ cup sugar.

*Add*_____¼ cup shortening
1 egg, unbeaten
½ cup milk
1 teaspoon vanilla.

*Beat*_____for 3 minutes, 150 strokes per minute, until batter is well blended. (With electric mixer blend at low speed, then beat at medium speed for 3 minutes.)

*Pour*_____into well-greased 8x8x2-inch pan.

*Bake*_____in moderate oven (350°F.) 35 to 40 minutes. Serve warm with spicy peach sauce.

SPICY PEACH SAUCE

BLEND together 2 tablespoons cornstarch and 1⅓ cups peach syrup, drained from peaches. Add ⅓ cup water, ¼ teaspoon cinnamon, ⅛ teaspoon cloves and ⅛ teaspoon nutmeg; cook until thick. Add 2 tablespoons butter, 1 tablespoon lemon juice and peach slices or halves (No. 2½ can), drained. Serve warm on warm cake.

CRÊPES SUZETTE

Here is a simple recipe for this famous French dessert. You roll
the wafer-thin pancakes and keep them warm in a tangy orange
sauce until serving time.

Serves 6

*Combine*_____½ cup enriched flour
½ teaspoon double-acting baking powder
½ teaspoon salt
1 cup milk
2 eggs, slightly beaten
½ teaspoon grated lemon rind.

*Bake*_____in small (7-inch) lightly greased frying
pan over direct heat. Use small amount
of batter and tilt pan so that pancake
batter will cover entire surface of pan
and will be very thin. Turn only once.

*Roll*_____each pancake and place in baking pan.
Cover with crepes suzette sauce. Keep in
warm oven until serving time.

SAUCE

BLEND together ½ cup butter, ½ cup sifted confectioners' sugar
and grated rind and juice of 1 orange. Heat and pour over rolled
pancakes.

Baked Alaska

BAKED ICE CREAM! *It seems unbelievable but you really can "bake" ice cream when you sandwich it between layers of sponge cake and seal it completely with mounds of meringue. The ice cream stays firm if you follow these suggestions:*

How to Make Perfect Baked Alaska

Preparation—Cut two layers of sponge cake one inch wider and longer than the brick of ice cream. Place a strip of heavy wrapping paper on a wooden cutting board. On the paper place one of the cake layers. Cover with a layer of ice cream and top with the second cake layer. Spread top and sides with meringue, sealing well.

Baking—Brown in hot oven as directed in recipe.

Serving—To transfer to serving dish, pull the paper strip and the baked Alaska with it. Decorate with berries, slice and serve immediately.

BAKED ALASKA

We think this chocolate baked Alaska is different, and so delicious!

Makes 9x4x3-inch cake

*Sift together*_____²⁄₃ cup sifted **enriched flour**
2 tablespoons **cocoa**
⅓ cup **sugar**
½ teaspoon double-acting **baking powder**
¼ teaspoon **soda**
¼ teaspoon **salt**.

*Combine*_____5 **egg yolks** and

2 tablespoons hot water; beat until light and foamy.

Add............1 tablespoon lemon juice; continue beating until thick and lemon colored.

Add gradually......¼ cup sugar, beating constantly, and ½ teaspoon vanilla.

Fold in............dry ingredients gently but thoroughly.

Pour............into 9x4x3-inch pan which has been greased and lined with waxed paper.

Bake............in moderate oven (350°F.) 30 to 35 minutes. Cool. Cut crosswise to make two layers.

Place............one layer on wooden cutting board covered with a strip of heavy wrapping paper.

Cover............with a 1-inch layer of peppermint ice cream, allowing cake to extend ½ inch on all sides. Top with remaining layer of cake.

Cover............cake and ice cream completely with meringue, sealing well. Bake in hot oven (450°F.) 5 minutes or until brown. Slice and serve immediately.

MERINGUE

BEAT 5 egg whites until they form mounds when beater is raised. Add ⅔ cup sugar, a tablespoon at a time, until dissolved. Continue beating until meringue stands in heavy, shiny peaks.

LUCY'S CARAMEL CUSTARD ICE CREAM

Pillsbury Contest Winner by Mrs. Carl Witt, Atchison, Kan.

This wonderful, homemade ice cream is made in an old-fashioned hand-turned freezer. This is a satin-smooth ice cream with caramelized brown sugar for real flavor. Add chopped pecans or walnuts, if you wish.

Makes 1 gallon

Melt............2 cups firmly packed **brown sugar** in heavy skillet over low heat until sugar is thoroughly caramelized. Stir constantly; be careful not to scorch.

Scald............4 cups (1 quart) **milk** in large saucepan. Remove from heat.

Combine............1 cup sifted **enriched flour**
2 cups sugar
3 well-beaten **eggs**. Mix thoroughly.

Add............egg-sugar mixture to milk, blending thoroughly. Return to heat and cook until thick, stirring constantly.

Combine............caramelized sugar and custard and cool thoroughly.

Add............4 cups (1 quart) **milk**
4 cups (1 quart) **whipping cream**
1 teaspoon **vanilla** to caramel mixture, blending well.

Pour............into ice cream freezer, 1-gallon size. Freeze to "mush" consistency.

Add............1 cup chopped **pecans** or walnuts.

Repack............freezer and freeze well. Remove dasher from ice cream freezer and pack well with ice and salt. Allow ice cream to stand in freezer about 3 hours before serving.

CHAPTER EIGHT

Pies

EVERYONE *has his own favorite kind of pie. Some people like a spicy apple pie best of all. Others would choose a fluffy lemon meringue pie—smooth, creamy custard pie—or rich mince pie, still warm from the oven. But one thing everyone agrees on is pie crust. Everyone likes light, delicate pastry— tender, golden-brown pie crust that falls into flakes at the first touch of a fork.*

You'll find our special tricks of pastry-making—and some of our favorite filling recipes on these pages. Try them, won't you?

What To Do with Pie Crust Trimmings

NEVER *reroll pie crust trimmings. Rerolling toughens the crust. Instead, cut the trimmings in strips, sprinkle with grated cheese or cinnamon and sugar, bake, and serve with salad or tea.*

How to Make Perfect Pastry

Fig. 1—Sift flour before measuring. Then sift together flour and salt.

Fig. 2—Cut in half of shortening until mixture resembles coarse meal—this makes pastry tender. Cut in remaining half until particles are size of large peas—this makes pastry flaky.

How to Make Perfect Pastry

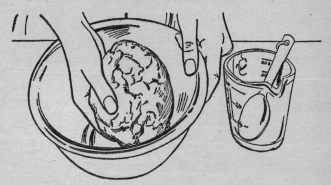

Fig. 3—Sprinkle water over mixture, a tablespoon at a time, mixing lightly with fork until dough is just moist enough to hold together. Too much water and too much handling make the crust tough. If you like, chill the dough before rolling.

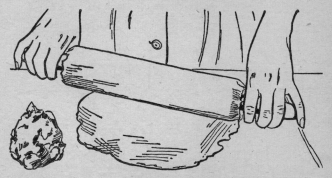

Fig. 4—Place one half the dough on lightly floured board or pastry canvas. (Pastry canvas and rolling pin cover make rolling out easier. You can use a minimum number of strokes which helps make crust more tender.) Roll dough a few strokes to flatten. Press edges together to keep dough in round shape. Then roll lightly from center to edge, lifting the rolling pin on each stroke as it nears the edge. Roll to about 1/8-inch thickness.

How to Make Perfect Pastry

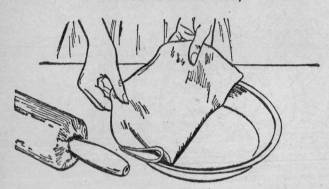

Fig. 5—Fold pastry in half, then in fourths. Place center of pastry in center of pie plate; unfold. (Or, dough may be rolled gently around rolling pin, lifted and carefully placed in pan.) Gently press out air pockets. Do not stretch! Stretching dough makes the pastry shrink during baking.

Fig. 6—For top crust; roll out remaining dough. Cut gashes for escape of steam. Fill bottom crust with desired filling. Place top crust over filling.

How to Make Perfect Pastry

Fig. 7—Trim edges so pastry extends ½-inch beyond rim of plate. Fold edge of top pastry under lower pastry. Flute by pinching dough with thumb and forefingers as shown. Bake as directed in recipe.

Fig. 8—For one-crust pastry shell, unfold pastry in pie plate and gently pat out air pockets. Trim and fold edge over, to form a standing rim. Flute edge by pinching dough with thumb and forefingers (see Fig. 7). Prick entire surface of pastry shell thoroughly with fork. Bake as directed. For a crisp, unsoaked pastry shell, cool both the filling and the pie crust before putting them together.

PASTRY FOR TWO-CRUST PIE

There are many methods and recipes for making pastry. We've tested many of them in our kitchen and feel that the following recipe is not only easy and quick but sure to turn out a light, flaky crust. This pastry may be used for all types of dessert pies and tarts—and as a meat pie topping, too. And notice how many ways the flavor may be varied! The addition of an ingredient or two can add a great deal of variety to your pie making.

Makes 2-crust 8 or 9-inch pie

*Sift together*_____2 cups sifted enriched flour
          1 teaspoon salt.

*Cut in*_____⅔ cup shortening until particles are the size of small peas.

*Sprinkle*_____5 to 6 tablespoons cold water over mixture, tossing lightly with fork until dough is moist enough to hold together.

*Divide*_____dough in half. Form into two balls. Roll out on floured board or pastry cloth to two 11-inch circles (10-inch circles for 8-inch pie).

*Fit*_____one circle of pastry loosely into pie pan. Gently pat out air pockets.

*Fill*_____with desired filling.

*Cut*_____slits in remaining circle of pastry to allow escape of steam. Place over filling. Fold edge of top pastry under lower pastry to form a standing rim; flute.

*Bake*_____as directed in recipe.

CHEESE PASTRY

PREPARE Pastry for Two-Crust Pie, adding ½ cup grated strong American cheese with shortening.

CHOCOLATE PASTRY

PREPARE Pastry for Two-Crust Pie, sifting 3 tablespoons cocoa and 2 tablespoons sugar with dry ingredients.

ORANGE PASTRY

PREPARE Pastry for Two-Crust Pie, adding 2 tablespoons grated orange rind with shortening.

SPICE PASTRY

PREPARE Pastry for Two-Crust Pie, sifting ½ teaspoon cinnamon, ¼ teaspoon nutmeg and ¼ teaspoon allspice with dry ingredients.

PASTRY FOR ONE-CRUST PIE

Makes 1-crust 8 or 9-inch pie shell

Sift together........1 cup sifted enriched flour
    ½ teaspoon salt.

Cut in................⅓ cup shortening until particles are the size of small peas.

Sprinkle........2 to 3 tablespoons cold water over mixture, tossing lightly with fork until dough is moist enough to hold together. Form into a ball.

Roll.................out on floured board or pastry cloth to an 11-inch circle (10-inch circle for 8-inch pie).

Fit..................pastry loosely into pie pan. Gently pat out air pockets. Fold edge to form standing rim; flute.

Bake................with or without filling as directed in recipe.

PASTRY FOR LATTICE PIE

Makes lattice-topped 8 or 9-inch pie

Prepare..............pastry dough following Pastry for Two-Crust Pie recipe. Roll out half of dough to fit pie pan.

Roll out..............remaining dough on floured board or pastry cloth to about ⅛-inch thickness. Cut into 10 strips, ½ inch wide.

Fill..............pastry-lined pan with desired filling.

Cross..............two longest strips over center of pie. Leave ends loose. Add remaining strips 1 inch apart, crisscross fashion, weaving under and over. Or twist each strip several times and place strips crisscross fashion over filling.

Seal..............ends to bottom crust and trim. Fold bottom crust to cover ends. Flute edge.

Bake..............as directed in recipe.

TART SHELLS

Makes 8 to 10 shells

Prepare..............pastry dough following Pastry for Two-Crust Pie recipe. Form into a ball.

Roll..............out on floured board or pastry cloth to about ⅛-inch thickness. Cut into 6-inch rounds.

Fit..............pastry rounds loosely into individual pie pans. (If individual pie pans are not available, cut smaller rounds to fit over backs of muffin pans.) Fold edge to form standing rim; flute. Prick crust generously with a fork.

Bake..............in hot oven (450°F.) 8 to 10 minutes.

MERINGUE

*Beat*_____3 egg whites with rotary or electric beater until they form slight mounds when beater is raised.

*Add*_____6 tablespoons sugar, a tablespoon at a time, beating until dissolved. Continue beating until meringue stands in lustrous heavy points.

*Spread*_____evenly over cooled pie filling.

*Brown*_____in moderate oven (350°F.) 15 minutes.

Hints on Making Meringue

BE SURE *to measure the sugar accurately and follow the instructions carefully. Beat in sugar after each addition until thoroughly dissolved. To prevent shrinkage, spread meringue so it touches and is sealed to edge of pastry. Leave meringue in uneven mounds for attractive finished pie. To help keep meringue from "weeping," cool at room temperature, away from drafts.*

Fruit Pies

APPLE PIE

Sometime—instead of serving cheese with this apple pie—put a little grated cheese in the pie crust. Delicious!

Makes 9-inch pie

*Prepare*_____Pastry for Two-Crust Pie. Line 9-inch pie pan with half of pastry.

*Combine*_____1 cup sugar
½ teaspoon cinnamon.

*Place*_____5 to 6 cups pared, sliced apples alternately in pastry-lined pie pan with cinnamon-sugar mixture.

Sprinkle................1 tablespoon lemon juice over apples. Dot with

2 tablespoons butter.

Place........................top crust over filling; seal and flute.

Bake........................in hot oven (450°F.) 10 minutes, then at 350°F. for 40 to 50 minutes.

FRENCH APPLE PIE

This delicious apple pie has a spicy golden-brown crumb topping.

Prepare....................Pastry for One-Crust Pie and line 9-inch pie pan.

Fill............................as for Apple Pie.

Combine..................1 cup enriched flour

¼ teaspoon salt

¼ cup sugar

	¼ cup brown sugar.
Cut in	½ cup butter.
Sprinkle	crumb mixture over top of pie filling.
Bake	in hot oven (450°F.) 10 minutes, then at 375°F. for 40 to 50 minutes.

BUTTERSCOTCH APPLE PIE

This apple pie is butterscotch flavored and has meringue on top.

Makes 9-inch pie

Prepare	Pastry for One-Crust Pie. Fit into 9-inch pie pan and prick generously with fork. Bake in a hot oven (450°F.) 10 to 12 minutes. Cool.
Combine	1 cup firmly packed brown sugar 1 cup water 1 teaspoon grated lemon rind in saucepan; heat to boiling.
Add	6 cups pared, sliced apples. Cook until tender. To keep apples from breaking, cover saucepan and cook slowly; turn apples occasionally.
Drain	syrup from apples into bowl.
Blend together	3 tablespoons melted butter ¼ cup enriched flour ¼ teaspoon salt in second saucepan.
Add	hot syrup and cook until thick, stirring constantly. Combine syrup and apples.
Turn	into baked pie shell. Spread meringue, page 311, over cooled filling and bake.

DEEP DISH APPLE PIE

There is a cinnamon-candy apple filling for this pie, and just one crust—a top crust! Make this deep dish apple pie in the traditional round 10-inch pan. Or, for variety, bake it in a square or rectangular pan and serve in squares topped with cream.

Makes 10-inch deep dish pie

*Prepare*_____Pastry for Two-Crust Pie, using all of pastry for one crust. Roll dough to extend 1-inch beyond rim of 10-inch pie pan. Cut slits to allow escape of steam.

*Melt*_____⅓ cup red cinnamon candies and
½ cup sugar in
½ cup water.

*Combine*_____6 cups pared, sliced apples
¼ cup enriched flour
½ cup sugar
½ teaspoon nutmeg
⅛ teaspoon salt.

*Pour*_____cinnamon syrup and
1 tablespoon lemon juice over apples. Blend until apples are coated with syrup.

*Turn*_____into 10x2-inch deep dish pie pan or 12x8x2-inch pan. Dot with
2 tablespoons butter.

*Place*_____crust over apples; seal and flute.

*Bake*_____in hot oven (450°F.) 10 minutes, then at 375°F. for 40 to 50 minutes or until apples are tender.

MELODY MINCE PIE

This rich blend of apples, prunes, molasses and nuts may remind you of old-fashioned mince pie. (This pie has a sugar-nut topping instead of a top crust.)

Makes 9-inch pie

Prepare................Pastry for One-Crust Pie. Fit into 9-inch pie pan.

Chop................1 cup cooked pitted prunes and 4 cups pared apples until fine.

Add................grated rind and juice of one small orange.

Blend together....½ teaspoon salt
⅔ cup sugar
2 tablespoons flour
¼ cup prune juice
¼ cup light molasses.

Combine................with fruit mixture and turn into pastry-lined pan.

Melt................1 tablespoon brown sugar and 2 tablespoons butter in saucepan. Add ¾ cup nuts. Sprinkle over filling.

Bake................in hot oven (450°F.) 10 minutes, then at 350°F. for 45 to 50 minutes. Cool. Serve with whipped cream.

CRANBERRY-RAISIN PIE

Red cranberries and raisins make a particularly colorful pie.

Makes 9-inch pie

Prepare................Pastry for Two-Crust Pie. Line 9-inch pie pan with half of pastry. Cut balance of rolled pastry in designs with fancy cooky cutter.

Blend together......2 tablespoons **flour**
            2 cups **sugar**
            ¼ teaspoon **salt**
            ⅔ cup **water**. Heat to boiling.
Add......................3 cups **cranberries**
            1 cup **raisins**
            2 teaspoons grated **lemon rind**.
Cook....................until berries start to pop, about 10 min.
Add......................2 tablespoons **butter**.
Turn.....................into pastry-lined pan.
Arrange................pastry cutouts on top of filling.
Bake.....................in moderately hot oven (400°F.) 35 to 40 minutes.

CRANBERRY-APPLE PIE

After testing this pie in our kitchen, we can't help feeling that
apples and cranberries belong together.

Makes 9-inch pie

Prepare .... Pastry for Lattice Pie. Line 9-inch pie
pan with half of pastry.

Cook .... 4 cups pared, sliced apples and
½ cup water in saucepan until apples are
partially tender.

Combine .... 1¾ cups sugar
2 tablespoons cornstarch
¼ teaspoon salt. Blend with apples.

Add .... 2½ cups cranberries
1 tablespoon grated orange rind and cook
until apples are tender and cranberries
start to pop.

Blend in .... 2 tablespoons butter. Cool.

Turn .... into pastry-lined pan.

Place .... lattice strips over filling; seal and flute.

Bake .... in hot oven (425°F.) 25 to 30 minutes.

APRICOT-RAISIN PIE

Here's a mid-winter fruit pie. Apricots and raisins make a colorful filling that tastes as good as it looks.

Makes 9-inch pie

Prepare .... Pastry for Lattice Pie. Line 9-inch pie
pan with half of pastry.

Cook .... 2 cups dried apricots until tender.

*Combine*_____2 tablespoons flour
　　　　　　　　　1 cup sugar
　　　　　　　　　¼ teaspoon salt.
*Add*_____1 cup water
　　　　　　　　　1 cup raisins
　　　　　　　　　2 teaspoons grated lemon rind
　　　　　　　　　2 tablespoons butter; cook until thickened.
　　　　　　　　　Add cooked apricots. Cool slightly.
*Turn*_____into pastry-lined pan.
*Place*_____lattice strips over filling; seal and flute.
*Bake*_____in hot oven (425°F.) 20 minutes.

RAISIN PIE

This is a real old-fashioned raisin pie. Ideal to top off a simple meal.

Makes 9-inch pie

*Prepare*_____Pastry for Two-Crust Pie. Line 9-inch
　　　　　　　　　pie pan with half of pastry.
*Combine*_____2½ cups raisins
　　　　　　　　　3 cups hot water
　　　　　　　　　1½ tablespoons grated lemon rind
　　　　　　　　　2 tablespoons lemon juice.
*Heat*_____to boiling; cook for 3 minutes.
*Combine*_____⅔ cup sugar
　　　　　　　　　¼ cup enriched flour
　　　　　　　　　¼ teaspoon cinnamon; add to raisin mix-
　　　　　　　　　ture.
*Cook*_____until thickened and clear, about 5 min-
　　　　　　　　　utes, stirring constantly.
*Turn*_____into pastry-lined pan.
*Place*_____top crust over filling; seal and flute.
*Bake*_____in hot oven (425°F.) 30 minutes.

STRAWBERRY GLACÉ PIE

This is our favorite way of making a fresh strawberry—or fresh raspberry—pie. You'll find that it retains all the delicate fresh flavor of the berries.

Makes 9-inch pie

Prepare................Pastry for One-Crust Pie. Fit into 9-inch pie pan and prick generously with fork.

Bake................in hot oven (450°F.) 10 to 12 minutes. Cool.

Line................baked pastry shell with 3 cups fresh **strawberries.**

Simmer................1 cup **strawberries** and ¾ cup **water** in saucepan about 3 to 4 minutes.

Combine................3 tablespoons **cornstarch** 1 cup **sugar**; add to cooked fruit.

Cook................until syrup is thick and clear, stirring constantly.

Add................1 teaspoon **lemon juice**; cool slightly. Pour over berries in pastry shell.

Chill................thoroughly. Decorate with sweetened whipped cream before serving.

RASPBERRY GLACÉ PIE

PREPARE Strawberry Glacé Pie, substituting raspberries for strawberries.

STRAWBERRY SOCIAL PIE

Pillsbury Contest Winner by T. O. Davis, Waynesboro, Miss.

Flaky pie crust . . . filling of fresh strawberries, marshmallows and fluffy whipped cream. Mr. Davis suggests that you make it in the cool of the morning and store it in the refrigerator until serving time.

Makes 9-inch pie

Prepare————————Pastry for One-Crust Pie. Fit into 9-inch pie pan and prick generously with fork.

Bake————————in hot oven (450°F.) 10 to 12 minutes. Cool.

Quarter————————10 fresh marshmallows.* Arrange in baked pie shell.

Spread————————1 cup sliced strawberries over marshmallows.

Beat————————⅔ cup whipping cream until stiff. Add ⅓ cup white corn syrup gradually; beat until mixture is very stiff.

Blend in————————¼ teaspoon almond extract and 10 fresh marshmallows, finely cut.*

Spread————————cream mixture over strawberries; seal to edge of pastry. Chill 6 to 8 hours before serving. Decorate with whole strawberries if desired.

---

*Marshmallows may be quartered and cut with scissors dipped in hot water.

STRAWBERRY-RHUBARB PIE

Strawberries and rhubarb—sweet and tart—how good they taste in a pie! The recipe is simple, too.

Makes 9-inch pie

Prepare................Pastry for Lattice Pie. Line 9-inch pie pan with half of pastry.

Combine................¼ cup **enriched flour**
1½ cups **sugar**
¼ teaspoon **salt**.

Add................2 cups fresh **strawberries**
3 cups diced fresh **rhubarb**;
combine thoroughly.

Turn................into pastry-lined pie pan. Dot with
1 tablespoon **butter**.

Place................lattice strips over filling; seal and flute.

Bake................in hot oven (450°F.) 10 minutes, then at 350°F. for 50 to 55 minutes.

FRESH RASPBERRY PIE

When fresh raspberries are in season, be sure to try this wonderful pie.

Makes 9-inch pie

Prepare................Pastry for Two-Crust Pie. Line 9-inch pie pan with half of pastry.

Combine................3 tablespoons **flour**
2 tablespoons **cornstarch**
⅛ teaspoon **salt**
1¼ cups **sugar**.

Add................4 cups fresh **raspberries**.
1 tablespoon **lemon juice**;
blend thoroughly.

Turn...............	into pastry-lined pan. Dot with
	1 tablespoon **butter**.
Place...............	top crust over filling; seal and flute.
Bake...............	in hot oven (450°F.) 10 minutes, then
	at 350°F. for 30 to 35 minutes.

SPRING FRESH RHUBARB PIE

There's all the rich juiciness of fresh rhubarb in this pie. Good
and a bit different, too.

Makes 9-inch pie

Prepare...............	Pastry for Lattice Pie. Line 9-inch pie pan with half of pastry.
Combine...............	4 cups **rhubarb**, cut into ½-inch pieces
	1 **egg**, slightly beaten
	1 tablespoon **lemon juice**
	½ teaspoon grated **lemon rind**.
Blend together.....	¼ cup **enriched flour**
	¼ teaspoon **salt**
	¼ teaspoon **nutmeg**
	1½ cups **sugar**.
Add...............	dry ingredients to rhubarb mixture; blend thoroughly.
Turn...............	into pastry-lined pan.
Place...............	lattice strips over filling; seal and flute.
Bake...............	in hot oven (450°F.) 10 minutes, then at 350°F. for 50 minutes.

CHERRY PIE

If you put a lattice-crust on top of this pie, the bright-red cherry filling shows through. Good to look at—and to eat.

Makes 8-inch pie

Prepare.................Pastry for Lattice Pie. Line 8-inch pie pan with half of pastry.

Blend together......2 tablespoons **cornstarch**
½ cup **sugar**
¼ teaspoon **salt**
¾ cup **cherry juice**; cook until thickened and clear, stirring constantly.

Add.................2 cups (No. 2 can) drained **cherries** and turn into pastry-lined pan. Dot with
2 tablespoons **butter**.

Place.................lattice strips over filling; seal and flute.

Bake.................in hot oven (450°F.) 10 minutes, then at 350°F. for 40 to 50 minutes.

BONNY BLUEBERRY PIE

Here is a really easy recipe for good old-fashioned blueberry pie.

Makes 9-inch pie

Prepare.................Pastry for Two-Crust Pie. Line 9-inch pie pan with half of pastry.

Combine.................¼ cup **enriched flour**
2 tablespoons **cornstarch**
1¼ cups **sugar**
¼ teaspoon **nutmeg**
⅛ teaspoon **salt**
1 teaspoon grated **lemon rind**.

Add............................4 cups fresh **blueberries**
                        1 tablespoon **lemon juice**;
                        blend thoroughly.
Turn............................into pastry-lined pan and dot with
                        1 tablespoon **butter**.
Place............................top crust over filling; seal and flute.
Bake............................in hot oven (450°F.) 10 minutes, then
                        at 350°F. for 35 to 40 minutes.

BOYSENBERRY PIE

You can make this pie with canned boysenberries, and serve it
any time of the year.

Makes 8-inch pie

Prepare............................Pastry for Two-Crust Pie. Line 8-inch
                        pie pan with half of pastry.
Combine............................2 tablespoons **cornstarch**
                        ¼ cup **sugar**
                        ¼ teaspoon **salt**
                        1 cup **boysenberry juice**; cook until thick
                        and clear, stirring constantly.
Add............................1 cup (No. 2 can) drained **boysenberries**.
Turn............................into pastry-lined pan.
Place............................top crust over filling; seal and flute.
Bake............................in hot oven (425°F.) 10 minutes, then
                        at 350°F. for 30 to 35 minutes.

FRESH BLACKBERRY PIE

Make this pie with big, fat fresh blackberries.

Makes 9-inch pie

Prepare............................Pastry for Two-Crust Pie. Line 9-inch
                        pie pan with half of pastry.

*Combine*_____ ¼ cup enriched flour
2 tablespoons cornstarch
⅛ teaspoon salt
1¼ cups sugar.

*Add*_____ 4 cups fresh blackberries;
blend thoroughly.

*Turn*_____ into pastry-lined pan.

*Place*_____ top crust over filling; seal and flute.

*Bake*_____ in hot oven (425°F.) 10 minutes, then
at 350°F. for 40 minutes.

GOOSEBERRY PIE

**There is just the right balance of sweetness and tartness in this
fresh gooseberry pie.**

Makes 9-inch pie

*Prepare*_____ Pastry for Two-Crust Pie. Line 9-inch
pie pan with half of pastry.

*Combine*_____ 4 cups gooseberries
1 egg, slighten beaten.

*Blend together*___ 2 tablespoons cornstarch
¼ cup enriched flour
¼ teaspoon salt
1½ cups sugar
¼ teaspoon nutmeg
¼ teaspoon cinnamon.

*Add*_____ to gooseberry mixture;
combine thoroughly.

*Turn*_____ into pastry-lined pan. Dot with
1 tablespoon butter.

*Place*_____ top crust over filling; seal and flute.

*Bake*_____ in hot oven (450°F.) 10 minutes, then
at 350°F. for 35 to 40 minutes.

PINEAPPLE PIE

It's so easy, yet so good. And adding just a hint of lemon brings
out the pineapple flavor.

Makes 8-inch pie

Prepare	Pastry for Two-Crust Pie. Line 8-inch pie pan with half of pastry.
Combine	2 tablespoons **cornstarch**
	½ cup **sugar**
	¼ teaspoon **salt**
	2⅓ cups (No. 2 can) crushed **pineapple**.
Cook	until thickened and clear, stirring constantly.
Add	1 tablespoon **butter**
	1 tablespoon **lemon juice**.
Turn	into pastry-lined pan.
Place	top crust over filling; seal and flute.
Bake	in hot oven (425°F.) 25 to 30 minutes.

PEACH-PINEAPPLE PIE

There are bits of golden pineapple and sliced peaches in the
filling of this pie. (This is a good "year around" recipe, because
it calls for canned pineapple and peaches.)

Makes 9-inch pie

Prepare	Pastry for Two-Crust Pie. Line 9-inch pie pan with half of pastry.
Combine	¼ cup sifted **enriched flour**
	½ cup firmly packed **brown sugar**
	¼ teaspoon **salt**.
Add	2 cups (No. 2½ can) sliced **peaches**, drained

1 cup crushed pineapple, drained;
blend thoroughly.

Turn............into pastry-lined pan.

Combine............¼ cup juice from fruit

1 tablespoon lemon juice

1 teaspoon grated lemon rind; pour over
fruit in pie pan. Dot with

1 tablespoon butter.

Place............top crust over filling; seal and flute.

Bake............in hot oven (450°F.) 10 minutes, then
at 350°F. for 30 minutes.

SUNNY PEACH PIE

**Golden, plump peach slices flavored with fresh orange juice
in a flaky pie shell. Top it off with whipped cream.**

Makes 9-inch pie

Prepare............Pastry for One-Crust Pie. Fit into 9-inch
pie pan and prick generously with fork.

Bake............in hot oven (450°F.) 10 to 12 minutes.
Cool.

Combine............¼ cup sugar and

3 tablespoons cornstarch in saucepan.

Add............1 cup syrup, drained from No. 2½ can
sliced peaches.

Cook............until thickened, stirring constantly. Remove from heat.

Add............¼ cup orange juice

1 teaspoon grated orange rind

1 tablespoon butter

⅛ teaspoon salt.

Blend in............sliced peaches.

Turn into............baked pie shell. Chill.

Top with whipped cream.

GOLDEN DREAM PEACH PIE

Pillsbury Contest Winner by Mrs. George B. Wesler, Milwaukee, Wis.

Use either fresh or canned freestone golden peach halves . . .
with caramel butter syrup and a touch of whipped cream. "This
recipe was given to me by a relative who is famous as a
hostess in her town," says Mrs. Wesler.

Makes 9-inch pie

Prepare................Pastry for One-Crust Pie. Fit into 9-inch
pie pan.

Arrange......10 to 14 fresh or canned peach halves,
well drained, in pastry-lined pan.
Place cut side up.

Combine............1 cup firmly packed brown sugar
⅓ cup enriched flour.

Cut in................3 tablespoons butter. Sprinkle evenly over
peaches.

Bake................in hot oven (450°F.) 10 to 12 minutes.
Cover pie with another pie plate or
aluminum foil. Then bake at 375°F.
for 35 to 40 minutes. Cool thoroughly.

Beat................½ pint (1 cup) whipping cream. Add
½ teaspoon vanilla and
1 tablespoon caramelized syrup from pie.
Place whipped cream around edge of
pie; sprinkle with nutmeg.

HAWAIIAN CONFECTION PIE

Pillsbury Contest Winner by H. B. Andrews, Inglewood, Calif.

A very rich fruit pie . . . . with a sweet, fluffy filling, spread
with pineapple and fresh strawberries.

Makes 10-inch pie

Sift together......1¼ cups sifted **enriched flour**
½ teaspoon **salt**.

Cut in..................½ cup **shortening** until particles are the
size of small peas.

Sprinkle............2 to 3 tablespoons cold **water** over mixture,
tossing lightly with fork until dough is
moist enough to hold together. Form
into a ball.

Roll.......................out on floured board or pastry cloth to
a 12-inch circle.

Fit........................pastry loosely into 10-inch pie pan. Fold
edge to form standing rim; flute. Prick
crust with fork.

Bake....................in hot oven (450°F.) 10 to 12 minutes.
Cool thoroughly.

Combine..............½ cup **sugar**
¼ cup light **corn syrup**
2 tablespoons **water** and boil until syrup
forms a thread (230° - 234°F.).

Beat....................2 **egg whites** until stiff.

Pour....................syrup slowly into beaten egg whites,
beating with electric mixer or rotary
beater until mixture stands in peaks.

Add....................1 teaspoon **vanilla**.

Spread................a thin layer of filling over surface of
cooled, baked pie shell.

*Combine*_____1 cup **pineapple chunks**, drained, and
1 cup sliced, sweetened **strawberries**.*
Spread over filling in pie shell and top
with remaining filling. Cool thoroughly
before serving.

_____

*If desired, one 12-oz. package frozen strawberries, well drained, may be used.

LEMON MERINGUE PIE

This good old favorite is cool, pretty—and will always have just the right amount of tang and sweetness to top off a generous meal.

Makes 8 or 9-inch pie

*Prepare*_____Pastry for One-Crust Pie. Fit into 8 or
9-inch pie pan and prick generously
with fork.

*Bake*_____in hot oven (450°F.) 10 to 12 minutes.
Cool.

*Combine*_____1 cup **sugar**
¼ cup **cornstarch**
½ teaspoon **salt**.

*Blend in*_____¼ cup cold **water**.

*Add*_____1¼ cups hot **water**.

*Cook*_____until thickened, stirring constantly. Continue cooking over low heat until clear
(5 to 8 minutes). Stir occasionally.

*Add*_____¼ cup **lemon juice** and
1 tablespoon grated **lemon rind**.
Cook 2 minutes.

*Blend*_____hot mixture slowly into
3 **egg yolks**, slightly beaten. Return to pan
and cook 2 minutes, stirring constantly.

Add.................2 tablespoons **butter**. Cool.

Turn.................into baked pie shell. Top with meringue, page 311.

ORANGE LEMONADE PIE

The combination of orange and lemon in this pie makes an unusually light, cool filling. Really refreshing!

Makes 8 or 9-inch pie

Prepare.................Pastry for One-Crust Pie. Fit into 8 or 9-inch pie pan and prick generously with fork.

Bake.................in hot oven (450°F.) 10 to 12 minutes. Cool.

Combine.................1 cup **sugar**
¼ cup **cornstarch**
½ teaspoon **salt**.

Blend in.................¼ cup cold **water**.

Add.................1 cup hot **water**.

Cook.................until thickened, stirring constantly. Continue cooking over low heat until clear (5 to 8 minutes). Stir occasionally.

Add.................¼ cup **lemon juice**
¼ cup **orange juice**
1 tablespoon grated **lemon rind**.
Cook 2 minutes.

Blend.................hot mixture slowly into
3 **egg yolks**, slightly beaten. Return to pan and cook 2 minutes, stirring constantly.

Add.................2 tablespoons **butter**. Cool.

Turn.................into baked pie shell. Top with meringue, page 311.

Cream Pies

CREAM PIE

This is a basic recipe for smooth, delicate cream pie. You can vary it to make banana cream, coconut cream, and many other cream pies.

Makes 9-inch pie

Prepare	Pastry for One-Crust Pie. Fit into 9-inch pie pan and prick generously with fork.
Bake	in hot oven (450° F.) 10 to 12 minutes. Cool.
Combine	⅓ cup enriched flour ½ cup sugar ⅛ teaspoon salt.
Blend in	2 cups scalded milk, gradually.
Cook	over boiling water until thickened, stirring constantly.
Blend	a little hot mixture into 3 slightly beaten egg yolks; return to double boiler.
Cook	about 2 minutes, stirring constantly.
Add	2 tablespoons butter and 1 teaspoon vanilla. Cool.
Turn	into baked pie shell. Top with meringue, page 311, or whipped cream.

BANANA CREAM PIE

PREPARE Cream Pie, slicing 3 bananas into baked pie shell before adding filling.

CHOCOLATE CREAM PIE

PREPARE Cream Pie, melting 2 squares (2 oz.) chocolate with scalded milk.

BUTTERSCOTCH CREAM PIE

PREPARE Cream Pie, substituting ¾ cup firmly packed brown sugar for ½ cup granulated sugar and increasing butter to 2 tablespoons.

COCONUT CREAM PIE

PREPARE Cream Pie, folding 1 cup grated coconut into cooled filling.

FRUIT SUNDAE PIE

Creamy filling—a topping of fresh berries and whipped cream —make this a particularly luscious pie. After the berry season is over, you can make it with fresh peaches and apricots.

Makes 9-inch pie

Prepare............Pastry for One-Crust Pie. Fit into 9-inch pie pan and prick generously with fork.

Bake..............in hot oven (450° F.) 10 to 12 minutes. Cool.

Combine............½ cup sifted **enriched flour**
¼ teaspoon **salt**
½ cup **sugar**.

Blend together......2 **egg yolks**, well beaten
¼ cup cold **water**;
combine with dry ingredients.

Add..............2 cups scalded **milk**
2 tablespoons **butter**.

Cook..............over direct heat until thickened, stirring constantly. Cool.

Add..............1½ teaspoons **vanilla**.

Turn..............into baked pie shell and top with fruit topping.

FRUIT TOPPING

COMBINE 1 tablespoon cornstarch and 1 cup fruit juice. Cook until thickened, stirring constantly. Add 1 cup fruit—fresh, frozen or canned. Spread over cream filling and top with whipped cream.

Chiffon Pies

CHOCOLATE-CRUSTED PIE

BEST OF CLASS WINNER
Pillsbury's 1st Recipe Contest
by Mrs. Robert Monroe, Atlantic City, New Jersey

The cooky-like crust for this pie is filled with a snowy chiffon filling. Whipped cream and chocolate crumbs go on top.

Makes 9-inch pie

*Sift together*____1¼ cups sifted enriched flour
⅓ cup sugar
¼ cup cocoa
½ teaspoon salt.

*Cut in*_____½ cup shortening until particles are the size of small peas.

*Add*_____½ teaspoon vanilla.

*Sprinkle*_____2 to 3 tablespoons cold water over mixture, tossing lightly with fork until dough is moist enough to hold together. Form into a ball.

*Roll*_____out on floured board or pastry cloth to an 11-inch circle.

*Fit*_____pastry loosely into 9-inch pie pan. Fold edge to form standing rim; flute. Prick crust with fork.

*Place*_____dough "trimmings" in second pie pan.

Bake	in moderately hot oven (400°F.) 8 to 10 minutes. Do not overbake. Cool.
Crumble	baked, cooled "trimmings" and save for crumb topping.

Vanilla Chiffon Filling

Soften	1 tablespoon (1 envelope) **gelatin** in ¼ cup **milk.**
Combine	4 **egg yolks**, slightly beaten 1¼ cups **milk** ⅓ cup **sugar** ½ teaspoon **salt.**
Cook	over boiling water until mixture thickens, stirring constantly. Remove from heat.
Add	1 teaspoon **vanilla** with softened gelatin and beat well with rotary beater. Chill until mixture begins to thicken.
Beat	4 **egg whites** until stiff. Beat in ¼ cup **sugar** gradually.
Fold	egg whites carefully into gelatin mixture. Pour into cooled, baked shell. Chill in refrigerator 3 to 5 hours.
Top with	1 cup **heavy cream**, whipped and sweetened. Sprinkle with the chocolate crumbs.

LEMON CHIFFON PIE

A delicious kind of lemon pie—fluffy, cool and light. Top it with whipped cream.

Makes 9-inch pie

Prepare	Pastry for One-Crust Pie. Fit into 9-inch pie pan and prick generously with fork.

Bake................in hot oven (450°F.) 10 to 12 minutes. Cool.

Soften................1 tablespoon (1 envelope) gelatin in ¼ cup cold water.

Combine................4 egg yolks, slightly beaten
½ cup sugar
1 teaspoon grated lemon rind
½ cup lemon juice
½ teaspoon salt.

Cook................over boiling water until thickened, stirring constantly. Remove from heat.

Add................softened gelatin and stir until dissolved.

Beat................4 egg whites until stiff but not dry. Beat in ½ cup sugar gradually.

Fold................egg whites carefully into gelatin mixture. Turn into baked pie shell. Chill in refrigerator until firm, 3 to 5 hours.

Top with................1 cup heavy cream, whipped and sweetened.

CHOCOLATE CHIFFON PIE

Here's rich chocolate in a light, fluffy filling. There's whipped cream in the filling, too. And a tender, flaky pie crust beneath it all.

Makes 9-inch pie

Prepare................Pastry for One-Crust Pie. Fit into 9-inch pie pan and prick generously with fork.

Bake................in hot oven (450°F.) 10 to 12 minutes. Cool.

Soften................1 tablespoon (1 envelope) gelatin in ¼ cup cold water.

Melt................2 squares (2 oz.) chocolate in 1 cup milk, stirring until smooth.

Add............................softened gelatin and stir until dissolved.

Beat...........................3 **egg yolks** until thick and lemon colored; gradually beat in

½ cup **sugar**

¼ teaspoon **salt**.

Add............................hot chocolate mixture, stirring until well blended. Chill until mixture begins to thicken.

Beat...........................3 **egg whites** until stiff but not dry. Beat in ¼ cup **sugar** gradually.

Fold...........................egg whites carefully into chocolate mixture.

Whip..........................½ cup **heavy cream**; add

1 teaspoon **vanilla** and fold into chocolate mixture.

Turn...........................into baked pie shell. Chill in refrigerator until firm, 3 to 5 hours. Top with sweetened whipped cream.

PEACH CHIFFON PIE

Peaches are folded through and through the billowy, delicately-flavored filling of this chiffon pie.

Makes 9-inch pie

Prepare.......................Pastry for One-Crust Pie. Fit into 9-inch pie pan and prick generously with fork.

Bake...........................in hot oven (450°F.) 10 to 12 minutes. Cool.

Dissolve......................1½ tablespoons (1½ envelopes) **gelatin** in ¼ cup cold **water**.

Combine......................3 **egg yolks**, slightly beaten

¼ cup **sugar**

⅓ cup **orange juice**

1 teaspoon grated **orange rind**

        ¼ teaspoon salt

        1⅔ cups peaches (No. 2½ can), sieved.

Cook............over boiling water until thickened, stirring constantly.

Add............softened gelatin and stir until dissolved. Remove from heat. Chill until mixture begins to thicken.

Beat............3 egg whites until stiff but not dry; gradually beat in

        ½ cup sugar.

Fold............gelatin mixture carefully into egg whites. Pour into baked pie shell. Chill in refrigerator until firm, 3 to 5 hours.

PUMPKIN CHIFFON TARTS

These tarts have the traditional flavor of old-fashioned pumpkin filling and the lightness of a chiffon pie. Make individual tarts or put the filling in a baked 9-inch pie shell if you wish.

Makes 8 to 10 tarts

Prepare............Tart Shells. Cool.

Soften............1 tablespoon (1 envelope) gelatin in

        ¼ cup cold water.

Beat............3 egg yolks with

        ½ cup sugar until thick.

Add............1⅓ cups mashed pumpkin, cooked or canned

        ⅓ cup milk

        ½ teaspoon salt

        ½ teaspoon cinnamon

        ½ teaspoon nutmeg

        ¼ teaspoon ginger.

Cook............until thickened, stirring constantly.

Add............softened gelatin, stirring until dissolved. Cool.

Beat .... 3 **egg whites** until stiff but not dry. Beat in
½ cup **sugar** gradually.

Fold .... egg whites into gelatin mixture.

Turn .... into baked tart shells. Chill in refrigerator until firm, 3 to 5 hours. Top with sweetened whipped cream.

Custard Pies

CUSTARD PIE

This pie is easy and quick to prepare and the filling always turns out creamy, smooth and delicate.

Makes 9-inch pie

Prepare .... Pastry for One-Crust Pie. Fit into 9-inch pie pan. Chill in refrigerator.

Scald .... 2½ cups **milk**.

Beat .... 3 **eggs** or 6 egg yolks slightly.

Add .... ½ cup **sugar**
¼ teaspoon **salt**
½ teaspoon **vanilla**
¼ teaspoon **nutmeg** and the scalded milk. Strain mixture.

Turn .... hot custard into chilled shell.

Bake .... in hot oven (425°F.) 10 to 12 minutes, then at 325°F. for 20 minutes or until a silver knife inserted about half way between the center and outside of the custard comes out clean.

AUNT MARY'S FAVORITE PIE

Pillsbury Contest Winner by Mrs. Drue Alexander, Russells Point, Ohio

This recipe is an old family favorite. It's an unusual custard
pie with a hint of spice. The crust is partially baked before
filling is added. Notice how the crust stays flaky and tender.

Makes 9-inch pie

Prepare................Pastry for One-Crust Pie. Fit into 9-inch
pie pan. Place waxed paper in the bot-
tom of pie shell and fill with dried beans
or place another pie plate inside shell to
retain shape during baking.

Bake................in hot oven (450°F.) 10 to 12 minutes.
Remove paper and beans from shell be-
fore filling.

Combine................4 **egg yolks**, slightly beaten
1¼ cups **milk**
1⅓ cups **sugar**
3 tablespoons melted **butter**
3 tablespoons **enriched flour**
½ teaspoon **cinnamon**
¼ teaspoon **nutmeg**
¼ teaspoon ground **cloves**. Mix well.

Beat................4 **egg whites**. Add
½ teaspoon **salt** and beat until stiff but not
dry. Fold gently into egg yolk mixture.
Pour filling into warm pie shell.

Bake................in moderate oven (350°F.) 40 to 50 min.

PUMPKIN PIE

This pumpkin pie can be served plain with whipped cream. Or try the special topping of brown sugar and pecans.

Makes 9-inch pie

Prepare—————— Pastry for One-Crust Pie. Fit into 9-inch pie pan.

Beat—————— 3 eggs slightly.

Blend in—————— ½ cup sugar

½ cup firmly packed **brown sugar**

1 tablespoon flour

½ teaspoon salt

½ teaspoon nutmeg

½ teaspoon allspice

1 teaspoon cinnamon.

Add—————— 1½ cups **pumpkin**, cooked or canned; mix well.

Add gradually— 1½ cups top milk, heated.

Turn—————— into pastry-lined pan.

Bake—————— in hot oven (450°F.) 10 minutes, then at 350°F. for 40 to 50 minutes or until a silver knife inserted about half way between the center and edge of filling comes out clean.

PECAN PUMPKIN PIE

*Prepare*_____Pumpkin Pie. Remove from oven at end of 30 minutes. Cover with the following pecan topping:

*Melt*_____1 tablespoon **brown sugar** and 2 tablespoons **butter** in saucepan.

*Add*_____¾ cup pecans.

*Place*_____on top of pie.

*Bake*_____in moderate oven (350°F.) 20 to 30 minutes or until a silver knife inserted about half way between the center and edge of filling comes out clean.

PRALINE PUMPKIN-CUSTARD PIE

Pillsbury Contest Winner by Mrs. W. W. Douglass, Searcy, Ark.

Pecan brown sugar crumbs form a layer beneath this pumpkin-custard filling. The pie shell stays dry and delicate.

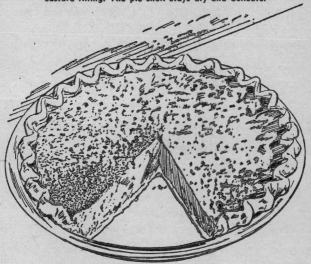

Makes 9-inch pie

*Prepare*_____Pastry for One-Crust Pie. Fit into 9-inch pie pan and prick generously with fork.

*Combine*_____⅓ cup finely ground pecans, packed
⅓ cup firmly packed brown sugar
2 tablespoons soft butter; press firmly into bottom of pie shell.

*Bake*_____in hot oven (450°F.) 10 minutes.

*Combine*_____2 eggs, well beaten
1 cup pumpkin, cooked or canned
⅔ cup firmly packed brown sugar
1 tablespoon flour

¼ teaspoon cloves
⅛ teaspoon mace
½ teaspoon each: salt, cinnamon, ginger.

*Blend in*_____1 cup coffee cream or undiluted evaporated milk, beating until smooth and creamy. Pour into partially baked shell.

*Bake*_____in slow oven (325°F.) 40 to 45 minutes.

SOUTHERN SUGAR PIE

Pillsbury Contest Winner by Mrs. D. F. Moss, Jamaica, Long Island, N. Y.

This chess pie has been a favorite in Mrs. Moss' family for nearly half a century. It's wonderfully rich and has a brown-sugar flavor.

Makes 10-inch pie

*Sift together*___1½ cups sifted enriched flour
½ teaspoon salt.

*Combine*_____3 tablespoons water and ¼ cup of the flour mixture to form a paste.

*Cut*_____½ cup shortening into remaining flour until particles are the size of small peas.

*Add*_____flour paste and mix until dough forms a ball.

*Roll*_____out on floured board or pastry cloth to a 12-inch circle.

*Fit*_____pastry loosely into 10-inch pie pan. Fold edge to form a standing rim; flute.

*Combine*_____1 cup sugar
1 cup firmly packed brown sugar
½ teaspoon salt
¼ cup enriched flour.

*Beat*_____4 eggs until thick and lemon colored. Add

dry ingredients gradually, beating until mixture is well blended.

Add gradually......½ cup melted **butter**

½ cup **milk**

1 tablespoon **vanilla**. Pour filling into un-baked pie shell.

Bake...............in moderate oven (350°F.) 50 to 55 min.

CUSTARD SNOW PIE

Pillsbury Contest Winner by Mrs. Lawson Odom Dailey, Dallas, Texas

"I persuaded an old lady—an excellent cook of the 'handful-and-pinch' school—to measure her custard pie ingredients for me to write down," says Mrs. Dailey. "I have used this custard for many original pies. This is one of them. You will like the crust with its tang of spice . . ."

Makes 9-inch pie

Prepare...............Pastry for One-Crust Pie. Fit into 9-inch pie pan and prick generously with fork.

Bake...............in hot oven (450°F.) 10 to 12 minutes.

Sift together........¼ cup **enriched flour**

½ teaspoon **salt**

1 cup **sugar**.

Beat...............3 **egg yolks** and

1 **egg** slightly. Add

½ cup cold **milk**. Blend into dry ingredients.

Add...............1 cup scalded **milk** slowly. Cook over boiling water until thick, stirring constantly. Remove from heat.

Add...............1 teaspoon **vanilla**. Cool.

Sprinkle...............1 cup moist **coconut** in bottom of baked pie shell. Pour cooled custard over coconut. Top with meringue, page 311; bake.

Special Pies

CHOCOLATE CREME MINT PIE

Pillsbury Contest Winner by Mrs. D. A. Rainey, Denver, Colo.

Here's a pie you'll serve often as company dessert. The chocolate filling has a hint of peppermint. (No cooking needed.)

Makes 8-inch pie

Sift together............1 cup sifted **enriched flour**
½ teaspoon **salt**.

Combine............2 tablespoons **water** and two tablespoons of the flour to form a thin paste.

Cut............⅓ cup **shortening** into remaining flour until particles are the size of small peas.

Add............flour paste and mix until dough forms a ball.

Roll............pastry on floured board or pastry cloth to a 10-inch circle.

Fit............pastry into 8-inch pie plate. Fold edge to form a standing rim; flute. Prick crust with fork.

Bake............in hot oven (450°F.) 10 to 12 minutes.

Cream............¾ cup **butter** thoroughly. Add
1 cup **sugar** gradually, creaming well.

Beat............3 **eggs** thoroughly. Blend into creamed mixture.

Blend in............3 squares (3 oz.) **chocolate**, melted and cooled. Beat until smooth.

Add............½ teaspoon **peppermint extract**. Pour mixture into baked, cooled pie shell. Chill several hours. Top with whipped cream before serving.

ICE CREAM PIE

You bake your pie shell first. When ready to serve, fill it with ice cream, and top it off with fluffy meringue. Brown it quickly in a hot oven. No trick at all to do—when you know how!

Makes 9-inch pie

Prepare................Pastry for One-Crust Pie. Fit into 9-inch pie pan. Prick generously with fork.

Bake................in hot oven (450°F.) 10 to 12 minutes. Cool.

Slice................1 quart hard ice cream and pack into baked pie shell. Chocolate or any desired flavor may be used.

Spread................meringue, page 311, over ice cream, sealing carefully to edge of crust.

Place................in very hot oven (500°F.) about 5 minutes until delicately browned. Serve immediately.

COMPANY'S-COMING CASHEW PIE

Pillsbury Contest Winner by Mrs. Hazel Frost, Chicago, Ill.

"This is one of several recipes I worked out to satisfy my husband's fondness for cashew nuts," says Mrs. Frost. "It is quickly and easily made—and is fool-proof—so makes a wonderful 'show-off' dessert."

Makes 9-inch pie

Sift together............1 cup sifted enriched flour
½ teaspoon salt.

Cut in................⅓ cup shortening until particles are the size of small peas.

Sprinkle................2 to 3 tablespoons cold milk over mixture, tossing lightly with fork until dough is moist enough to hold together. Form into a ball.

Roll_____out on floured board or pastry cloth to an 11-inch circle.

Fit_____pastry loosely into 9-inch pie pan. Fold edge to form standing rim; flute.

Cream_____1 cup firmly packed brown sugar
3 tablespoons soft butter.

Combine_____¾ cup light corn syrup
1 teaspoon vanilla. Add to creamed mixture, blending well.

Blend in_____3 eggs, well beaten.

Add_____1 cup (4½ oz.) crushed, salted cashew nuts. Pour into unbaked pie shell.

Bake_____in moderate oven (350°F.) 50 to 55 min.

SOUTHERN PECAN PIE

Pecans, butter and brown sugar give this pie a delicious and
rich flavor.

Makes 9-inch pie

Prepare_____Pastry for One-Crust Pie. Fit into 9-inch pie pan.

Cream_____⅓ cup butter; add gradually
½ cup firmly packed brown sugar, creaming well.

Blend in_____1 cup light corn syrup and
1 teaspoon vanilla; mix thoroughly.

Add_____3 eggs, slightly beaten
1 cup chopped pecans.

Turn_____into pastry-lined pan.

Bake_____in hot oven (450°F.) 10 minutes, then at 350°F. for 25 minutes.

MINCEMEAT PIE

Most people like this spicy, mellow-flavored mince pie best when served warm and fragrant—fresh from the oven.

Makes 8 or 9-inch pie

Prepare................Pastry for Two-Crust Pie. Line 8 or 9-inch pie pan with half of pastry.

Combine............2 cups prepared mincemeat
1 to 2 cups pared apples, finely chopped
1 teaspoon lemon rind
2 tablespoons lemon juice.

Turn....................into pastry-lined pan.

Place..................top crust over filling; seal and flute.

Bake..................in moderately hot oven (425°F.) 30 to 40 minutes.

Accompaniments

PARTY PASTRY TREATS

These straws and turnovers may be prepared in advance and chilled. Bake them just before serving.

Prepare................Pastry for Two-Crust Pie, adding
1 cup grated cheddar cheese with shortening.

Roll....................out on floured board to ⅛-inch thickness. Make cups, turnovers or straws.

Bake..................in hot oven (425°F.) 10 to 12 minutes.

Pastry Cups........Cut pastry into rounds with 3-inch round cutter. Fit rounds into small ungreased muffin pans; prick with fork. Bake. Fill

with chicken, tuna or sea food salad.
Decorate with stuffed olive or pickle.

Miniature
*Turnovers*_____Cut pastry into 3-inch squares. Place a
teaspoon of deviled ham, potted meat or
fish filling on each square. Fold over to
form triangle. Seal edges with fork and
prick top. Bake. Serve warm.

*Cheese Straws*_____Cut pastry into 5x½-inch strips. Place on
ungreased baking sheet, twisting each
strip several times. Bake. Serve warm.

CHEESE TEMPTERS

To make these hors d'oeuvres add a dash of herbs, a bit of
Worcestershire sauce as in this pastry recipe. Cut it into rounds
the size of a nickle for tangy bite-size tempters.

Makes about 11 dozen wafers

*Sift together*_____2 cups sifted enriched flour
1½ teaspoons salt
½ teaspoon paprika
⅛ teaspoon dry mustard.

*Cut in*_____⅔ cup shortening
1¼ cups (¼ pound) grated nippy cheese
until particles are the size of small peas.

*Combine*_____⅓ cup cream and
½ teaspoon Worcestershire sauce; sprinkle
over flour mixture, tossing lightly with
fork until dough is moist enough to hold
together.

*Roll*_____out on floured board or pastry cloth to
¼-inch thickness. Cut into ½-inch

squares or into 1-inch rounds with small cutter.

Bake————————in hot oven (450°F.) 10 to 12 minutes.

ORANGE PASTRY TARTLETS

These dainty little tarts are made from orange-flavored pastry and filled with jam and marmalade.

Sift together————2 cups sifted enriched flour
1 teaspoon salt.

Cut in————————⅔ cup shortening
2 teaspoons grated orange rind until particles are the size of small peas.

Sprinkle————5 to 6 tablespoons orange juice over mixture, tossing lightly with fork until dough is moist enough to hold together.

Roll————————out on floured board to ⅛-inch thickness. Make cups or tartlets.

Bake————————in hot oven (425°F.) 10 to 12 minutes.

Pastry Cups————Cut pastry into rounds with 3-inch round cutter. (A scalloped cutter makes a dainty edge.) Fit rounds into ungreased muffin pans; prick with fork. Bake. Fill with favorite jam, marmalade or mincemeat and top with nuts.

Round Tartlets————Cut pastry into rounds with 2½-inch round cutter. Place a teaspoon of jam or marmalade in center, top with a round of pastry cut with doughnut cutter so that filling can be seen. Seal edges with fork and bake.

CHAPTER NINE

Baking Terms
Techniques and Measurements

What Baking Terms Mean

Bake................................To cook by dry heat, usually in the oven.

Beat..................................To make a mixture smooth or to introduce air by using a brisk, regular motion that lifts the mixture over and over.

Blend or Combine.....To mix thoroughly two or more ingredients.

Caramelize....................To slowly heat sugar until it becomes brown in color. The darker the color, the stronger the flavor.

Cream............................To work one or more foods until soft and creamy, using the hands or a spoon or another implement. This generally applies to shortening and sugar.

Cut..................................To incorporate shortening into dry ingredients with least amount of blending.

Dissolve.........................To make a solution from a dry and liquid ingredient.

Fold................................To combine by using two motions, cutting vertically through the mixture and turning over and over by sliding the implement across the bottom of the mixing bowl with each turn.

Knead............................To work and press dough with the palms and heels of the hands.

Melt	To change a solid to a liquid by heating.
Sauté	To brown or cook quickly in a small amount of fat.
Scald	To heat a liquid to just below the boiling point.
Sift	To put dry ingredients through a sieve.
Steam	To cook by contact with live steam in a closed container.
Stir	To mix using a circular motion.
Whip	To beat rapidly to incorporate air and increase volume.

Measurements and Equivalents

Dash	less than 1/8 teaspoon
3 teaspoons	1 tablespoon
4 tablespoons	1/4 cup
5 1/3 tablespoons	1/3 cup
16 tablespoons	1 cup - 8 ounces
2 cups	1 pint - 16 ounces
4 cups	1 quart - 32 ounces

★   ★   ★

4 cups sifted flour	1 pound
1 pound granulated sugar	2 1/4 cups
1 pound brown sugar	2 cups
1 pound sifted confectioners' sugar	3 1/2 cups
1 pound butter or shortening	2 cups
1 square chocolate	1 ounce
1/4 cup cocoa and 2 teaspoons shortening	1 oz. or 1 square chocolate
1 cup eggs	5 medium eggs
1 cup egg whites	7 to 9 medium eggs

1 cup egg yolks	12 to 14 medium eggs
1 cup coconut	3 ounces
1 pound cheese	4 cups grated
1 pound rice	4 cups. One cup uncooked rice measures 3 cups when cooked.
1 pound apples	3 cups pared and sliced
1 pound dried apricots	about 56 halves—5 cups cooked
1 pound bananas	1¼ cups—3 to 4 bananas
1 pound cranberries	4¾ cups—3 to 3½ cups of sauce
1 pound unpitted dates	1¾ cups
1 pound pitted dates	2½ cups
1 pound nuts	4 cups chopped (approximately)
1 15-ounce package raisins	2½ cups
1 medium lemon	3 tablespoons juice (approximately)
1 medium orange	½ cup juice (approximately)
½ pint whipping cream	2 cups whipped cream

Oven Temperatures

Very Hot	{ 500° F. { 475° F.	Moderately Hot	400° F.
Hot	{ 450° F. { 425° F.	Moderate	{ 375° F. { 350° F.
		Slow	{ 325° F. { 250° F.

Deep Fat Frying Temperatures

Croquettes and other cooked foods	375° - 385° F.	40 seconds to brown 1-inch cube of bread
Doughnuts, fritters	355° - 375° F.	60 seconds to brown 1-inch cube of bread

Can Sizes

No. ½	1	cup
No. 1 tall	2	cups
No. 2	2½	cups
No. 2½	3½	cups
No. 3	4	cups
No. 5	7	cups
No. 10	13	cups

Ingredients and How to Measure

Flour—Always sift flour once before measuring, then spoon flour lightly into cup and level top by scraping with edge of spatula. *Never pack flour in cup,* and don't yield to the temptation to add that extra touch for good measure!

Sugar—If sugar is lumpy, sift before measuring. Brown sugar may be pressed through a coarse sieve and measured by packing firmly in cup. Store brown sugar in the bread box or keep half an apple or slice of fresh bread in the brown sugar can to keep it moist. Confectioners' sugar should always be sifted before measuring.

Shortening—Be sure to use high-quality shortening. Shortening may be measured in two ways. It may be packed firmly into cup or spoon measures and leveled by scraping with edge of spatula. Shortening may also be measured by the water displacement method. For instance— to measure ½ cup shortening, fill a measuring cup to the ½ cup level with water. Add shortening until the water level reaches the 1 cup mark, then pour off water.

Butter, margarine, lard or vegetable shortening may be used interchangeably unless hydrogenated shortening is specified.

When using melted shortening, allow it to cool before adding to the other ingredients. Salad oil may be used when melted shortening is specified.

Salt—The most accurate measuring and the highest quality
  ingredients cannot assure satisfying flavor without salt.

Liquids—All liquids should be at room temperature when
  used unless otherwise specified in the recipe. A glass
  measuring cup marked off in quarters and thirds is useful for measuring liquids. For accurate measurements,
  read at eye level. Before measuring honey, syrup, or
  molasses, grease the inside of the measuring cup.

  Buttermilk and sour milk may be used interchangeably. If sour milk is not available, add 1 tablespoon
  lemon juice or vinegar to 1 cup sweet milk; let stand
  5 minutes.

Eggs—Because eggs vary in size, it is advisable to use cup
  measurements for yolks or whites when recipes require
  four or more eggs. For best results, eggs should be at
  room temperature. Eggs beat much better if allowed to
  stand at room temperature several hours before they
  are used.

Baking Powder—There are two common types of baking
  powders: double-acting and single-acting. Double-
  acting—or SAS-phosphate—is in more general use. It
  yields a small amount of its gas when combined with
  liquid and the remainder when the batter is exposed to
  heat. Single-acting—or tartrate—reacts when liquid is
  added, and the gas expands when heated.

  The recipes in this book call for double-acting baking
  powder unless otherwise specified. If you use single-
  acting baking powder, substitute 1½ teaspoons for each
  teaspoon of double-acting listed in recipe.

Soda—It is generally advisable to sift soda with the dry
  ingredients.

Chocolate—Always melt chocolate over hot water—in a pan,
  bowl, or on a piece of aluminum foil. Cool before using.
  It is not necessary to cut chocolate into small pieces before melting.

Cocoa—When substituting cocoa for chocolate, use ¼ cup cocoa plus 2 teaspoons shortening for each ounce (1 square) of chocolate.

Yeast—In this book the recipes calling for "one cake compressed yeast" refer to the small, individually wrapped cakes of yeast—approximately 3/5 ounce in size. "One package" refers to one small packet of dry granular yeast.

Cakes of yeast should be dissolved as directed in each recipe. Dry yeast must be dissolved as directed on the package, and the amount of water in which it is dissolved deducted from the total amount of liquid specified in the recipe.

Dates, Raisins, and Other Dried Fruits—Cut dates and other sticky fruits with wet or greased scissors.

Nuts—Chopping: Nuts may be chopped by cutting with a long knife on a cutting board, using a chopping bowl and chopper, a mechanical nut chopper, or crushing with a rolling pin.

—Blanching: To blanch nuts, cover with boiling water and let stand until skins wrinkle—about 3 minutes. Drain and plunge into cold water. Rub with fingers or the dull side of knife to remove the skins.

—Toasting: To toast nuts, spread in shallow pan with a small amount of butter or shortening. Place under broiler for a few minutes to brown, stirring occasionally.

Coconut—If coconut shreds are long, cut into shorter lengths before using. To toast coconut, sprinkle in shallow pan and place in heated oven until golden brown.

Onion Juice—To extract onion juice, cut onion in half and scrape the cut side with the edge of a spoon or with a fine grater.

Equipment and How to Use It

Flour Sifter—Always sift flour before measuring.

Standard Measuring Cups and Spoons—Accurate measurements call for standard size measuring cups and spoons. All measurements should be level. Never pack ingredients except those specified in recipe.

A nest of graduated measuring cups—consisting of ¼, ⅓, ½ and 1 cup measures—is most accurate for measuring dry ingredients. For liquids, a glass measuring cup marked off in quarters and thirds is convenient and makes for easy reading.

A cup with a rim above the 1 cup line avoids spilling. Read at eye level.

A set of measuring spoons should include spoons measuring ¼ teaspoon, ½ teaspoon, 1 teaspoon and 1 tablespoon. An accurate set measures 48 teaspoons or 16 tablespoons per cup.

Mixing Bowl—Bowl should be large enough to allow dough or batter to be mixed with sweeping strokes.

Mixers—Use a good, easy-to-handle wooden spoon for mixing by hand. A sturdy rotary beater is handy for beating eggs, frostings, meringues and thin batters, such as pancakes and popovers. In this book the recipes specify when an electric mixer may be used.

Spatula—A good flexible spatula is very useful. Level ingredients with edge of spatula when measuring. Use spatula when releasing baked products from sides of pans, also for frosting cakes.

Rubber Scraper—When using an electric mixer, guide batter or dough into beaters with a rubber scraper and scrape sides of bowl frequently. It is an excellent tool for scraping all of batter or dough from bowl into pans.

Pans—Use size pan specified in recipe. Measure top inside length and width and inside perpendicular depth. The recipes in this book specify whether pans should or should not be greased.

—**Metal Pans:** New metal baking pans should be scoured thoroughly with soap and a mild abrasive before using. To season, place in a hot oven for a few minutes, then cool.

—**Oven Glassware Pans:** When glass baking pans are used for cakes, reduce the oven temperature by 25°F.

Pastry Cloth and Stocking—A canvas pastry cloth and cotton rolling pin cover make it easier to roll pastry, biscuit doughs and cookies. Flour the cloth and rolling pin lightly.

Oven—Always bake near the center of the oven and use only one rack if possible. Pans should not touch each other or the sides of the oven. If it is necessary to use more than one rack, do not set pans on the top rack directly above those on the lower rack. Stagger them to permit an even distribution of heat.

Thermometers—Use a thermometer to measure temperature accurately in baking, candy cooking and deep fat frying. An oven thermometer is especially useful if the oven does not have a temperature control.

How to Freeze Baked Foods

Advantages of Freezing—Many baked foods may be frozen
and stored in your freezer ready to serve. There is no
need to worry about what to serve expected or unex-
pected company with your freezer full of pies, cakes
and other foods. No need to have stale bread or cake
—these may be frozen in family-size portions.

Freezing saves time—prepare meals in advance in
large quantities. Then complete meals can be on the
table ready for eating in less than an hour. A month's
supply of baked foods can be prepared in two or three
days and frozen for future use. Marketing can be done
occasionally instead of daily.

Foods to be Frozen—Cakes, cookies, yeast breads, quick
breads and most pies may be frozen satisfactorily. Usually results are best if these foods are baked and cooled
thoroughly before being frozen.

Packaging—Proper packaging is essential to satisfactory
freezing.
   —Materials: Materials should have the following
   characteristics:
      1. Moisture-vapor-proof
      2. Strong and tough
      3. Odorless and tasteless
      4. Ease of handling, sealing and labeling.
   Aluminum foil, polyethylene and pliofilm, easily obtainable at your hardware or department
   store, are among the best. Most of the frozen
   food containers on the market are also very good.
   —Wrapping: Foods should be wrapped very
   tightly. The "druggists' wrap" is the easiest way
   to make tight folds and a close wrap. The "butch-
   er's wrap" is also effective. Except for aluminum
   foil, which is self-sealing, use freezer tape to seal.

Pies—Fruit pies, mince pies, vegetable pies such as pumpkin, and chocolate and lemon chiffon pies freeze well. Meringue toppings shrink and become tough and custard pies also do not freeze satisfactorily. Pies are easier to wrap after they are frozen. They may be stored up to 8 weeks. Thaw at room temperature about two hours or in a moderate oven 30 to 40 minutes.

Cakes—Freeze cakes unfrosted or frosted with a confectioners' sugar frosting. Freeze before wrapping and thaw in original wrapping to prevent moisture from forming on surface. Two hours at room temperature or a few minutes in a slow oven are sufficient for thawing. They may be stored up to 3 to 4 months.

Cookies—Cookies may be frozen baked or unbaked. Freezing cooky dough is simpler and takes less freezer space but requires more work after thawing. Freeze baked cookies in covered containers and thaw in original container at room temperature for about 30 minutes. They may be stored up to 3 months.

Breads—Bake, cool and wrap yeast and quick breads before freezing. Thaw in wrapper at room temperature for 45 minutes to 1 hour or in slow oven for 10 to 15 minutes. Slices of frozen bread or frozen waffles may be dropped into the toaster without previous thawing. They may be stored up to 3 months. Doughnuts may be frozen but should be stored only 3 weeks.

INDEX

GENUINE **POCKET** BOOK BEST SELLERS

Many hours of reading enjoyment await you in these recent
POCKET BOOK *titles. Ask for them now at your local dealer.*

*If your dealer does not have the title or titles you
want, you can get them for the usual newsstand price
plus 5 cents to cover the cost of mailing by writing to:*
POCKET BOOKS, INC., Rockefeller Center, New York 20, N.Y.

---

796. FOR DOCTORS ONLY

by Dr. Francis Leo Golden. From the most ludicrous
aspects of human frailty come these hilarious bits
about anatomy, psychiatry, surgery, gynecology,
obstetrics, sex, pediatrics and all other fields of medi-
cal practice. In these happy pages the whole scope
of human existence unfolds as seen through the whim-
sical eyes of men of medicine.

---

782. DIALOGUES OF PLATO

selected and with prefatory notes by J. D. Kaplan.
This selection includes four complete dialogues—
APOLOGY, CRITO, PHAEDO, SYMPOSIUM—and the most
famous passages from the REPUBLIC. These fascinating dialogues have been read by millions of people
over the years as an answer to many everyday ques-
tions.

---

730. THIS IS AMERICA

edited by Max J. Herzberg. This fascinating antholo-
gy of famous American state papers, stories, biogra-
phies, essays, sayings and orations reveals the found-
ing and making of the United States and its history in
peace and war. It includes the Bill of Rights, the
Gettysburg Address, Patrick Henry's LIBERTY OR
DEATH and F.D.R.'s APPEAL TO THE NATIONS.

POCKET BOOK

THIS SYMBOL GUARANTEES

THE BEST IN READING